The City that Bleeds

Race, History and the Death of Baltimore

Paul Kersey

Paul Kersey

Dedicated to Anna Sowers and the children she never raised with her late husband Zach[1]

---

[1] http://pages.jh.edu/~jhumag/0608web/sowers.html

Table of Contents

The Most Enduring Symbol of the Civil Rights Movement – Plexiglas... p. 11

The Desolation of Baltimore... p. 17

Days of Future Past... p. 28

Johns Hopkins Trauma Center Stunting Evolution? ... p. 36

Homicide: A Year on the Killing Streets... p. 41

Desperate Measures... p. 47

Shoe Is On the Other Foot... p. 54

Last Days of Disco... p. 65

Indianapolis vs. Baltimore... p. 70

Mirror, Mirror... p. 75

Rowhouses... p. 79

God's Gonna Sit This One Out p. 83

War Zone, USA... p. 87

Baltimore City, You're Breaking My Heart... p. 95

Baltimore's "Alamo"... p. 103

Real Gun Control ... p. 109

Kimberley Leto... p. 119

Norplant Solution... p. 123

Life in Baltimore's White Minority... p. 132

America's Monrovia... p. 142

Portlandia vs. *The Wire*... p. 148

Quoth the Raven... p. 153

Year-Round Curfew Centers... p. 158

Control: Ultimate Goal of Civil Rights Movement. p. 169

The History of Residential Segregation (Restrictive Covenants) in Baltimore... and Why They Were Necessary...p. 186

Lynchings in USA vs. Black-on-Black Homicide in Baltimore... p. 228

Life During Wartime (Baltimore Public Schools)... p. 237

State of the City...p. 242

"No Snitching"... p. 250

Kurt Schmoke... p. 253

Tracey Halvorsen... p. 258

Primal Anger... p. 268

An Equation for the Madness... p. 273

Paul Kersey

Baltimore's Population by Decade: Broken Down by Race

Year	Total Population	White Population	White Total (%)	Black Population	Black Total (%)
1910	558,000	473,000	85%	85,000	15%
1920	733,826	625,130	85%	108,322	15%
1930	804,874	662,124	82%	142,106	18%
1940	859,100	692,705	81%	165,843	19%
1950	949,748	723,655	76%	225,099	24%
1960	939,024	610,608	65%	325,589	35%
1970	905,759	479,837	54%	420,210	46%
1980	786,775	346,692	45%	430,934	55%
1990	736,014	287,933	41%	435,619	59%
2000	651,154	205,982	31.60%	418,951	64.3%
2010	620,961	183,830	28%	395,781	63.6%

(Source: U.S. Census Bureau and *Black Social Capital: The Politics of School Reform in Baltimore, 1986-1998*, p. 65)

From 85 percent white in 1910 to 28 percent white in 2010

THE CITY THAT BLEEDS

The Most Enduring Symbol of the Civil Rights Movement -- Plexiglas

It's illegal to discriminate as an official business practice. You can't deny anyone service at your restaurant or keep a person from entering your store on the basis of race, sex, sexual orientation, or handicap.

America is now officially in the business of waging war on those who dare stand in the way of equality, freedom, and tolerance, meaning any form of discrimination is reason for unleashing an army of lawyers, armed police/SWAT, and the full fury of the fourth estate (the state-controlled media).

Surprisingly, the most enduring symbol (the ultimate legacy) of the civil rights movement (you know, that epoch in history that forever destroyed a private citizen's right to run their privately-held company/business/property) isn't white flight from urban areas.

Nor is it a black man at 1600 Pennsylvania Avenue.

It's transparent thermoplastic, a security measure required to protect those employees (and property) of business owners who still dare try and turn a profit in cities like Newark, Camden, Birmingham, Detroit, and Baltimore.

Though the lingering evidence of civilization in these cities can be discerned in the empty skyscrapers jettisoning into the air (that same air is routinely pierced with the sound of gunshots), those merchants sticking behind to gobble-up easy food stamp/EBT money are required to ensconce their employees, as well as much of their merchandise, behind impenetrable Plexiglas.

Plexiglas.

Though Black History Month celebrations this February will spend considerable amount of time detailing the horrors of segregation, such as whites-only seating/water fountains and the unspeakable evil of a business owner denying black people service, there exists no symbol more powerful than the erection of Plexiglas at a place of business to protect employees from the black customers it serves.

11

No symbol.

The purest legacy of civil rights, for nothing can forestall the natural inclinations of a people who believe they're entitled to anything and everything like a wall of bullet-proof material.

The Johns Hopkins Bloomberg School of Public Health Center for a Livable Future issued a study where the authors bemoaned the Baltimore City food environment as one in which "behind-glass stores" was an omnipresent, ubiquitous reminder of racial differences in behavior (they didn't actually use those words, but Plexiglas at a business has a harsh way of saying nothing, but speaking to power everything):

> The final category of stores, behind-glass stores, is an important subset of corner stores. They are characterized by having barriers of Plexiglas walls separating the consumer on one side from the retail items and owner/workers on the other side.
> Behind-Glass Stores: Small corner stores (found almost exclusively in Baltimore's poorer, African American neighborhoods) in which all access to goods is limited by thick walls of Plexiglas serving as a barrier between the customers on one side and the cashiers and merchandise on the other. Considered a necessary safety measure by many store owners, behind-glass stores have the lowest availability of healthy foods in Baltimore as measured by the Healthy Food Availability Index ratings.[2]

A "revolving Plexiglas pass-through" - where customers exchange money for a good (so that no physical contact between employee can occur) - is a hallmark of the Behind-Glass store.[3]

As Afro.com laments, "*Imagine living in an area where the only sources of food within blocks are canned products bought through*

---

[2] http://www.jhsph.edu/research/centers-and-institutes/johns-hopkins-center-for-a-livable-future/_pdf/research/clf_reports/BaltimoreCityFoodEnvironment.pdf

[3] http://www.baltimorebrew.com/2013/04/04/lifting-up-park-heights-by-cracking-down-on-liquor-stores/

Plexiglas partitions, from seedy corner joints, or convenience stores."[4]

Well, you live in an area where the shadow of the post-civil rights era has smiled.

This story is the true legacy of the civil rights movement. [Storeowner reopens store after relative was murdered: Jose Melo's wife was also injured in the Jan. 9 shooting; police say they identified a suspect, Baltimore Sun, 1-20-2014]:

> Recovering from four bullet wounds, Jose Melo's wife begged him not to go on Monday, but he would not hear of it.
> Eleven days had passed since Melo last worked at his small corner store in Southwest Baltimore. On that day — Jan. 9 — he had come out of the bathroom hearing gunshots and screaming only to see a hooded gunman fire one more shot into his wife before fleeing. Her brother, who helped out behind the counter, was slumped next to her, fatally shot in the chest.

> He wasn't scared, Melo told his wife, Irkania Moran, repeatedly. God would protect him, he said.

> Melo, 52, reopened the Latino American Deli & Grocery at the corner of Christian and South Smallwood streets on Martin Luther King Jr. Day, determined to be free of fear. He walked past aisles of Gerber baby food and Glory collard greens to the rear deli where he makes the $3.75 subs he's known for around the Carrollton Ridge neighborhood. He threw out expired gallons of milk and stuffed stale rolls and loaves of white bread into a black trash bag and went to work.

> Eighteen people have been killed in Baltimore this year, a bloody start after homicides rose 8 percent in 2013 — the second consecutive year of increases.

> Baltimore police said they were expanding the footprints of heavily patrolled "hot zone" violent crime areas, and every few hours a uniformed police officer stepped into Melo's store Monday to check on him.

> There was never another choice but to reopen, Melo said. He had to support his wife and their two children, and he wasn't

---

[4]

http://www.afro.com/sections/news/baltimore/story.htm?storyid=7606
8

about to give up on the store he had purchased more than a year ago, plunking down more than $25,000 just to remodel the abandoned space.

He worked seven days a week, 12 hours a day. His first quarter earned is taped to the counter near a pile of Charleston Chews, and his first dollar hangs behind a Plexiglas wall with a few words written on it:

"Buena Suerte! Dios se lo bendiga. Genesis." Good luck. God bless you.[5]

God doesn't bless fools. The novelist, Madison Smartt Bell, wrote a walking history of Baltimore for the Crown Journey's imprint in 2007. *Charm City: A Walk Through Baltimore*, offers a glimpse of once prosperous civilization in sorrowful decay. And, yes, he encounters plenty of Plexiglas:

> The amber sunset light is glorious – a light that finds beauty in everything it touches. I'm on the wrong side of the street, however – I have become part of that Hopperesque view, when I would rather be appreciating it.
> The sun is low, and shining in my eyes. I trudge past the Agape Christian Church, a storefront much like the restaurants and shops along this stretch of road. Oasis appears a couple doors south in the form of Wozi's Lounge.
>
> Inside the front door is kind of an airlock, a space about the size of an elevator, hemmed in by thick Plexiglas, blacked out by stickers and hand-lettered posters, the few clear areas opaque from scratches.
>
> I've tripped a bell coming in, and presently a shadow appears at the cash registered on the other side of the Plexiglas hatch through which I could buy a six-pack or a short dog, were that my mission, but instead I jerk my thumb at the inner door. For sure, I'm not their usual customer, but I must not look too much like an armed robber, either, because after forty seconds of scrutiny, the shadow punches the buzzer and lets me in.[6]

---

[5] http://articles.baltimoresun.com/2014-01-20/news/bs-md-ci-corner-store-reopens-20140117_1_southwest-baltimore-store-monday-carrollton-ridge

[6] Bell, Madison Smartt. *Charm City: a walk through Baltimore*. New

Continuing his journey through Baltimore, Bell writes:

> By this time, having walked close to five miles at a swinging pace, I am thirsty again. At the top of the next rise, just past the graveyard wall, another oasis appears on the opposite corner: Avenue Liquors and Bar, promising "package goods, ice, open 7 days..."
>
> I nudge Eric, and we climb the steps and pop into another Plexiglas holding tank, similar to Wozi's in its basic design, though a little larger and better lit. The heavy plastic partitions are so yellowed and scarred you can barely see through them; the Korean cashier on the other side looks blurry as a ghost.
>
> There's a black couple ahead of us, clad in matching fuzzy white sweat suits, negotiating their rations of grog. The drill is to lay your money down in the compartment of a Plexiglas lazy Susan that's open to you, while the proprietor places your bottle of choice in the opposite compartment facing him.
>
> A quick rotation of the cylinder exchanges payment for goods with next to no compromise of security. To enter the back-room bar, you must pass a visual inspection. Apparently, Eric and I will do, for after the Korean gentleman gives us a good looking over, he buzzes us through.
>
> The bar is atypically bright, with an extension of the cashier's counter cutting a short diagonal across it, and cluttered with cardboard packing cases. Eric and I about fill the place up. Behind the counter is an array of little airline liquor bottles on a small set of shelves, and a glass-front refrigerator full of beer. But the owner is still serving street-side customer through the lazy Susan to our left.[7]

Plexiglas, a constant reminder that the civil rights movement unleashed something... unmentionable. [What's best in Baltimore taxis: shields or security cameras?: Local company wants cameras instead of bullet-resistant panels, Baltimore Sun, 3-5-2012]:

York: Crown Journeys, 2007. p. 33-34

[7] Ibid. p. 49-50

Step into a cab in many major cities, including Baltimore, and you'll wind up sitting behind a clear, bullet-resistant shield that separates you from the driver.

But one taxicab company operating in Baltimore wants to replace the state-mandated protective guard with security cameras. Baltimore Taxi Affiliation Services, which operates 100 cabs under the Arrow Cab and Baltimore City Taxi brands, recently asked the Maryland Public Service Commission to consider amending state regulations to allow for either a shield or a camera in Baltimore cabs.

About 1,150 taxicabs are licensed to operate in Baltimore City, where shields became mandatory in 1995. The partition is not required in Baltimore County cabs.

Meanwhile, the idea of replacing partitions with security cameras appears not to have wide support in the local taxi and driver community.

"Shield is protection," said Tsegaye Yitbarek, who has been a taxi driver in the city for 15 years. "Camera is a witness."

Other drivers and companies also expressed concern about the cost of installing cameras, especially as drivers are now paying more for gas. And some say plainly that shields are the best prevention against crime.

The Public Service Commission's staff said in a report last month that it was "not convinced that the security camera will reduce crime as effectively as the mandated partition given the fact that a perpetrator's opportunity for harm increases without the barrier of the partition."[8]

Social capital vanishes when such security precautions are necessary to maintain the safety of employees in an area we call at a 'food desert'.

So, this Black History Month, let's all travel to convenience stores in our Whitopia's and shake the hands of the gas station clerk. Note Plexiglas partitions aren't necessary.

---

[8] http://articles.baltimoresun.com/2012-03-05/business/bs-bz-taxi-security-cameras-20120305_1_security-cameras-baltimore-taxis-cabs

But in urban America, the most enduring symbol of the civil rights movement is an ever-present reminder that the past is never dead.

The Desolation of Baltimore: How David Simon's *The Corner* Inadvertently Blames the Demise of Baltimore on Black Migrants from the South

David Simon, co-creator of the immensely popular HBO show *The Wire* and chronicler of all things black in Baltimore (via his two books, *Homicide: A Year on the Killing Streets* and *The Corner*) has spent a career romanticizing black people.

Attempting to humanize the black underclass, decrying the "War on Drugs" as the fundamental reason this demographic group can't assimilate to the American Dream, Simon has completely acclimated to the terrifying culture only the black population of Baltimore's biology could manifest.

In the words of *Baltimore Sun* editor, Simon's work "ennobled criminals," the very black underclass that was making Baltimore an inhospitable, dangerous place to live for individuals and driving away businesses for safer real estate. [Who Gets to Tell a Black Story?, New York Times, 6-11-2000][9]

---

[9] http://www.nytimes.com/2000/06/11/us/who-gets-to-tell-a-black-story.html?pagewanted=all&src=pm

Perhaps a passage from *The Corner* might shed some light into a brief moment of sanity Mr. Simon encountered, when he cited the Great Migration of blacks from the Southern portion of the United States with drastically altering the future of Baltimore:

> It was 1942 and William McCullough, at the age of fourteen, was a small but committed part of the largest ethnic migration in American history. It was larger than the flight of the starving Irish a century before, larger still than the succeeding waves of Eastern European and Italian immigrants who later crowded the halls of Ellis Island and Castle Garden. The black exodus from the rural South in this century would utterly transform the American cities of the East and Midwest. In the Mississippi Valley, the northward migration brought thousands of southern blacks to Memphis, Kansas City, St. Louis, and ultimately, to the terminus cities of Chicago and Detroit. In the East, the same phenomenon brought waves of migrants to Baltimore and Washington, Philadelphia and New York.
>
> There was nothing surprising about this. Mechanization was changing the agrarian economy of the South, with the sharecropping and tenant farming that characterized so much of the black rural life increasingly marginalized. By the early 1940s, even the farming of cotton- the most labor-intensive of the Southern crops – was being transformed as mechanical cotton pickers were perfected and marketed. Once the South had staked both its society and economy on black labor; by World War II, the same labor force was expendable.
>
> To the north, the smoking cities of the American industrial belt offered an alternative. Even in the Depression years, the pages of the black community newspaper in the McCullough hometown of Winnsboro were littered with the notices of a generation inexorably drifting northward: "We regret to report another departure for Baltimore..."
> "Mr. Hill, a Winnsboro native and lifelong resident of the county, will leave to join relatives in Philadelphia."
> "On Sunday last, a good-bye picnic was held for the Singletary family..."

"... the young gentleman will be departing our community next month with friends to pursue prospects in Washington..."

Baltimore siphoned from the rural black population of both Carolinas and the Virginia tidewater. Southern whites- those with any sense of the future anyway- began to see the migration as beneficial, a pressure valve on their demographic time bomb. Though increasingly superfluous in the wake of mechanized agriculture, the black population had become a majority in many rural counties, a growing threat to the world of Jim that might one day require a reckoning. Now, through migration, much of that reckoning would come in the North.[10]

Baltimore was 81 percent white in 1940; today, it's 65 percent black.[11]

The day of reckoning did come, and it is further proof that demography is destiny. Whereas wave after wave of European immigrants through Ellis Island enriched America, there is no documented beneficial net-gain found in New York City, Philadelphia, Chicago, Detroit, or Baltimore via the Great Migration of blacks (a "superfluous population" according to Simon) from the South.

The professional sports industry doesn't count, nor does growth in the security industry from their presence. Here is an example of the type of boost the civilization in Baltimore received with an infusion of blacks from the South. In a pictorial essay at the Baltimore Sun's web site – The Faces of Summer Violence: The Fury of the Season's Bloody Crime Spike Casts a Shadow Over the Entire City and its Residents – a journalist at the paper offers a glimpse into the sunk cost that is the black population of Maryland's largest city[At violent summer's end, weary city grapples with the toll, Baltimore Sun, 8-31-2013]:

---

[10] Simon, David, and Edward Burns. *The corner: a year in the life of an inner-city neighborhood.* New York: Broadway Books, 1997. p. 88-89

[11] Baum, Howell S.. *Brown in Baltimore: school desegregation and the limits of liberalism.* Ithaca: Cornell University Press, 2010. p. 212

The rapper

Cornelius Owens stood alone on a West Baltimore corner, his usual hangout. In front of him mostly vacant row houses reflected the bleak opportunities provided by a life on the street. A block away, a makeshift memorial for his slain teenage friend represented a common, and fatal, dead end.

Owens, 21, lives nearby on West Lexington Street but violence isn't going to make him move from the neighborhood. He pulled out a battered smartphone, and found a music track: So stuck in my ways, get the [expletive] out of my way ...

The tinny speakers blasted the rap song he recorded, a street-hustling anthem as well as a personal statement. He vowed not to be taken from his corner, his way of life, his goals or the 1-year-old son who bears his name.

It's brash talk considering gunfire has taken three friends in three years. "Only certain ones survive," he said. "The good ones, they get took."

Deshaun "Lor D'Shaun" Jones was one of them, a teen who helped make up a group of amateur rappers. They included Owens — who goes by "C" — "Icon" and "Lor David" — Jones' brother, all plying their trade on YouTube and at area clubs with some success.

Jones, just 15, was one of the best, Owens said. He was killed Aug. 24 when, police say, someone shot up a dice game, wounding six others, near North Gilmor and West Fayette Streets.

"He was a 'hood legend," Owens said. His videos have amassed more than 16,000 online views. Rumors have surfaced since his death that a nationally known rapper was starting to take an interest in his music.

It's something the entire group dreams of.

"I'm trying to put it all in my music, so I won't have to be in the streets," said Kevin "Icon" Ben. "I love my city but it's quicksand."

Owens loves Franklin Square, too — his "hood," his community. But he wants to rise out of it, as well. He is proud that he graduated from high school last year at 20. He had almost given up when a two-month stint in jail for assault put him too far behind to stay with his class.

He's reluctant to abandon his home even after losing two other friends: David Mitchell, 16, in 2010 and Davon Dorsey, 18, "shot in the head" in 2011.

"The last couple of years, you have seen the violence rise," he said. "East Baltimore, West Baltimore, Cherry Hill. ... For all the little kids around here and my son, of course I'm scared."

Had Owens not been working a day-labor job, hauling junk and abandoned mattresses out of an East Baltimore yard, he said, he would've been with Jones that fatal summer night.

"Probably would be a victim myself. Probably wouldn't be standing here," he said.

Owens said he knows what's causing the violence. It's not drugs or money, though they are fuel. Triggers are pulled over "respect" — and it doesn't take much.
"It can be words," he said. "It can be eyes. Eyes can be disrespectful. I know it sounds crazy but it's true."

Turn the other cheek today and someone will take advantage of you tomorrow.
"At the end of the day, if someone feels disrespected, what's the first thing they think about?" he said.

"They have to respond to disrespect. You can't walk away from where you live at."
We do this every day, every day we live ...

The song "Stuck in My Ways" on Owens' phone ends abruptly. Jones was supposed to go to a studio and rap the last verse.

"Didn't get the chance to be on it," Owens said. "So we had to end it right there."[12]

Environments do not create individuals; Baltimore was a thriving city prior to the arrival of blacks from the South as part of the "Great Migration"; the biological reality of race dictated that, once white people left Baltimore, the city would become just another outward phenotype of the majority-black population found there. [2 slayings push toll in 1990 to 296, most since early 1970s, Baltimore Sun, by David Simon, 12-24-1990]:

---

[12] http://darkroom.baltimoresun.com/2013/08/crime-story/#1

An article in yesterday's editions of The Sun reported incorrectly that 296 people had been murdered in Baltimore in 1990. In fact, the number of violent deaths officially classified as murders at that time was 294, according to the police.

The Sun regrets the error.

A pair of shootings early yesterday pushed Baltimore's 1990 murder count near the 300 mark -- a level of violence that the city has not encountered in almost two decades.

Yesterday's slayings -- one in an argument over a woman, the other in apparent retaliation for the theft of drugs -- were the 295th and 296th of the year.

The numbers confirm 1990 as the most violent year since Maryland's renowned shock-trauma system was organized in the early 1970s.

It was in 1971 and 1972 that the city posted its highest murder totals -- 323 and 330, respectively -- after which the emergency medical system became fully operational and the homicide rate fell dramatically, reaching a low of 171 in 1977.

But for the last three years, the city's murder rate has climbed steadily, dovetailing with a national trend that has produced record homicide totals in more than a dozen other U.S. cities this year.

Nationally, police generally attribute the increase to the burgeoning inner-city drug trade and the proliferation of firearms, particularly semiautomatic handguns. Locally, homicide detectives are saying pretty much the same thing.

"We've had 18 murders in the last two weeks," said Kevin Davis, a veteran homicide detective. "It's the guns and the drugs and the general lack of respect for human life that's keeping us busy this holiday season."

The city homicide unit has solved about 67 percent of this year's homicides.

Officially, the city unit's current clearance rate is 75.9 percent, taking into account the 23 murders from previous years that were solved in 1990 -- a statistical system permitted under federal crime reporting guidelines. The Baltimore rate is better than the national average of about 70 percent.

Police officials and city prosecutors acknowledge, however, that the increasing violence is straining the criminal-justice system by burdening investigators, clogging courtrooms and producing backlogs in the trace evidence, ballistics and fingerprint sections of the city crime laboratory.

As in past years, the 1990 murder toll has fallen disproportionately on young black men, who accounted for the great majority of both victims and suspects and for whom homicide has become the leading cause of death nationwide.

Almost 93 percent of the city's murder victims this year were black, 85 percent were male, and 58 percent were 29 or younger. Police records show that the first 74 homicide victims of 1990 were black.

Similarly, of 300 suspects currently identified in connection with the year's murders, more than 91 percent are black, 90 percent are male, and 58 percent are 25 or younger.[13]

The first 74 homicide victims of 1990 were black.

Let that sink in for a second.

It didn't get any better in 1991, with the "Day of Reckoning" (the surplus black population) coming to the black community, courtesy of the black community [Baltimore homicides for 1991 reach 304, 1 under '90 record Shooting of woman marks first of '92, Baltimore Sun, 1-2-1992]:

> It was the last day of 1990. The killings in Baltimore had hit 305 and the mayor was talking tough.
>
> "We are going to lower the number of murders next year," Kurt L. Schmoke insisted. "We just can't repeat 1990."
>
> We didn't, but we came close. Baltimore closed out 1991 with 304 homicides, one fewer than the city recorded in 1990. At least 12 had been children under 9 years old.
>
> At the close of 1990, Baltimore recorded more homicides than any year since 1972, when 330 persons were killed in Baltimore. For more than a decade after that, improvements in Baltimore's emergency medical services brought the number of killings down, reaching a low of 171 in 1977.

---

[13] 2 slayings push toll in 1990 to 296, most since early 1970s, Baltimore Sun, by David Simon, 12-24-1990

While the numbers have been steadily increasing for the past three years, homicide detectives say it might have been even higher except for the emergency medical services.

"The only thing we can do is thank God for our medical personnel in Baltimore City, our outstanding medical personnel," said Sgt. Jay Landsman, a veteran homicide detective.

In this majority-black city, young black men have dominated the homicide roster in recent years, and 1991 was no exception.

As of Nov. 30, when The Sun put the year-to-date killings at 269, 62.8 percent of homicide victims -- or 169 -- were black men between the ages of 20-39. When blacks between the ages of 10 and 20 were included, the percentage of victims who were black and male increased to 75 percent.

All of the slain children were black. Among them was 6-year-old Tiffany Smith, who was killed late one summer evening when she was visiting a young friend overnight in the Walbrook area of West Baltimore. She stepped into the path of a shootout between two men. And there was Renae Hicks, an 11-month-old baby allegedly beaten to death last month by her mother and her mother's boyfriend.[14]

This is the culture black people brought with them from the South, where demographic changes ensure Baltimore became a city ruled with the iron fist of black supremacy.

Baltimore's homicide problem isn't related to drugs; it's related to blacks.

The homicide problem in 2008 Baltimore was still black[15]; in 2012, it was black, black, and black.[16]

---

[14] http://articles.baltimoresun.com/1992-01-02/news/1992002004_1_homicide-detectives-number-of-homicides-homicide-rate

[15]http://weblogs.baltimoresun.com/news/crime/blog/2009/01/homicide_by_number.html

[16] http://articles.baltimoresun.com/2013-01-01/news/bal-

As David Simon wrote in *The Corner*, the desolation of Baltimore is the end-result of individual – superfluous - black people migrating from the South; their lives (and contributions to the city) aggregated together spell nothing but doom for the civilization that whites created there.

Evan Serpick, writing for *City Paper* in Baltimore, would have you believe every murder is a tragedy.

The evidence has clearly shown, however, that Serpick is wrong: if life, black life, was actually valued by black people in Baltimore, the carnage would stop.

It is not.

Serpick writes:

> In the past couple months since I started as editor of *City Paper*, one of my grimmer duties has been to edit Anna Ditkoff's Murder Ink column. Every week, in an effort to make sure our readers are aware of the weekly toll of deadly violence, she details the facts of every murder that takes place in Baltimore City—128 so far this year. Among those details, she includes the race of every person murdered, and, when applicable, the race of people arrested for those murders, which demonstrates that African-Americans are the overwhelming victims of murder in Baltimore City: Of 128 people murdered in Baltimore so far this year, 125 have been African-American. The people arrested for those murders are also overwhelmingly African-American.

> Last week, Joseph "Alex" Ulrich Jr. was killed, making him the third white person killed in Baltimore this year. I didn't know Ulrich any more than I knew any of the other 127 victims. But, now that I've been following the stories of those murdered week in and week out, I'm struck by the drastic difference in the public reaction to this death and virtually all the others.

> The vast media coverage as well as the attention on social

demographics-of-2012-baltimore-homicides-20121231_1_drug-arrests-baltimore-homicides-gun-crimes media and at a well-attended vigil in Mt. Vernon last night, where the shooting took place (depicted in a front-page photo in the *Sun* today), are a striking contrast to coverage of other murders, which sometimes merit no more than a *Sun* blog post.

Even more striking, I think, are the comments and actions of the police in response to the murder. Immediately after the shooting, the Baltimore Police Department announced that they would step up foot, mounted, and bicycle patrols in Mt. Vernon. That certainly sounds like a good idea, but I wonder if police responded in a similar way after the other 127 murders this year, many of which also involved wholly innocent victims, like Ulrich. In a *Sun* story yesterday, police spokesman Anthony Guglielmi commented on the incident, saying, "The community needs a show of force, and we need to find out who's responsible for this violence. We'll pour in everything we can to figure that out." Again, I wonder if other neighborhoods got the same show of force after murders there, or whether police promised to "pour in everything we can" to solve the other 127 murders. I certainly haven't heard a police representative say so.

It's a familiar pattern to anyone who follows crime news in Baltimore City. Week in, week out, people are killed—seven people were murdered in Baltimore City in the week before Ulrich was killed. The stories are given little coverage in the local media—did you hear anything about those seven people killed last week? If I wasn't editing Murder Ink, I'm pretty sure I wouldn't have. But when a white person is killed or is the victim of a serious crime, as with the hapless tourist whose beating and robbery were captured on downtown security cameras earlier this year, it is front-page news, and the source of angst: Is our city safe? It's hard not to translate the subtext of that angst to, Is our city safe for white people? Because if the general population was concerned about whether or not the city was safe for black people, there would be a whole lot more vigils and angst.[17]

The city isn't safe for black OR white people, precisely because black people's criminality, and particularly high rates of black-on-black

---

[17] http://blogs.citypaper.com/index.php/2012/08/every-murder-is-a-tragedy/

crime, convinced white people to flee to the suburbs. It's why in 1992, at an event celebrating the Emancipation Proclamation, the speeches focused on the high rate of black-in-origin homicide:

> By the time city officials gathered last Sunday for the annual ceremony commemorating the Emancipation Proclamation abolishing slavery, Baltimore had already witnessed its seventh homicide of the new year. The carnage prompted Mayor Schmoke to drop his prepared remarks and ask rhetorically, "Why are we killing ourselves like this?"

> The vast majority of homicide victims in Baltimore are young and poor and black. A widely publicized study last year reported that homicide is the leading cause of death among young black men, who die overwhelmingly at the hands of other young black men.

> But while it was entirely appropriate to address the problem of black-on-black violence on the day commemorating blacks' emancipation from slavery, it also was somewhat misleading. "Can you imagine the hurt and anguish our ancestors feel looking down on us in 1992?" Baltimore Rep. Kweisi Mfume asked the assembled crowd. Well, yes we can -- but no more so than we can imagine that of the ancestors of children living in, say, Medellin, Colombia, or any other other impoverished Third World city where similar conditions exist. It is not race or previous condition of servitude but the pervasive poverty and hopelessness under which people live that drive them to commit desperate acts.[18]

A third world population – black migrants from the South (what Simon noted in *The Corner* were "superfluous" to the new economy there) – have remade the once flourishing, first world city of Baltimore in their image.

---

[18] http://articles.baltimoresun.com/1992-01-08/news/1992008146_1_young-black-men-emancipation-homicide

Days of the Future Past: When "Stop and Frisk" Becomes "Investigative Stops" in Baltimore, Civilization is Nearing Death

Its no secret Baltimore is one of America's hotbeds for black murder, mayhem and dysfunction [Baltimore murder victims, suspects share ties to criminal justice system: Slayings down but trends continue, Baltimore Sun, 1-2-2012].[19]

It's also no secret that Del. Pat McDonough was correct when he chided black youths for being solely responsible for the crime in the city's Inner Harbor area [Delegate warns of "black youth mobs" in Baltimore's Inner Harbor: Comment brings sharp criticism, ABC2NEWS.com, 5-17-2012].

The greater crime/sin in the incident wasn't the abhorrent crime level itself; it was McDonough daring to notice and publicly comment on what we all know to be true. Incidentally, police did strengthen patrols in the Inner Harbor area only a month after his 'racially insensitive' comments [Baltimore Leaders Increase Security At Inner Harbor, CBS Baltimore, 6-21-12].[20]

Murder and gun-crime, just like in New York City, is almost entirely the avocation/vocation of non-whites in Baltimore (specifically, blacks).

---

[19] http://articles.baltimoresun.com/2012-01-02/news/bs-md-ci-homicide-analysis-20120102_1_killings-stanley-brunson-baltimore-murder-victims

[20] http://baltimore.cbslocal.com/2012/05/21/baltimore-leaders-increase-security-at-inner-harbor/

Which might be why the news of Baltimore running a "stop and frisk" program is so encouraging, though a name change (purely for positive public relations reasons...) still has raised the blood pressure of the ACLU to an unhealthy level. [ACLU slams Baltimore Police over 'stop and frisk' name change, Baltimore Sun, 9-25-13]:

> The ACLU of Maryland is criticizing the Baltimore Police Department's decision to change the name of its "stop and frisk" procedures and said they receive regular complaints from citizens about such stops.
>
> Last month, the ACLU filed a public records request with police seeking detailed records covering citizen encounters with police and was recently told the agency needed more time as it revises its general orders relating to "stop and frisks." The Sun reported this week that the agency has changed the name of "stop and frisks" to "investigative stops," in an effort by the agency to distance itself from controversy over the stops in New York City. City attorney Christopher Lundy told the ACLU that the new term was "more proper" way to refer to stops "motivated by reasonable articulable suspicion."
>
> The ACLU posted its request, and the BPD's response, here.
>
> Sonia Kumar, a staff attorney with the ACLU, said in a statement:
>
> "Whether we call it 'stop and frisk' or something else makes no difference to the Baltimore residents stopped and searched without any reasonable suspicion that they have done something wrong. The problem isn't the name - it's how police are treating people.
>
> "By law, an officer must have reasonable suspicion that someone has committed or is about to commit a crime before stopping him or her. But that suspicion alone is not enough to justify a frisk during the stop. In order to frisk, an officer must also reasonably suspect that the person stopped is armed.

"Yet, as deployed in Baltimore and around the country, people of color who are totally innocent of any wrongdoing have been subjected to totally baseless stops and searches by police who are on fishing expeditions. The ACLU routinely hears from Baltimore residents whose rights have been violated in this way. Not only are such stops illegal, but they also corrode the relationship between police and the people whose help they need to keep everyone safe."[21]

David Simon's book *Homicide* clearly shows cops in Baltimore understand they are on their own, hated by the black population in the city and only one difficult arrest away from a public demonstration (against police brutality/racism) and losing their badge.

Though most of the large-scale public housing no longer exists in Baltimore (strategically condensing crime to high-rise buildings gave way to the novel idea of exporting it throughout Baltimore via Section 8 vouchers), life in these formally all-black, taxpayer-supported enclaves was a 24/7/365 war-zone.

No story illustrates the type of world black people create better than one from 1992 in Baltimore, when an armored vehicle was called in to save 10 officers pinned down by black snipers [10 officers rescued in latest of city-housing problems, Baltimore Sun, 8-21-1992]:

The latest from Baltimore's public high-rise housing projects: 10 police officers, pinned down by sniper fire, had to be rescued yesterday by an armored car as gunmen fired shots from upper floors.

A week earlier, 9-year-old Ebony Scott was murdered and left in a trash bin at George B. Murphy Homes, another city-owned housing project. And a week before that, a drug user

21 http://www.baltimoresun.com/news/maryland/crime/blog/bal-aclu-slams-baltimore-police-stop-and-frisk-name-change-20130925,0,872250.story

was shot to death in a robbery at the same building.
This year, at least six people have been slain at city high-rise projects.

Residents at Murphy Homes even marched to City Hall Wednesday to demand better security.

But for housing officials, who say they are trying to come up with ways to battle the rampant crime, it seems to be a losing cause.

"What can we do? When you have police officers pinned down by snipers firing automatic weapons, and it takes a tank to rescue them, what the hell do you do?" said one city housing official, who asked not to be identified. The same official has been dealing with security concerns from Ebony Scott's murder. "This is a massive, massive problem that we cannot control," the official said.

When police made it inside Flag House Courts yesterday, along the 100 block of Albemarle St., the snipers had fled – almost surely to their apartments, police said.

Police said they believe about a half-dozen shots were fired from two of the Flag House Courts buildings, apparently in protest of officers who made a minor drug arrest at 1:30 a.m. on the street below.

An armored vehicle from the Prince George's County Police Department was brought in to help rescue the officers, eight from the city Police Department and two from the city Housing Authority, during a standoff that lasted about five hours.

The vehicle, similar to ones sent to the Persian Gulf war last year, was used "just to insure there was a safe evacuation of those officers," police spokesman Sam Ringgold said.

Bill Toohey, a city Housing Authority spokesman,

acknowledged that crime problems have reached a serious level at the four city-owned high-rises: Flag House in East Baltimore, Murphy Homes and Lexington Terrace in West Baltimore, and Lafayette Courts in East Baltimore.

He said the small Housing Authority police force -- he refused to specify their numbers -- is overwhelmed by the drug-related crime.

A private, unarmed security force was removed last year from the buildings because it had no effect on crime, Mr. Toohey said. In fact, drug dealers often fired at the guards sitting behind bulletproof glass, and from time to time, they punctured the glass, Mr. Toohey said.[22]

Sterilization/birth control of anyone receiving government benefits would seem to be one solution; repatriation another. Instead, those supported by the taxpayer are encouraged to continue the dysgenic policy of having more children (virtually unwanted and uncared biological detritus that guarantees greater lucre per month).

What would Inner Harbor and Baltimore look like today such a policy had been put in place in the early 1990s? Would black youths be terrorizing the Inner Harbor if, one generation ago, a sensible reproductive strategy had been employed to reduce the black birth rate in Baltimore, especially those living off of government handouts?

Instead, the first black mayor of Baltimore awarded a racially-motivated contract to the Nation of Islam to patrol the 'projects.[Muslim Guards To Stop Work In Baltimore, New York Times, 11-10-1995]:

Federal officials have ordered Baltimore to sever its contract with the Nation of Islam Security Agency and award it to another company, Mayor Kurt Schmoke said today.

---

[22] http://articles.baltimoresun.com/1992-08-21/news/1992234096_1_police-department-city-police-snipers

It was not welcome news for the Mayor, who said violent crime had fallen in the last two years at the public housing units, where the security agency has been patrolling.

He said the decision, by the Department of Housing and Urban Development, was motivated by concerns about the security agency's ties to Louis Farrakhan, leader of the Nation of Islam. Mr. Farrakhan, who called the Million Man March on Washington in October, is widely accused of anti-Semitism.

"This is tremendously disappointing to me," Mayor Schmoke said. "We do not do this voluntarily."

A spokesman for the Federal housing agency, Alex Sachs, said the order stemmed from a review showing that the city had arbitrarily rated Nation of Islam Security above Wells Fargo, even though the latter had offered a bid about $1 million lower. He said the decision had not been influenced by political pressure or an investigation into the use of the agency in several cities.[23]

What exactly do individuals realistically believe a future America, devoid of white people, will look like?

In places like Baltimore, the non-white future is today.

Twenty years ago, black snipers pinned down police with a barrage of gunfire merely for arresting a brother on drug charges; today, the economic vitality of the city is at stake because of our leaders' refusal to address the onus of crime in the city on black people.

Instead, every attempt imaginable to placate this population has occurred (the creation of Jazz Festivals),[24] with extra security/police

---

[23] http://www.nytimes.com/1995/11/10/us/muslim-guards-to-stop-work-in-baltimore.html

[24] http://articles.baltimoresun.com/1995-04-18/news/1995108045_1_harborplace-jazz-easter

deployed to ensure black youth are free to drive away commerce and scare away potential tourists during such celebrations as the traditional "Easter" black celebration [Security tightened for Easter events at Inner Harbor Officials seek to prevent rowdiness by teens, Baltimore Sun, 5-5-1996].[25]

Baltimore officials, in their endless efforts to appease the black population, even goes so far as to claim these events didn't happen – before the advent of World Star Hip Hop could confirm what elected officials in the city didn't want you to know [Mayor dismisses reports of downtown rowdiness, Baltimore Sun, 5-18-1995]:

> Rodney A. Orange, president of the Baltimore chapter of the National Association for the Advancement of Colored People, said black teens have complained to him that "they feel stereotyped. They only want to enjoy their evening, wherever they are going, but very often they're looked at suspiciously."[26]

Were the city of Baltimore to have a population that was 63 percent white (instead of 63.6 percent black and 28.2 percent white in 2010), would the ACLU be attacking the police for changing the name of "stop and frisk"? Would white people, living in public housing, have ever utilized sniping techniques to pin down police officers making a routine drug arrest?

Would white teens/youths, engaging in flash mob attacks, turn the Inner Harbor into a no-go zone for tourists?

Would the Nation of Islam ever have been awarded a contract for anything in the city, let alone providing security?

No to all of the above.

---

[25] http://articles.baltimoresun.com/1996-04-05/news/1996096051_1_easter-schmoke-harbor

[26] http://articles.baltimoresun.com/1995-04-18/news/1995108045_1_harborplace-jazz-easter

Baltimore would be a thriving city, able to attract foreign investors and compete with other major cities as a viable metropolis to relocate corporate offices.

But the Kerner Commission Report ensured that 'white racism' would always be the safety valve when discussing black failure/dysfunction/pathology/crime/incompetence.

So, Baltimore will remain one of America's hotbeds for black murder, mayhem and dysfunction – 'white racism' will be to blame, of course.

What Would the Murder Rate in Baltimore be Without the Johns Hopkins Trauma Center Stunting Evolution?

$10. The latest multiple homicide and shooting in Baltimore was over $10 [Pigtown shooting stemmed from dispute over $10, Baltimore Sun, 8-21-13].[27]

Ten dollars.

That's what life is worth in a 64 percent black city (28 percent white), where there have been twenty shootings in an 80-hour time span. [Fatal Pigtown shooting brings city count to 20 in 80 hours: Suspect in custody; two others taken to area hospitals, Baltimore Sun, 8-21-13]:

> An infant child was found next to her dying mother just before dawn Tuesday after police say a man broke into a Pigtown home, killed a young couple and shot two others — a grisly scene that brought to 20 the number of people shot in the city in a span of 80 hours.
>
> Police said they had charged 35-year-old Melville Mason, who they said was caught trying to escape the home. The arrest came as officials sought to address concerns about spiking crime amid a violent summer and a recent outburst of street robberies throughout the city.[28]

Not even the prospect of getting a free laptop in exchange for your

---

[27] http://www.baltimoresun.com/news/maryland/crime/blog/bal-pigtown-shooting-stemmed-from-dispute-over-10-20130821,0,4616385.story

[28] http://www.baltimoresun.com/news/maryland/crime/blog/bs-md-pigtown-shooting-20130820,0,7475756.story#ixzz2cccxZVKG

firearm (a program called "Stop Shooting, Start Coding")[29] could stem the rising tide of black mayhem castigating all the citizens of Baltimore; a city where electronic doors and bulletproof Plexiglas protect store owners from their primarily-black customer base [Liquor store owner kills gunman in W. Baltimore, Baltimore Sun, 12-18-1990].[30]

Black crime (and incredibly high murder rates) in Baltimore was the primary reason law-abiding citizens vacated the city, where immigrant traders erected bunkers to ply their capitalistic ventures in a Mahogany War-Zone [Trade Barriers Community: From behind the protective glass, Korean-American grocers Ki and Sung Yi cast a wary eye on crime in the city., Baltimore Sun, 2-8-1997]:

> In their corner grocery in East Baltimore, Ki Nam Yi and his wife, Sung Cha Yi, measure out their 13-hour days in small sales of soda pop and potato chips, white bread and homemade iced tea, candy and cigarettes.
>
> The first-floor windows of the worn old rowhouse at the corner of Luzerne Avenue and Preston Street are boarded up. The overhead sign still says Green's Grocery; in the early '60s, a couple of guys named Isadore and Ruben Green owned the store, and nobody's bothered to change the sign since. A variety groceries and confectioneries have occupied this corner for at least 50 years.
>
> In their windowless store, the Yis work behind a locked door and Plexiglas shielding that gives the shop the atmosphere of a bunker or a guard post, a checkpoint on some hostile border.
>
> The Yis deal with their customers through rotating Plexiglas windows, like monks withdrawn to a cloistered monastery, getting paid before handing over an order.

---

[29] http://www.baltimorebrew.com/2013/07/14/baltimore-residents-line-up-to-get-laptops-in-exchange-for-guns/

[30] http://articles.baltimoresun.com/1990-12-18/news/1990352117_1_ray-liquor-store-owner-bulletproof

Behind their murky Plexiglas they seem watery and
indistinct as creatures in an aquarium. Beyond the barriers,
their customers seem equally remote and shadowy.[31]

Ladies and gentlemen, welcome to how commerce is done in a black
metropolis -- behind Plexiglas.

Baltimore's murder rate would be much, much higher, were it not for
the incredibly talented trauma surgeons at Johns Hopkins Hospital,
which stands in the way of the evolutionary zeal with which black
people endeavor to voluntarily cull their own population

David Simon's 1991 book, *Homicide: A Year on the Killing Streets*
(which chronicles his following Baltimore homicide detectives for one
year) sees him make a hilarious admission regarding why murder
rates have declined in Baltimore.

Remember, this is the same Baltimore where U.S. Military surgeons
are trained before war-zone deployments, and you'll get the joke
Simon inadvertently tells in *Homicide:*

> But for the rest of the homicide unit, it's business as usual.
> For much of the decade, homicide detectives in Baltimore
> have believed that the law of averages will guarantee
> somewhere between 200 and 250 murders a year, a total that
> shakes out to about two homicides every three days. The
> unit's institutional memory includes a few 300-plus years in
> the early 1970s, but the rate declined abruptly when the
> state's shock-trauma medical system came on line and the
> emergency rooms at Hopkins and University started saving
> some of the bleeders. For the last two years, the body count
> has edged slightly higher, cresting at 226 in 1987, but the
> trend is nothing that makes the act of murder in Baltimore
> seem like anything more than a point on the probability
> curve.
>
> On Friday afternoons, the nightshift detectives can watch

---

[31] http://articles.baltimoresun.com/1997-02-
08/features/1997039092_1_yis-korean-liquor-stores

Kim and Linda, the admin secretaries, stamp case numbers on empty red binders-88041, 88042, 88043-and know with fat, happy confidence that somewhere on the streets of the city, several victims-to-be are stumbling toward oblivion. The veteran detectives will joke about it: Hell, the case numbers are probably tattooed on the backsides of doomed men in ultraviolet ink. If you put one through a postage meter, if you showed him the 88041 stenciled on his right cheek and told him what it meant, the poor fuck would change his name, lock himself in his basement, or jump the first Greyhound to Akron or Oklahoma City or any other spot a thousand miles away. But they never do; the math remains absolute.

Of course, within the confines of the established rate, statistical fluctuation permits the slow weekend due to rain, snow or a pennant race in the American League East. Also permitted is the aberrant full-moon midnight shift, when every other right-thinking Baltimorean reaches for a revolver, or those occasional and unexplained homicidal binges in which the city seems hell-bent on depopulating itself in the briefest time span possible.[32]

"City seems hell-bent on depopulating itself in the briefest time span possible," is a beautiful way to surmise the black-on-black (and black-on-anyone) violence destroying Baltimore.

However, the New York Times would have you believe Malt Liquor is the reason law-abiding citizens are hiring private security[33] to

---

[32] Simon, David. *Homicide: a year on the killing streets.* Boston:

Houghton Mifflin, 1991. p. 431-432

[33] http://www.foxbaltimore.com/news/features/top-stories/stories/baltimore-neighborhoods-look-private-security-21733.shtml#.UhUsz3_EY12

protect themselves from the ravishment of spontaneous blackness [Beers Implicated in Emergency Room Visits, New York Times, 8-19-2013]:

> The study, carried out over the course of a year at the Johns Hopkins Hospital in Baltimore, found that five beer brands were consumed most often by people who ended up in the emergency room. They were Budweiser, Steel Reserve, Colt 45, Bud Ice and Bud Light.
>
> Three of the brands are malt liquors, which typically contain more alcohol than regular beer. Four malt liquors accounted for nearly half of the beer consumption by emergency room patients, even though they account for less than 3 percent of beer consumption in the general population.
>
> Previous studies have found that alcohol frequently plays a role in emergency room admissions, especially those stemming from car accidents, falls, homicides, and drownings, said the lead author of the study, David H. Jernigan of the Johns Hopkins Bloomberg School of Public Health. The new study, published in the journal Substance Use and Misuse, is the first to look at whether certain brands or types of liquor are overrepresented.
>
> Dr. Jernigan said that the breakdown of liquor consumption in the study may be particular to Baltimore, and that he and his colleagues are hoping to study other cities as well. The findings could have policy implications, potentially influencing labeling requirements and marketing for higher-alcohol beers, Dr. Jernigan said.[34]

Dr. Jernigan, the reason liquor stores in Baltimore are protected by Plexiglas windows is so customers can't kill employees over a $10 bottle of vodka or a $10 12-pack of malt liquor.

---

[34] http://well.blogs.nytimes.com/2013/08/19/beers-implicated-in-emergency-room-visits/?ref=health?src=dayp&_r=2

You keep talking about American Exceptionalism, please.

Please.

And Baltimore will continue to die, courtesy of blacks willing to kill one another over ten bucks.

David Simon's "Homicide: A Year on the Killing Streets": The Book That Explains why 2013 Baltimore is on the Verge of Death

The city of Baltimore (out of nearly 620,000 people, the city is 63 percent black) will spend $22 million to tear down 1,500 blighted houses, the visible, tangible reminder that Mother Nature has a sense of humor.
[City to raze hundreds of vacant houses in stepped-up plan: Vacants to Value programs gets an infusion of cash, Baltimore Sun, 8-17-13].

> Boarded-up and falling down, hundreds of Baltimore's vacant and blighted rowhouses are scheduled for demolition in coming months in a stepped-up effort to rid the city of its most visible sign of decades of urban decay.
>
> Over the next 2 1/2 years, the city is budgeted to spend nearly $22 million to tear down 1,500 abandoned houses — a move urban planners say could transform Baltimore visually and clear a path for struggling neighborhoods to attract future development. Previously, the city had been spending about $2.5 million a year on demolition.[35]

---

[35] http://www.baltimoresun.com/news/maryland/baltimore-city/bs-md-ci-vacants-demolition-20130816,0,5409448.story#ixzz2cGP3Aj8d

Those houses were once occupied (and built) by a people representing a far different civilization than the one that now finds itself the demographic Hegemon in Baltimore -- the vacant and blighted rowhouses, "visible sign of decades of urban decay," are the visual manifestation of the immutable laws of race.

It's a fact David Simon, the creator of HBO's *The Wire*, would gladly throw a brick at (as he suggested 'people of color' do to the Sanford Court House after the George Zimmerman verdict), though the immutable laws of race would only laugh at such missile lobbed from one of America's great white apologists for black crime/dysfunction/misery.[36]

Simon's best known for *The Wire*, but he emerged on the map with his 1991 book *Homicide: A Year on the Killing Streets,* which is an account of shadowing the detectives on the Baltimore police force for one year.

It is in this book the chaos of Black Run America (BRA) emerges, with Simon inadvertently documenting in vivid detail why the level of blight in the city is so severe, it justifies the $22 million price tag to tear it down.

So, instead of reading the nearly-600-page book, here's the SBPDL Racial Notes of Simon's
Homicide: A Year on the Killing Streets. A melancholy picture of life in post-white, majority black Baltimore should quickly emerge, helping explain why so much of the city has blight (because so little of the city is now white).

What happens when a major metropolitan city (whose infrastructure, institutions, and laws were birthed by whites) undergoes white flight, resulting in black control of city hall, the court system, the police,

---

[36] http://tv.yahoo.com/blogs/tv-news/-the-wire--creator-david-simon-on-trayvon-martin-case---ashamed--to-be-an-american-011408813.html

and the political direction of the municipality?

What happens to those whites who stayed behind?

Simon's book delineates this:

> Commanding the homicide unit's two shifts of eighteen detectives and detective sergeants are a pair of long-suffering lieutenants who answer to the captain in charge of the Crimes Against Persons section. The captain, who wishes to retire with a major's pension, does not want his name associated with anything that gives pain to the colonel in charge of the Criminal Investigation Division. That is not just because the colonel is well liked, intelligent, and black, and stands a good chance of getting kicked upstairs to a deputy commissioner's post or higher in a city with a new black mayor and a majority black population that has little faith in, or regard for, its police department.[37]

> As a supervisor, Gary D'Addario is generally regarded by his sergeants and detectives as a prince, a benevolent autocrat who asks only competence and loyalty. In return, he provides his shift with unstinting support and sanctuary from the worst whims and fancies of the command staff. A tall man with thinning tufts of silver-gray hair and a quietly dignified manner, D'Addario is one of the last survivors of the Italian caliphate that briefly ruled the department after a long Irish dynasty. It was a respite that began with Frank Battaglia's ascension to the commissioner's post and continued until membership in the Sons of Italy was as much a prerequisite for elevation as the sergeant's test. But the Holy Roman Empire lasted less than four years; in 1985, the mayor

---

[37] Simon, David. *Homicide: a year on the killing streets.* Boston:

Houghton Mifflin, 1991. p. 18

acknowledged the city's changing demographics by dragging Battaglia into a well-paid consultant's position and giving the black community a firm lock on the upper tiers of the police department.[38]

But times had changed. A quarter century ago, an American law officer could fire his weapon without worrying whether the entrance wound would be anterior or posterior. Now, the officer faces the risk of civil liability and possible criminal prosecution increases every time he unholsters a weapon; what could once be justified by an earlier generation of patrolmen is now enough to get the next generation indicted. In Baltimore, as in every American city, the rules have changed because the streets have changed, because the police department isn't what it used to be. Nor, for that matter, is the city itself.

In 1962, when Donald Worden came out of the academy, the code was understood by the players on both sides. Break bad on a police, and there was a good chance that the cop would use his gun and use it with impunity. The code was especially clear in the case of anyone foolish enough to shoot at police. Such a suspect had one chance and one chance only. If he could get to a police district, he would live. He would be beaten, but he would live. If he tried to run and was found on the street in circumstances that could be made to look good on paper, he would not.

But that was a different era, a time when a Baltimore cop could say, with conviction, that he was a member of the biggest, toughest, best-armed gang on the block. Those were the days before the heroin and cocaine trade became the predominant economy of the ghetto, before every other seventeen-year-old corner boy could be a walking sociopath with a 9mm in the waistband of his sweats, before the department began conceding to the drug trade whole tracts of

[38] Ibid. p. 37-38

the inner city. Those were also the days when Baltimore was still a segregated city, when the civil rights movement was little more than an angry whisper.[39]

For the public, and the black community in particular, the shooting of Ja-Wan McGee became a long-awaited victory over a police department that had for generations devalued black life. It was, in that sense, the inevitable consequence of too much evil justified for too long. It made no difference that Scotty McCown was neither incompetent nor racist; in Baltimore, as in other police departments nationwide, the sons would be made to pay for their fathers' crimes.

For cops on the street, white and black, the McGee shooting became proof positive that they were now alone, that the system could no longer protect them. To preserve its authority, the department would be required to destroy not only those men who used and believed in brutality, but also those who chose wrongly when confronted with a sudden, terrifying decision. If the shooting was good, you were covered, though even the most justified use of force could no longer occur in Baltimore without someone, somewhere, getting in front of a television camera to say that police murdered the man. And if the shooting was borderline, you were probably still covered, provided you knew how to write the report. But if the shooting was bad, you were expendable.[40]

As with every other part of the criminal justice machine, racial issues permeate the jury system in Baltimore. Given that the vast majority of urban violence is black-on-black crime, and given that the pool of possible jurors is 60 to 70 percent black, Baltimore prosecutors take almost every case

---

[39] Ibid. p. 104

[40] Ibid. p. 109

into court with the knowledge that the crime will be seen through the lens of the black community's historical suspicion of a white-controlled police department and court system. The testimony of a black officer or detective is therefore considered necessary in many cases, a counterweight to the young defendant who, following his attorney's advice, is wearing his Sunday best and carrying the family Bible to and from court. That the victims are also black matters less; after all, they're not around to set such a good example in front of the jurors.

The effect of race on the judicial system is freely acknowledged by prosecutors and defense attorneys- black and white alike-although the issue is rarely raised directly in court. The better lawyers, whatever their color, refuse to manipulate jurors through racial distinctions; the others can do so with even the most indirect suggestions. Race is instead a tacit presence that accompanies almost every panel of twelve into a Baltimore jury room. Once, in a rare display, a black defense attorney actually pointed to her own forearm while giving closing arguments to an all-black panel: "Brothers and sisters," she said, as two white detectives went out of their minds in the back row of the gallery, "I think we all know what this case is about." (p.455)

Even the best white cop feels the distance when he works with black victims and black suspects; to him they are otherworldly, as if their tragedy is the result of a ghetto pathology against which he is fully immunized. Working in a city where nearly 90 percent of all murder is black-on-black, a white detective might understand the nature of a black victim's tragedy. He might carefully differentiate between good people to be avenged and bad people to be pursued. But, ultimately, he never responds with the same intensity; his most innocent victims bring empathy, not anguish; his most ruthless suspects bring contempt, not rage.[41]

---

[41] Ibid. p. 506

The city of Baltimore (out of nearly 620,000 people, the city is 63 percent black) will spend $22 million to tear down 1,500 blighted houses, the visible, tangible reminder that Mother Nature has a sense of humor.

The portions of David Simon's book, excerpted above, should explain why the city is dying.

Desperate Measures -- Black Violence in Baltimore Requires "Police Surge" to Protect Citizens over July Fourth Holiday

Before Kurt Schmoke's election as Baltimore's first black mayor, an editorial in the Baltimore Afro-American painted a bright picture of the prospect of black political control of Baltimore. Concluding that control of the 'political levers' would have a decisive effect upon the quality of life in the black community, the Afro called upon the black community to elect "highly able, qualified, and esteemed blacks" to positions of authority and power. Electing such people, the Afro continued, would pay great dividends in "black pride, self-respect, and motivation."[42]

---

[42] McDougall, Harold A.. *Black Baltimore: a new theory of*

So wrote Harold McDougall in the book *Black Baltimore: A New Theory of Community*,

After decades of black political rule, the city of Baltimore is on the verge of financial Armageddon. Those political levers of power were granted to black individuals who treated the government like a retiree treats a slot machine lever in Las Vegas after they've won a big jackpot.[43]

The election of blacks has had virtually no effect on black self-respect, though black pride (perhaps stubbornness?) continues to haunt a city that was once considered among America's greatest achievements.

Now, the city is busy covering up black crime in the Inner Harbor,[44] and any attempt to address the problem is quickly denounced, treated as a more serious offense than the black mobs attacking tourists and driving away business. An increase in security is the only "solution" the black leaders have proposed thus far (logically, an outright banning of blacks from the Inner Harbor would solve the problem).

With July 4 approaching (what, exactly, are we American's celebrating again? Freedom, that which directly resulted in the ruinous state of our major cities?), the violence of the black community in Baltimore is reaching levels not seen in years... perhaps since the crack epidemics of the 1980s.

---

community. Philadelphia: Temple University Press, 1993.

p.91

[43] http://www.foxnews.com/politics/2013/02/06/city-baltimore-is-on-path-to-financial-ruin-report-says/?intcmp=trending

[44] http://www.baltimoresun.com/news/maryland/sun-investigates/bs-md-ci-violence-downtown-police-20120420,0,6678578.story

Twenty-nine shot, 10 dead in a span of six days.[45] Welcome to life in a city driven by black political power.[Baltimore police promise 'dramatic increase' in presence through July 4: Weeklong spike in shootings, homicides spurs law enforcement partnerships, Baltimore Sun, June 28, 2013]:

> Residents can expect to see a "dramatic" law enforcement increase this weekend and through the July Fourth holiday, as city and police officials search for ways to tamp down a spree of deadly violence.
>
> Police officials vowed to deploy up to three times the number of officers typically on the streets over the weekend, with the city's patrol forces being joined by officers from the Maryland State Police, the Maryland Transportation Authority and the Baltimore City sheriff's office.
>
> In another show of police force, authorities made the rare move Friday of closing off a city block on Bennett Place with metal fences, allowing only residents from the block to enter after a third person was shot and killed in the area since February.
>
> A total of 35 people have been shot in the city since June 21.
>
> "We are increasing our deployments throughout all of the hot spots over the course of the week," said Sgt. Eric Kowalczyk, a Baltimore police spokesman.
>
> But some questioned the so-called saturation patrols. The increased presence comes at a time when the Police Department is on track to exceed its overtime budget for the fiscal year, which comes to a close after this weekend. The department also exceeded its budget last year.
>
> Fraternal Order of Police President Robert F. Cherry Jr. said

---

[45] http://www.baltimoresun.com/entertainment/tv/z-on-tv-blog/bal-baltimore-bloody-summer-shootings-tv-coverage-20130628,0,3772338.story

the saturation plan is not sustainable, while City Councilman James Kraft questioned whether it would sap resources from some neighborhoods to flood troubled ones.

Police Commissioner Anthony W. Batts attributed the crime spike on Friday to warring gangs, retaliatory shootings and club violence. He also said conflicts at the city jail — in the spotlight for a scandal involving corrections officers allegedly working with gang members — may be playing out in city neighborhoods.

"There are some issues that are taking place inside the jail facility that are spilling out to the streets," he said in an interview with Baltimore Sun columnist Dan Rodricks on WYPR-FM. "We believe there's a connection at the jail that's spilling out on the street. But I don't want to get too much more into that."

Batts also questioned the effectiveness of the court system as a deterrent.

"Our criminals on the streets are more willing to take a charge on murder because they think they can get off with our juries," he said.

The violence continued to play out as the weekend neared.

Just after 9 p.m. Thursday, between 50 and 100 residents on Elmora Avenue in the Four by Four neighborhood of Northeast Baltimore milled around outdoors in small cliques and circles, arguing among themselves in what police would later describe as a "community altercation."

Suddenly, police said, bullets were fired into the crowd, and three women were injured. One, 21-year-old Gennie Shird of Pen Lucy, was pronounced dead before 10 p.m.[46]

---

[46] http://www.baltimoresun.com/news/maryland/crime/blog/bs-md-ci-death-toll-20130628,0,4686445.story#ixzz2XcnP8BSr

In 2012, 94 percent of murder victims in Baltimore were black (217 murders, with a clearance rate of 47 percent); 79 percent of known suspects had a criminal record, with 82 percent of the victims also having a criminal record.[47]

An internecine war among the underclass black population is dragging the entire city to a layer of hell not even Dante could have endured.

The Baltimore Sun publishes an interactive map that shows the race of murder victims (and where they were murdered) going back to 2007. Go ahead and look at the reality of crime in the city of Baltimore.[48]

Calling the black violence 'gang-related' is a disservice to the intensity (and random) nature of black violence in the city:

> Maria Whiting's Northeast Baltimore home is immaculate. The dining room table is set with gold chargers beneath each plate and matching gold napkins at each setting. The white couches, covered in artfully arranged throw pillows, are so fluffy and pristine it seems impossible that anyone has ever sat on them. Whiting herself is equally put together and looks far younger than her 50 years. It's hard to believe that this friendly, soft-spoken woman has seen so much tragedy.
>
> In 1995 her eldest son, Valgene Donte Alston, was heading home after playing basketball when a man with a gun mistook him for someone he had fought with earlier that day.

---

[47] http://articles.baltimoresun.com/2013-01-01/news/bal-demographics-of-2012-baltimore-homicides-20121231_1_drug-arrests-baltimore-homicides-gun-crimes

[48] http://data.baltimoresun.com/bing-maps/homicides/?range=none&district=all&zipcode=all&age=all&gender=all&race=all&cause=all&article=all&show_results=Show+Results

According to Whiting, the man stood over her son, a good kid who had never been in trouble, and shot him twice in the head. "When he walked away one of the guys said, `Oh, I shot the wrong black nigger,'" Whiting says. Donte was 22.[49]

A case of mistaken identity -- perhaps all blacks look alike to black people?

The reason Baltimore is dying is simple -- it's black population (the city was 81 percent white in 1950, with the black population - courtesy of Manifest Destruction - rising from 142,000 in 1930 to 326,000 in 1960) successfully drove out whites through the 1960s, '70s, '80s, '90s, and well into the 2000s, because the fear of what happened to Valgene Alston wasn't something white people wanted to deal with on a regular basis.

So how did that whole "black-political-power-translates-into-self-respect-and-black-pride" idea turn out? Just look at the body count black people racked up in 2007:

A Breakdown Of Baltimore City's 2007 Homicide Statistics

Total number of victims: 282

Victims by Race:

African-American: 261

Asian: 1

Caucasian: 14

Hispanic: 4

Other: 2

Percentage of victims who were African-American: 92.6 percent

---

[49] http://www2.citypaper.com/news/story.asp?id=15142

Percentage of the city's population who are African-American:
64.8 percent

Per capita homicide rate: 44 per 100,000

Per capita homicide rate for African-American men in their
20s: 460 per 100,000[50]

And it's not just Baltimore that black people are directly
transforming into just another version of Port-au-Prince, Haiti,
within the city limits of a once-thriving American city.

Milwaukee, Chicago, Indianapolis, and St. Louis are all black war
zones (courtesy of the so-called "Great Migration"); the dwindling,
terrified white population left behind are saddled with declining
property values and the prospect of a Detroit 2013 scenario hanging
over their heads like a guillotine.

What are *you* celebrating this July 4th?

Seriously?

---

[50] http://www2.citypaper.com/news/story.asp?id=15147

Paul Kersey

"Now the shoe is on the other foot. See how you like it." How a 1991 Quote About Rising Black Political Power in Baltimore Predicted the Future Demise of the City

There's no romanticism here.

None of that "if only they'd leave the liberal plantation" mentality.

Runaway slave?

Good, keep running.

Don't stop.

Baltimore Homicides by Race (2007 – 2013*)

	2007	2008	2009	2010	2011	2012	2013
Homicides	282	234	240	224	197	217	117
White	14	8	19	13	5	11	7
Black	252	114	203	203	183	203	109
Hispanic	2	1	8	5	6	2	0
Asian	0	0	1	1	2	1	0
Unknown	14	111	9	2	1	0	1

(Source: Baltimore Sun – Homicide Victim Map. * - 2013 data is through July 1)

From the Baltimore Sun's interactive homicide map, a breakdown of victims by race. Suspects in Baltimore homicide are, axiomatically, black (not all the time, but most).

The above mindset is an attempt to absolve black individuals from their actions and self-created dysfunction, as if some imaginary, racist form of 'the force' from *Star Wars* keeps them from displaying some form of impulse control or future time-orientation thinking.

You see, it's clearly understood the mindset of former black Baltimore Mayor Sheila Dixon is the predominant view of black people across the nation when it comes to what 'democracy' means: racial democracy. [Council tries to mend fences on changing boundaries Recalling the night that Sheila Dixon let the shoe drop, Baltimore Sun, March 21, 1991]:

> When time mercifully causes all else to fade from memory about the great racial debate of 1991, the vision of a shoeless Sheila Dixon will unfortunately remain.
> While the city councilwoman from West Baltimore did not literally put her foot in her mouth the other night, she did remove her shoe and wave it in the faces of her white colleagues and declare:
>
> *"You've been running things for the last 20 years. Now the shoe is on the other foot. See how you like it."*
>
> In so doing, Dixon performed that rare feat of saying exactly the right thing in exactly the wrong manner -- and thus pointed out the festering sore that race relations still remain, years after many imagined it would heal itself through hard work and good will and diplomacy.
>
> Dixon, who is black, spoke bluntly of an undeniable truth: As the city of Baltimore has shifted over the past 25 years from majority white to majority black, its political representation has unfairly stayed majority white.[51]

---

[51] http://articles.baltimoresun.com/1991-03-

It's been 22 years since Dixon took her shoe off and said in racially explicit terms, "*Now the shoe is on the other foot. See how you like it.*"

The shoe has been on the black foot for more than a score in Baltimore; remove the shoe, and the stench of a failed, third-world state is overpowering.

Acrid.

Gun crime in Baltimore is almost exclusively black, with a smattering of white homicide victims thrown in for good measure.[52] The late Lawrence Auster dubbed it "Black Baltimore's Youth Intifada," but such a title fails to take into consideration that the internecine black-on-black (and tragic black-on-white) crime in the city has helped make Baltimore one of America's least desirable places to live.

This exponential rise in black violent crime occurred, oddly enough, during the time of black political power, as Sheila Dixon pointed out, back in 1991 when she did her black-power impression of Khrushchev banging a shoe.

In a sane world, no government would tax its most productive citizens to provide welfare, EBT/Food Stamps, Section 8 Housing vouchers, etc., to ensure the proliferation of its *least* productive, most violent citizens (it would do everything humanely possible to decrease the number of its least productive members, and everything possible to increase the number of productive citizens).

Such is the case in Baltimore, where the least productive demographic group has all but driven out the most productive population (and its tax dollars) from the city. In the process, black

---

21/news/1991080063_1_sheila-dixon-northeast-baltimore-white-council

[52] http://www.amnation.com/vfr/archives/012129.html

politicians like Dixon have been elected to represent the remaining black underclass.

An underclass where yet another aspiring black rapper has become just another statistic, another homicide victim to add to the growing tally for the year. [Teen killed in weekend city shooting was an aspiring rapper: Baltimore police investigating incident that hit seven people, Baltimore Sun, 8-27-13]:

> Fifteen-year-old Deshaun Jones had spent much of the summer hanging out in the neighborhood where he died last weekend, gunned down as he sat on a porch just before his first day at Frederick Douglass High School.
>
> The teen was among seven people shot in a single incident Saturday in Franklin Square. On Monday, when he was to have begun his freshman year, red, white and blue balloons were left at the shooting scene, along with a stuffed toy animal. The other victims — all adults — are expected to survive.
>
> Jones was an aspiring rapper who went by the name Lor D'Shaun. "His biggest dream was to make it. To move out of this 'hood," said his mother, Shanika Harris.
>
> In one song, he says, "At a young age you turn into a man out here/Cuz these n----s on the street don't play out here."
>
> In another track, he sounds a combative message. He waves around a gun in a video called "Bodie 'Em" and taunts his rivals. "Run up on them with that Ruger/they don't even know who did it/hit the target, hit the witness/I ain't trying see the prisons."
>
> Harris said her son had never been violent, but he wrote about a subject that hit close to home.
>
> "It was like re-enacting life, what he saw in the neighborhood," she said of her son's lyrics.
>
> The shooting was the latest in what Commissioner Anthony

W. Batts has called "cluster" shootings, where multiple victims are left injured. In an interview with WJZ-TV on Monday, Mayor Stephanie Rawlings-Blake called the culprit in Saturday's shooting an "idiot coward."

Police have not announced any arrests in the incident.

Police said there have been 287 nonfatal shootings this year, up from 237 at this time last year — a 21 percent increase. So far, 150 homicides have been reported, which is 10 more than at this time last year and a 7 percent increase.

Batts has said hundreds of officers were deployed in the neighborhood where the shooting took place Saturday night, though many of them were dealing with a nearby block party at the time.

The gunfire broke out after a conflict over a dice game, police said.[53]

Another rapper, dead.

Sure Ms. Shanika Harris, your son was never violent (forget the video proof of his violent tendencies; he was just a thespian portraying Lor D'Shaun...).

What's most striking in the above *Baltimore Sun* article is the admission by Baltimore Police Chief Batts that "hundreds of officers were deployed in the neighborhood" where Jones was gunned down.

There's an ongoing evolutionary war in Baltimore between black individuals and their genetics, which unfortunately aren't compatible with the laws governing public behavior established by those dead white males who created our civilization.

Take a look at this breakdown of violence in London, England (and

---

[53] http://www.baltimoresun.com/news/breaking/bs-md-ci-deshaun-jones-follow-20130826,0,5754627.story#ixzz2dCnS5EN4

the monetary resources/officers necessary to investigate it) versus that of Baltimore. [London and Gun Crime, Baltimore Sun, November 27, 2009]:

> The Sun's Justin Fenton, having recently returned from our reporter exchange in London, brings us a story today about a murder investigation and a special squad of British cops called Trident. What strikes me is that they've got 40 cops assigned to one killing.
>
> The Trident unit has 300 officers and a $44 million budget. Baltimore cops have about 70 homicide detectives investigating murder; the homicide unit has a budget of $5.3 million (the Criminal Investigation Division's budget is $38 million).
>
> London, a city of about 7.5 million, has had 110 homicides this year, 17 of which involved guns. Baltimore, a city of about 640,000 has had 208 slayings so far this year, most with guns.
>
> It's impressive that London puts so many resources into homicide, and this unit specifically targets black-on-black gun murders in London's ethnic neighborhoods, where police, as in Baltimore, complain that distrust of law enforcement hampers their ability to solve crime.[54]

We know from reading David Simon's *Homicide* that the black population of Baltimore views the police as some sort of occupying force, protectors of some draconian sense of law and order that isn't shared by the majority demographic group in the city.

Yet Baltimore boasts nearly *twice* the number of murders than London, a city more than an order of magnitude bigger (population-wise) than Baltimore! No allocation of monetary resources or extra

---

[54]

http://weblogs.baltimoresun.com/news/crime/blog/2009/11/london_and _gun_crime.html police units on patrol in violent-crime hotspots will deter Baltimore's criminal underclass from wreaking havoc and misery on the city. The only real way to stop the violence in Baltimore is to reduce the black population.

The Baltimore Sun provides an interactive homicide map (going back to 2007), allowing the end-user to plot homicides in the city by location, day, month, year, and, most importantly, by racial group as well.

SBPDL broke out the data for you (pictured above), but it showcases a fact no plantation could hide: even the ascension of black political power - the shoe on the other foot, if you will - hasn't stopped black individuals from collectively engaging in chaotic, anarchic behavior that threatens the stability of the entire city of Baltimore.

"Now the shoe is on the other foot. see how you like it."

Don't romanticize black people.

Baltimore is what happens when runaway slaves congregate together, a reminder that when the 'shoe' of political authority is on a black foot, instinctively it goes directly on stomping whites down ("If you want a vision of the future, imagine a boot stamping on a white face - forever").

Permanently.

This 'victory' over apartheid, white supremacy, racism, Jim Crow, or white privilege is short-lived, with the advances made by the former white population immediately wiped out by the combined efforts of black elected officials and those blacks who elect them.

It's a city where blacks have organized an exclusively, blacks-only, police union (Vanguard Justice Society) and a blacks-only fire union to promote the collective interests of only black firefighters (Vulcan Blazers). Perhaps Walter Williams can do us justice [Racial Hoaxes and the NAACP, Creators.com, 12-12-2007]:

Last May, firefighters at a Baltimore, Md., fire station came under scrutiny for displaying a deer with an afro wig, gold tooth, gold chain and a cigarette hanging from its mouth.

Marvin "Doc" Cheatham, president of the Baltimore chapter of the NAACP, went ballistic, charging, "There is now and has been a culture of racism and white supremacy within the Baltimore City Fire Department."

As it turns out, it was a black fireman who dressed up the critter. Cheatham refused to apologize for his accusations of fire department racism, maintaining "there is now and has been a culture of racism and white supremacy within the Baltimore City Fire Department."

On Nov. 21, a hangman's noose was found at the fire station with a note, "We can't hang the cheaters, but we can hang the failures. No EMT-1, NO JOB." The noose and note turned up on the heels of an investigation into allegations of cheating on the test that emergency medical technicians must take for certification.

Baltimore Mayor Sheila Dixon, a black, in a written statement said, "I am outraged by this deplorable act of hatred and intimidation. Threats and racial attacks are unacceptable anywhere, especially in a firehouse." Doc Cheatham said, "We're going to demand that this be handled as a hate crime. This thing really needs to end here in Baltimore city." The incident prompted a federal investigation.

Last week, Donald Maynard, a black firefighter-paramedic, confessed to having placed the noose, note and drawing depicting a lynching on a bunk in the firehouse.

City officials said Maynard was recently suspended, prior to his confession, from the department Friday for failing to meet requirements for advanced life-saving training. A spokesman for Mayor Dixon said there would be no criminal charges filed.

In response to Maynard's confession, NAACP President Cheatham still blamed white racism, saying, "It really saddens us to hear that evidently things have reached a stage that even an African-American does an injustice to himself and his own people as a result of a negative culture in that department."[55]

The promotion of black power via politics (as state policy) is the equivalent of an electromagnetic pulse being detonated over the city/state/nation where this idea is loudly, proudly, and vividly expressed -- after all, the major airport in Baltimore is named after the first black Supreme Court Justice, Thurgood Marshall, who famously declared about racial discrimination, "You guys have been practicing discrimination for years, now it's our turn."

Funny: when whites advance white power/supremacy as a policy of the state, we made it all the way to the moon. Yet the abrupt repudiation of such arguably successful policy and, in its place, the implementation of black power/supremacy in cities like Baltimore and Detroit brought about scenarios no horror/science-fiction writer could ever hope to replicate.

Chang-rae Lee _On Such a Full Sea_ is a look at the future of Baltimore.

It's dystopian fiction by a Korean immigrant to America, documenting a future unburdened by the chaos caused by white privilege; it's a society that has completely collapsed.

Chang-rae Lee is attempting to take a stab at a less-than-utopian view of post-white America, set in a city overflowing with shouts of black pride and black power... Baltimore. [A novelist's view of a future dystopian "B-mor": How Chang-rae Lee imagines America hundreds of years from now — kind of like the Baltimore of today,

---

[55] http://www.creators.com/opinion/walter-williams/racial-hoaxes-and-the-naacp.html

Baltimore's vacant rowhouses have spawned lawsuits,
catchily-named mayoral initiatives, slumlord-shaming
projects (that have landed their arch perpetrator in court and,
most recently, in *The Wall Street Journal*) and, for the people
who live near them, a day-to-day headache in the form of
trash, rats and crime.

Now they have inspired a sprawling dystopian novel that is
the literary darling of the new year: *On Such a Full Sea* by
Chang-rae Lee.

Lee has said he got the idea while riding on Amtrak trains
between D.C. and New York and seeing the bombed-out-
looking landscape of East Baltimore.

In his book set hundreds of years in the future, the U.S.
government has collapsed, the population dispersed, and
immigrant workers largely from China have come to labor in
the former Baltimore, now named B-mor.

The kind of deserted areas Lee saw through the train window
are re-purposed here for the production of fish and organic
vegetables for the spoiled and indifferent elites called
"Charters."

In Lee's 352-page epic, the continent once known as China
has been rendered unlivable by pollution. In B-mor, along
with these onetime Chinese villagers and their snooty
Charter overlords, are the wild and banished dwellers in the
"Outer Counties."

Upending our current class landscape, the book casts places
like present-day Harford County and chi-chi Columbia as the
territory of hard-scrabble bands of outlaws.

Lee, a frequent train rider apparently, hit upon the idea in a
kind of epiphany one day looking down out of the window at
"the same ghetto neighborhood of East Baltimore" he'd passed
over for the last 35 years, he said in a Q&A with *NPR*'s

Rachel Martin:

And separately I thought, you know, it's just a pity that this neighborhood has been abandoned and rehabitated and abandoned again, serially over all these years, and I thought, why can't just some — I don't know — village from China settle this place, and I was just idly thinking that, and I thought, oh gee, well what would happen if such a thing happened? What a crazy, crazy idea!

The book doesn't seem to have too much literal connection to the Baltimore of 2014, other than the general post-apocalyptic look of our 16,000-plus vacant houses.

There are African-American characters (the heroine is Chinese and her boyfriend is black), and it makes some references to our current streetscape:

But hold on, you might say. On our street, once called North Milton Avenue and renamed Longevity Way by our predecessors, who saw the nearly three-kilometer run of ruler-straight road and couldn't help but think of wondrously extended, if not eternal, life, the main infractions are spitting or littering or publicly relieving oneself, most always perpetrated by the very old and very young and those who overindulge on nights before their free-day.

Through a Train Window

Lee is not the first creative to cruise through Baltimore on Amtrak's Northeast Corridor and come up with a good idea.

Singer-songwriter Randy Newman said he got the idea for his song "Baltimore," from the same train-rider's-view of East Baltimore, obviously just as depressing and vacant-looking in the 1970s as it is today judging by his dirge-like lyrics.

Hooker on the corner Waitin' for a train Drunk lyin' on the sidewalk Sleepin' in the rain
And they hide their faces And they hide their eyes 'Cause the city's dyin' And they don't know why

'Cause the city's dyin'; And they don't know why.. [56].

Oh, we know why Baltimore died.

Four letters, that when combined, elicit a predetermined, visceral response: R-A-C-E.

The shoe's on the black foot, yet no dares point out it was the foot that squashed the civilization of Baltimore.

The Last Days of Disco

Cancelled leave. All police officers were on duty.

Every single one of them.

Ladies and gentlemen, *this* is how you achieve a peaceful Independence Day celebration in Baltimore.

By saturating the entire city with every police officer available, Baltimore officials attempted to demonstrate that the state still maintains the monopoly on violence in a metropolis overrun with black criminality [Baltimore Fourth of July to feature heavy police presence: All officers ordered to report, state law enforcement agencies coming in, Baltimore Sun, July 4, 2013]:

> Baltimore police ordered every officer to work July 4 and will rely heavily on reinforcements from state law enforcement agencies, an effort intended to keep Inner Harbor visitors safe while maintaining a strong presence in areas besieged by

---

[56] http://www.baltimorebrew.com/2014/01/07/a-novelists-view-of-a-future-dystopian-b-mor/

recent violence.

The city has traditionally packed downtown with officers for Independence Day celebrations like the one planned for Thursday. But this year police are also stepping up their presence in neighborhoods across the city that have been rocked by more than 40 shootings and 16 homicides since June 21.

"The Inner Harbor is going to be safe on the Fourth of July," Lt. Col. Darryl DeSousa declared at a news conference.

DeSousa promised an "overflood" of officers downtown and said that all police districts would be at full strength, because the department has canceled leave for the holiday.

A visible army of city and state police, city sheriff's deputies and Maryland Transportation Authority Police officers will be posted downtown as about 200,000 people fill the Inner Harbor at dusk to watch fireworks burst over the water.

Revelers will see police on foot and on horseback, patrolling in cars and peering from helicopters. Undercover officers will mix with the throngs while investigators monitor multiple angles from overhead CitiWatch cameras and "surveillance" stages.

The Inner Harbor celebration runs from 4 p.m. to 10 p.m. The fireworks display is scheduled for 9:30 p.m.

While city police have been grappling with a persistent deficit of officers due to retirements, defections and suspensions, Mayor Stephanie Rawlings-Blake has made it clear to Police Commissioner Anthony W. Batts that he has her "full support," mayoral spokesman Ryan O'Doherty said.

O'Doherty said police would have technological resources needed "to target repeat violent offenders, gangs, and illegal guns while keeping our streets — including downtown — safe." He noted that the CitiWatch camera network, which the mayor has expanded, acts as a "force multiplier" that helps officers with more eyes on the street.

As the city seeks to balance the needs of well-off enclaves with those of troubled neighborhoods, community leaders said the holiday represents one of the biggest tactical challenges Batts has faced since being hired last fall.

"This may be the real first test of whether downtown and uptown Baltimore is covered as well as all areas," said former Baltimore NAACP president Dr. Marvin L. "Doc" Cheatham Sr.[57]

But why would 'all areas' need to covered Mr. Former Baltimore NAACP president? Haven't colored people advanced the city of Baltimore to a point where police are unnecessary, a superfluous reminder of the discriminatory past?

No.

Every officer had to be called to work on July 4, 2013 in Baltimore (imagine the overtime/holiday pay), because the threat of black violence was that great.

Meanwhile, the slow death of a great American city was accelerated on Independence Day 2013. [Teen fatally shot in crowd after Downtown fireworks; faith leader calls incident 'frightening, unsettling', Indy Star, July 5, 2013]:

> The shooting death of a 16-year-old after Thursday's Downtown fireworks has raised concern this morning among community leaders.
>
> "It's frightening and unsettling in that something like that could occur in the context of what has been a safe activity," said the Rev. Charles Ellis, pastor at 25th Street Baptist Church and interim director of the Indianapolis Ten Point

---

[57] http://www.baltimoresun.com/news/maryland/crime/blog/bs-md-ci-july-4-safety-20130702,0,7622786.story#ixzz2YBF8idmv

Coalition, a local outreach group trying to quell violence.

"The reality is until some of the really root problems are addressed," Ellis said, "violence can continue to happen."

According to Ellis, those issues include the state's gun laws and the city's rates of poverty and education.

Ellis said in these cases, the coalition is usually called to talk with family members or others involved and ease tensions in the community.

"We typically begin to find the person's connections and try to stem the tide of retaliation," he said.

While the shooting death was the first seen in Indianapolis this July, it follows a month where 16 people were killed -- and comes a week before thousands begin arriving Downtown for Indiana Black Expo's Summer Celebration.

IMPD Police Chief Rick Hite said this morning that police had no suspects and were investigating if the victim was targeted.

"It could have been a number of things," Hite said. "It could have been a shot at distance. It could have been random shots."[58]

Is there anything in life more feckless than a black 'community leader' or black 'faith leader' attempting to be a shepherd to their unruly, uncontrollable flock?

You could cancel leave for all police officers employed by the city of Indianapolis, and the same violent situation will flare up like a case

---

[58]

http://www.indystar.com/article/20130705/NEWS02/307050013/Teen-fatally-shot-crowd-after-Downtown-fireworks-faith-leader-calls-incident-frightening-unsettling-?odyssey=mod%7Cbreaking%7Ctext%7CIndyStar.com of herpes again and again.

War zones.

The threat of a war zone, requiring the deployment of all officers (and the cancellation of Independence Day leave) employed by the city...

It's not Islamic Fundamentalist engaged in some Holy War against the Great Satan that requires such a mass concentration of police to ensure some semblance of order; it's the Black Terror that has already claimed such cities as Birmingham and Detroit, New Orleans and Memphis.

With the threat of riots - in response to the acquittal of George Zimmerman - already an established reality (a reality the police department of Sanford, Florida is preparing in earnest to combat), the instruments of our liberation lie in wait.

Watching.

And never yielding.

We still live in a world where the Kerner Commission dictates how we view black criminality (especially its origins).

We've been dancing to that same tune for fifty years.

But the music is starting to fade out.

What's the Difference Between the Conditions of a 27% Black City and a 64% Black City?

Indianapolis

Population: 834, 852

Black percentage of population: 27.5%

Percent of Black population on EBT/Food Stamps (as of 2009): 34% of blacks in Marion County on Food Stamps.

Baltimore

Population: 621, 342

Black percentage of population: 63.6%

Percent of Black population on EBT/Food Stamps (as of 2009): 32% of blacks in Baltimore on food stamps.

So Baltimore has 403,998 blacks, compared to Indianapolis' 240,789.

The violence in both cities is almost entirely due to these population groups. Though the black population of Indianapolis is less than two-thirds that of Baltimore, it's already reached the tipping point. Now Indianapolis is on a fast track toward Baltimore's current reality: where a peaceful downtown Independence Day celebration will require the type of police-state we saw in H.L. Mencken's hometown in 2013.

Baltimore blacks recently marched in solidarity after an impressively Chicagoan spate of black violence rocked the city. Of course, it did nothing to deter the violence: Not two days after the march, a double-shooting claimed another life only blocks from where the Nubian "peace" rally was held.

Black clergy promised to try and get a handle on the black violence that's quickly turning Baltimore into more than just a proverbial 'ghost town'; but an actual city where the ghostly apparitions of a once-thriving society (the white man's skyscrapers) stand as silent witnesses to the black community engaged in fratricide. [A new level of outrage brings hope after a violent stretch: Organizers, officials looking to channel and sustain community activity, Baltimore Sun, July 8, 2013]:

> On Monday, a group of ministers promised to take on a bigger role in violence prevention and activists held a peace rally and barbecue in East Baltimore. Recent days have seen a citywide prayer tour and calls for a 24-hour Baltimore "cease fire."

> The most visible example of the increased passion came Friday night, when organizers said 600 men walked the length of North Avenue and back — about 10 miles — to protest violence. Among those who attended was 66-year-old Cornell Rigby of Northwest Baltimore, who said he came to the event after hearing about it on the radio.

> "If we don't demonstrate, it's like saying [the gun violence] is OK, that society is accepting of it," said Rigby, who led call-and-response chants during the march.

> "We're redeeming ourselves, because we've been quiet too long."

> Those involved in the efforts say many people don't pay attention to crime until an incident hits close to home. Others might want to get involved but have trouble figuring out how.

> "It's just so challenging to figure out what to do," said the Rev. Scott Slater, of the Episcopal Diocese of Maryland, at a

71

ceremony Monday in East Baltimore to dedicate a peace mural. The Rev. Willie Ray has been trying to galvanize residents for decades, including an annual event that sought to get people to link hands along the length of North Avenue — but which sometimes drew only a handful of participants.

"It's a slow process, and you have to go with the flow," Ray said. "You find a few people that's going in your direction, and you roll with it."

At the corner of Broadway and North Avenue, where Marques Dent sold snow cones for three summers as a child, the former Air Force captain threw a peace rally on Monday afternoon complete with a DJ, grilled hot dogs and drinks.

"Baltimore's small," said Dent, who grew up in the area and started an IT job-training nonprofit when he got out of the Air Force in January. "It might not be my cousin, but it might be the cousin of someone I know. I have several friends who have been affected. They say, 'I'm tired of going to funerals.'"

Dent said the violence has shaken Baltimore because it seems to be on the uptick, with few answers as to why.

"People are upset — they're upset with our law enforcement, they're upset with our legislature, they're upset with our community leaders," he said. "People can't be dropping like flies just because it's hot outside."[59]

The key take-away from the quoted material is that *for decades*, Rev. Willie Ray had tried to galvanize blacks to do something, anything, to try and convince the black community of Baltimore to cease fire.

Even with the 'peace rally' and Nubian marches, black people are still dropping like flies in Baltimore.

The same is now true of Indianapolis, where in a span of a day, two

[59] http://www.baltimoresun.com/news/maryland/crime/blog/bs-md-ci-crime-response-20130708,0,4960036.story#ixzz2YaIDcQQJ

black people were gunned down (by other blacks). [Man holding baby dies in overnight shooting; had survived earlier Indianapolis shooting, Indy Star, July 9, 2013] and [Teenager dies in Eastside Indianapolis shooting, Indy Star, July 8, 2013].

The former story helps establish why white families chose to vacate a community/neighborhood that starts being overwhelmed by the black undertow: a shooting at a park, a black kid gunned down next to a swing set just before 3 p.m. on a Monday...; a row of 8 IMPD officers lined up watching as a crowd of blacks gathered, and eventually fights erupting.

The very same conditions of 64 percent black Baltimore (and the type of communities blacks create), found in a city only 27.5 percent black.

Erika Smith, writing at the *Indy Star*, noted 90 percent of the city of Indianapolis and Marion County's budget goes to public safety. How much of the overall budget would go towards public safety if, say, there were no blacks in Marion County or Indianapolis? [Erika D. Smith: It will take more than police to stop violence in Indianapolis, Indy Star, July 9, 2013]:

> If suburbanites were uneasy about venturing into the "dangerous" city before, gun-toting gang members are working overtime to validate their fears.

> Collectively, city and county governments spend about 90 percent of their budgets on public safety. That's correct — about 90 percent!

> The other 10 percent pays for things that actually make cities attractive and livable: parks, infrastructure, transportation options.

> Indianapolis needs to find a way to even out the ratio. We can't keep spending more and more money to lock people up. It's expensive, and the cycle will only continue to repeat itself with each new generation.

> Because one of the reasons why we have so much crime is

because we spend so much money trying to punish people after they commit crimes instead of investing in things that will prevent crime and help people find other ways to live.

Every high-crime neighborhood where IMPD will send more officers is a neighborhood also plagued with poor schools, rundown parks and crumbling infrastructure. Abandoned houses, by the thousands, are falling apart in these areas.

Overgrown lots are filled with weeds, rodents and other vermin. Streets flood when it rains. Sidewalks are turning into gravel and dust. And the city's grossly underfunded bus service is of limited use at best in getting to and from employment centers that pay livable wages.[60]

What Erika Smith can't write and what the *Indy Star* won't print is that every high-crime neighborhood where IMPD must send more officers is black; it is black children who are the students at schools that are deemed 'poor'; it is the conduct of black individuals who collectively run down city parks and assist in 'blighting' (or, her words, 'crumbling') the infrastructure.

The abandoned houses in Indianapolis are empty because black individuals moving into a formerly flourishing neighborhood drove down property value so much that their white owners couldn't give them away. Weeds overgrow the lots because black people willfully refuse to take ownership of their surroundings (especially when it comes to admitting that it's black dysfunction causing the collapse of the community). Most black individuals lack the qualifications for high-paying jobs – outside of the public sector – and business owners locate their companies/corporations in areas where their employees will feel safe.

---

[60]

http://www.indystar.com/article/20130708/NEWS19/307080060/Erika -D-Smith-It-will-take-more-than-police-to-stop-violence-in-Indianapolis

Were white people to occupy the same communities currently targeted by the IMPD's for their "show of force" (Project 46218) in an effort to regain control of their city, weeds would be cut; schools would be free of excessive discipline action while test scores and graduation rates would rise; parks would be overflowing with young white families; sidewalks would be pristine, with people walking their dogs and bikers aggressively riding past them; abandoned houses would be filled with the laughter of children.

If HBO wants to resurrect another season of *The Wire*, why not just do a spinoff set in Indianapolis?

Mirror, Mirror on the Wall...

A superpower? A First-World Nation?

Come on now.

Don't be silly.

This experiment is nearly over.

It's living on borrowed time. [Baltimore Men March to Stem Violence, *Baltimore Sun*, July 6, 2013]:

> On a day when at least four people were shot in Baltimore before dinner time — two of them fatally —hundreds of city men took to the streets in a planned 10-mile march along North Avenue, shutting down portions of the thoroughfare, to protest the recent spike in gun violence.
>
> "There's a war going on in our streets" that "starts and ends with our young black men," City Councilman Brandon Scott told the crowd, which included the mayor and police commissioner. "We're going to take our city back. ... We can

no longer stand on the backs of the women."

Scott and family friend Munir Bahar, who was in trouble as a kid but turned his life around to mentor other city kids, organized the 300 Man March. It was modeled after the 1995 Million Man March in Washington D.C., a massive show of solidarity among African-American men.

The idea was to stir Baltimore's men to action in their own neighborhoods and homes to stop the cycle of violence so frequently driven by drugs and gangs. While many have called on authorities to stem the tide, this was the first time the larger community has come together to fight back.

More than 40 people have been shot since summer began, with 20 of them struck in a single weekend. On Friday, at least four more people were shot by late afternoon.

In an impassioned speech before the march, Police Commissioner Anthony W. Batts implored those within earshot to take action, saying repeatedly that this wasn't about numbers for him, but about faces.

There are "just too many black faces dying on the streets," he said. "This is not a game to me. This is not a rally to me. ... The time for talk is over."

Men, mostly African-American, shouted their support as he spoke.

As the only female speaker, Mayor Stephanie Rawlings-Blake said she spoke on behalf of the women, the many single mothers working multiple jobs to take care of their children — or their children's children — often without help from the fathers.

"We'll do it because we have to, but not because we want to," she said of the hard-working women. "We want to be in partnership with the men in our lives."

As the marchers gathered at the 3400 block of North Ave.,

bound for a turning point at the intersection with Milton Street five miles away, women lined up on either side of them, clapping and shouting in support.

"Black men and unity are words that typically don't go together," said one marcher, Paz Morris, 37. "Black men and drugs, black men and violence" — that's what some in the city are used to hearing, he said. "But black men and unity I think is what you're witnessing here."

Richard Thornton Jr., a minister, called the event a "first step."

"Sometimes, with things like this, if you just show up and participate, it can lead to other things," said Thornton, 58.

The city's violence is largely contained to its poorer areas, those blighted by drugs and gang activity, Places it can be too easy to write off, some said.

"It's easy to get numb to" the violence until it hits home, said O'Neill McDaniels Jr., 39. Three women were shot in late June, one fatally, in the northeast neighborhood he grew up in.[61]

Borrowed time indeed; two more people were killed on the same day of the march.[62]

At least no one dared to pull a Ray Nagin, who in 2007 seemed to endorse the idea of crime in the *Crescent City* [Mayor: Crime Part of New Orleans `brand', Washington Post, August 10, 2007]:

Mayor Ray Nagin said he worries that slayings in the city make it seem dangerous, but news of such crimes "keeps the

---

[61] http://www.baltimoresun.com/news/maryland/crime/blog/bs-md-ci-300-man-march-20130705,0,824262.story#ixzz2YHJ4UsZZ

[62] http://baltimore.cbslocal.com/2013/07/05/2-more-killed-in-baltimore-city-as-hundreds-gather-for-ten-mile-march-to-stop-the-violence/

New Orleans brand out there."

In a city where the tourism industry is the lifeblood of a fragile economy, the wave of violence threatens to derail efforts to bring visitors _ and former residents _ back. Yet Nagin, at a bricklaying ceremony Thursday, told reporters it's a "two-edged sword."

"It's not good for us, but it also keeps the New Orleans brand out there, and it keeps people thinking about our needs and what we need to bring this community back," he said. "Sure it hurts, but we have to keep working every day to make the city better."[63]

Someone cue up the James Brown: We're all just *living in America...*

Crime has been particularly bad, then, for the "branding" of Baltimore as a tourist destination, with the 2012 St. Patrick's Day black mob violence at the Inner Harbor covered up by police[64] and the media denouncing anyone for noticing the violence was all perpetrated by 'black youths.'[65]

Violence is not good for the viability, or "branding", of any city, especially one like 63 percent black Baltimore.

---

[63] http://www.washingtonpost.com/wp-dyn/content/article/2007/08/10/AR2007081001649.html

[64] http://articles.baltimoresun.com/2012-05-12/news/bs-md-ci-violence-downtown-police-20120420_1_pratt-and-light-youths-police-commander

[65] http://articles.baltimoresun.com/2012-05-17/news/bs-ed-mcdonough-20120517_1_baltimore-county-delegate-criminal-behavior-baltimore-officials

Have You Forgotten When Those (Row) Towers Fell?

No.

This is not about 9/11.

It's about Baltimore.

A city where the "shoe of power" is now firmly on a black foot.

Beneath the weight of this boot, true civilization (abandoned by whites when black criminality became an untenable reality) has been all but demolished. [Last houses standing: The beautiful row houses once part of sprawling tenements that illustrate Baltimore's urban decay, *Daily Mail*, September 3, 2013]:

> One of the architectural quirks of certain cities on the eastern seaboard of the U.S. is the solo row house.

> Standing alone, in some of the worst neighborhoods, these nineteenth century structures were once attached to similar row houses that made up entire city blocks.

> Time and major demographic changes have resulted in the decay and demolition of many such blocks.

> Occasionally, one house is spared - literally cut off from its neighbors and left to the elements with whatever time it has left.

> Still retaining traces of its former glory, the last house

standing is often still occupied.[66]

The Daily Mail teased the reason those 'row towers' fell: demographic change. But we'll make it explicit: white people, the engine that kept civilization powered in Baltimore, was extinguished by a demographic Electro Magnetic Pulse (EMP) when the black population reached a point where "democracy" smiled upon their majority numbers.

Well, the late Ron Smith - a long-time radio personality in Baltimore - identified the real reason why those row towers fell. Thanks to Lawrence Auster for archiving this column [The Column the Baltimore Sun Would Not Publish, June 05, 2009, Amnation.com]:

> *Here is the column that was submitted by Ron Smith, a weekly Baltimore Sun columnist, to the newspaper. However, The Sun decided not to run the piece today for various reasons. Decide for yourself whether the decision makers at The Sun made the right decision.*
>
> Because of all the reports I've read and conversations I've had on the radio this week about Baltimore's notorious violence being directed these days randomly at people going about their daily business even in the supposedly safe "touristy" areas of the city, I reached for my copy of Anthropologist Jack Weatherford's book, "Savages and Civilization: Who Will Survive?"
>
> Weatherford has traveled just about everywhere in his long and distinguished career and during his research began to perceive that the modern world was near its end. He argues that cities, the centers of civilization, are inherently destructive.
>
> "They consume the areas around themselves," he writes, "and

---

[66] http://www.dailymail.co.uk/news/article-2408624/Baltimores-houses-standing-The-beautiful-row-houses-sprawling-tenements.html#ixzz2eco5fXxy

if they cannot find new materials, they die." Think of it this way: the discipline of archeology arose from what? From the study of dead cities, strewn about the landscape of the world.

What kills them? He says the cause is the extravagant habits of consumption and destruction that are at the heart of civilization. Everything is eventually consumed.

The forests are denuded. Water, plants, stone, metal, animals, even the land itself is used up. It took thousands of years to consume and destroy the birthplace of civilization in Mesopotamia, and then the pattern continued in the Mediterranean and Europe, with the eventual need to find vast new areas, the Americas and Australia, in order to obtain the resources to replace that which had been consumed.

That game is now over. What can be civilized has been. How, you might wonder, does this tie into the increasing violence in our big cities? I'll tell you. Jack Weatherford is an expert on tribal cultures.

He has written books about the epic clash between the Native American and European cultures during the 300 years of warfare between the two. Civilized people have defeated the tribal peoples of the world, who have been killed or scattered. But the tribal people who survived have been moving en masse into the worlds' major urban areas.

And as he notes, "Neither the classless society of communism nor the global village of capitalism managed to homogenize the world during the twentieth century." Group conflict, far from being eradicated, has been heightened in modern times.

The nation-state swallowed the remaining tribal people but could not digest them.
And that brings us to this startling observation from Mr. Weatherford after spending some time doing field research in Washington, D.C.: "Nowhere in the world had I witnessed as much savagery, brutality, crime and cruelty as I did on the

streets of the capital city of the United States."

He worked at a bookstore.

The clerk who worked at it before him was shot in the head and killed. The clerk who replaced him was beaten with a metal pipe and left for dead. "On the streets of Washington," he writes, "I saw forms of social organization and culture that I had never seen among any tribal people. Everywhere in the world, tribal life centers on the family and family units, but in the center cities of America, the family has broken down." The welfare state put the finishing touches on the destruction of the family.

In the fifteen years since his book was published, we can safely assume things have degenerated even more. Young males in the inner cities pursue their lives and interests separate from the females with whom they beget children.

"Much of the male activity," Weatherford observes, "varies between idle boredom and fierce violence." The males coalesce into gangs that operate with warrior bravado. This is the reality: "Aside from a few exclusive and heavily guarded enclaves, the central city is home to the lost." And the lost are lashing out at the rest of us. Wherever uncontrolled crime appears, vigilantism soon follows.

"Soon," writes Weatherford, "it becomes difficult to distinguish one group from the other as the criminals and vigilantes both operate outside the law...in their struggle for control of the streets and the neighborhoods."

Strange things are happening. Unease is widespread.[67]

Unease is widespread.

---

[67] http://www.amnation.com/vfr/archives/013361.html

Unanswered Prayers (Even of the Voodoo Variety) = Continuation of Black Crime

Burlap sacks and ashes didn't stop the killing in Birmingham (strangely, the deployment of such novel crime fighting tactics were only needed in the black community); no amount of voodoo dances and conjuring of Haitian spirits can save New Orleans from the same type of crime vexing Birmingham [New Orleans Conjures Old Spirits Against Modern Woes, *New York Times*, August 18, 1995]:

> The voodoo priestess used a mix of gunpowder and old graveyard dirt to draw a magic symbol on a crossroads in the Bywater neighborhood, opening a spiritual door through which a fearsome deity could pass and save her community from the evil of crack cocaine.

> For two hours on Wednesday night, as drums pounded along Piety Street and orange flames of fire-eaters and torch carriers danced in the dark, the white-gowned priestess, Sallie Ann Glassman, enticed Ogoun La Flambeau, a voodoo god of war and fire, to prowl among the rows of shotgun houses and punish the dope peddlers and other criminals.

> She offered rum, cigars, incense and music, and called out to him in French, respectfully but firmly, since it is unwise to appear weak-willed in the presence of spirits. "Great gods cannot ride little horses," she said.

> Sometime after 10 P.M., as a circle of sweat-slick dancers and voodoo drummers seemed about to collapse in the sticky heat, Ogoun showed himself to her, the priestess said.

> "I can see him and feel him. He is here," said Ms. Glassman. His feet, she said, were on the street, and the rest of him rose up, high into the dark. "I can see him now, hovering over us," she said.

Even in New Orleans, where there is magic in many things and weirdness in most, this does not happen every day.

The ceremony was born in the frustration of residents in the racially and economically diverse neighborhood on the edge of the French Quarter, said Ms. Glassman and others who live here. They said the New Orleans Police Department had been ineffectual at best in dealing with blatant drug traffic, burglaries, prostitution, robberies and assaults.

"This is not frivolous," said James Smith, a writer who lives in Bywater, who came to lend his support to the ceremony.

"It has to work better than the legal system," in frightening away some of the criminals who make a living here, Mr. Smith said. "Because New Orleans is a very superstitious place."[68]

The voodoo chants have yet to ward off any of the black criminality in the Crescent City, the exact same result the burlap bag wearing, ashes-on-the-forehead crowd in Birmingham achieved when their divine intervention was requested to assist a certain community in being violence free.

Now, violence in Baltimore (courtesy of the same racial demographic that drove citizens of Birmingham and New Orleans toward such different types of prayer to try and stop) [Baltimore Officials & Clergy Ask For Help After Dozens Killed, CBS Baltimore, June 30, 2013]:

The surge in violence continues in Baltimore as the police report more shootings, the last of which happened late Saturday in Northeast Baltimore.

Christie Ileto has more on how clergy and lawmakers are trying to calm anxious residents.

At least 40 shootings have happened in the last 10 days and 16 of them were deadly.

---

[68] http://www.nytimes.com/1995/08/18/us/new-orleans-conjures-old-spirits-against-modern-woes.html

Police have stepped up their presence on the streets in response to a surge in violence that included 11 fatal shootings in the span of a week. Commissioner Anthony Batts has said nearly three times the usual number of officers would be on the streets this weekend.

City clergy are now asking residents to step up and end this violent trend.

City clergy and members of 120 churches are rallying and praying this weekend for peace.

Even a 21-car motorcade drives through the city showing just how deadly this violent trend is becoming.

"If you put a police officer in every block, you still could not solve the program when the problem is inside of the individual, " said Bishop Angel L. Nunez of Bilingual Christian Church.

This recent surge in shootings highlights the city's problem with gun violence and homicide rate. So far this year, there have been around 117 homicides, the highest in six years.[69]

Of course, in Detroit, the exact same community which appealed to a Higher Power for intervention in the violent crime of Baltimore, New Orleans, and Birmingham, chose to send a hearse motorcade around the city.

Yes.

A hearse motorcade paraded around the city, a macabre warning to the residents of the 90 percent black city to stop the violence.

---

[69] http://baltimore.cbslocal.com/2013/06/30/baltimore-officials-clergy-ask-for-help-after-dozens-killed/

Perhaps its time for a voodoo parade, led by hearses, and driven by

individuals wearing burlap sacks, to finally end the plague of black

crime infecting these four cities?

The Baltimore Sun provides the most impressive newspaper database
for researching homicide in the city (available here[70]); you can access
all murders between 2007 and July 1, 2013 - by race, weapon used,
and where in the city it happened - by inputting various searches
within the tabs.

Since 2007, there have been 1511 murders in the city of Baltimore. Of
these, 1267 were black and 77 were white (inexplicably, in 2008, 111
of the murder victims are listed as "race unknown").

Most interesting, however, is a feature that allows you to see if a
news story was published at the Baltimore Sun about the murder
victim.

In two of the cases of white murder victims, we learn the story is of
the black-on-white variety: Dr. Peter Marvit,[71] a researcher at the
National Institute of Health, was murdered in 2012 by two "light-
skinned black males"; in 2008, 16-year-old Matthew Scarborough was
killed by a black male during a home invasion. [Murder Ink., City
Paper, 9/10/2008]:

> Willondon Pettiford, a 17-year-old African-American male,
> was indicted by the Baltimore City Grand Jury on Sept. 4 for
> the murder of Matthew Scarborough. According to the
> Baltimore State's Attorney's Office, Scarborough, a 16-year-
> old Caucasian male, was in an apartment with four other
> people in the 500 block of Castle Drive in North Baltimore's
> Lake Walker neighborhood on Aug. 7 when they were

---

[70] http://data.baltimoresun.com/bing-maps/homicides/

[71] http://www.wbaltv.com/news/maryland/baltimore-city/People-of-
interest-sought-in-NIH-researcher-s-death/-/10131532/16997434/-
/4575mtz/-/index.html

allegedly robbed at gunpoint by Pettiford and unidentified others. According to the State's Attorney's Office, Pettiford shot Scarborough when he did not respond quickly enough to his demands.[72]

How many more of the white murder victims in the city of Baltimore had a black killer?

Prayers won't work.

Burlap sacks and ashes won't work.

A parade of hearses won't work.

Voodoo won't work.

What will work?

An admission of vast racial differences in both behavior and intelligence would be a good, rational first step.

(Makes more sense than voodoo...)

War Zone, USA: The Black Undertow Provides Multiple Cities the Opportunity to Train Military

---

[72] http://www2.citypaper.com/news/story.asp?id=16294

Emergency Personnel to Deal with the Horrors of War

Here are two SBPDL truths that must be stated:

1. Distinct racial groups create their own "culture": with that stated, Black people can assimilate to what is commonly known as "white culture" (though they will be shunned by their own community for 'acting white'), or white people can assimilate to "Black culture" (though they will be widely identified as 'wiggers').
2. Black people, in all cases, can neither create "white culture" nor sustain "white culture" independently of whites; instead, they can be expected to "revert to type". However, white people, while unable to *create* "Black culture," can, through gentrification, remove negative elements of "Black culture" that blighted a city or neighborhood and depreciated property value. "Black Culture" follows Black people wherever they go, even if they attempt to assimilate to "white culture" (this is called the Black Undertow and it creates *Climate Change*).

You always hear Disingenuous White Liberals (DWLs) and Professional Black Agitators claim that criminality is a byproduct of poverty, not race, yet hospitals and medical centers located in predominately white cities (or suburban areas) do not serve as training ground for doctors who will serve in the various branches of the United States Military.

We already know that the University of Cincinnati College of Medicine, University Hospital, and United States Air Force train emergency teams on how to evacuate wounded personnel in combat zones in Afghanistan and Iraq by treating the cities' Black gunshot and knife-attack victims. The victims of the Black Undertow in Cincinnati provide the perfect opportunity and war zone atmosphere to prepare emergency crews for dealing with the horrors of war abroad. (Here you can read how the Institute for Military Medicine brags about the partnership with the University of Cincinnati, and how the city's Black Undertow prepares emergency teams for horrors seen in war by supplying the trauma center with civilian casualties on a daily basis.[73])

Cincinnati isn't the only city struggling under conditions - courtesy of the Black Undertow, a byproduct of "Black culture' - resembling a war zone. The University of Maryland Shock Trauma Center in Baltimore also serves as training ground for military doctors, because Baltimore's Black population engages in bellicose behavior frighteningly similar to the conditions our troops will face overseas in hostile territory:

> CNN Pentagon correspondent Barbara Starr reported this weekend on a program used to train military doctors for the fast-paced and bloody environment found in war zone hospitals — namely, America's inner cities.
>
> Starr follows a rotation of military doctors who are preparing for their deployment at the University of Maryland Shock Trauma Center in Baltimore. The program director told Starr that the hospital is the closest to a war zone hospital he has seen:
>
> COL. DAVID POWERS: The injuries that I've treated here and that I see here at this hospital are the closest thing to the injuries I saw in Iraq that I've experienced in the continental United States.
>
> While the program is no doubt useful for preparing doctors for the high-intensity environments overseas and likewise giving doctors broad sets of skills they can use at home, that doctors can train for war zones through the crush of patients with, among other injuries, stabbing and gunshot wounds serve as a powerful reminder that as the wars overseas wind down, problems at home remain.
>
> The total spending on the U.S.' wars now exceeds $1.2 trillion.

73

http://surgery.uc.edu/divisions/centers/InstituteForMilitary/Institute ForMilitary.html

The Pentagon budget passed by the House earlier this month allocated nearly $200 billion this year for the wars in Iraq and Afghanistan. Meanwhile, Baltimore ranks as the eighth most dangerous city, second in its reported HIV/AIDS rate, and is the heroin capital of the country.[74]

No mention, of course, that Baltimore is a Black Undertow city, or that it is Black people and their "culture" that makes the city unlivable. Nor does it identify Black people (primarily Black homosexual males infecting Black females and each other) as the cause for its staggeringly high HIV/AIDS rate. Nevertheless, the Black inhabitants of Baltimore provide military doctors with real-life trauma experience that fully prepares them to psychologically survive the horrors of war as they repair the bodies of our soldiers. (After all, they have survived the horrors of Baltimore.)

Unfortunately, it's not just Cincinnati and Baltimore. The United States Air Force also utilizes St. Louis, another American city labeled "worst" and "most dangerous" (courtesy of the Black Undertow) to train surgeons and emergency personnel. The US Army? They use Miami, where the Black Undertow - mixed with a lethal and combustible cocktail of Haitian, Cuban, and other immigrants from less-developed (i.e., non-white) nations – supplies the carnage for trauma surgeons and emergency personnel that would scare even George Romero and John Carpenter:

> MIAMI — The trauma center's radio crackles an alert: A 34-year-old woman injured in an auto wreck is being brought in by helicopter. Parts of her scalp have been torn back, exposing her skull. Broken bones may be sticking out through the skin of her left leg. Her injuries may help save the lives of U.S. soldiers in Iraq.
>
> For two weeks, 28 Army medics, nurses, doctors and nurse anesthetists have been learning trauma medicine and teamwork under pressure at the Ryder Trauma Center at

---

[74] http://thinkprogress.org/security/2011/07/18/271790/baltimore-war-zone-hospital/

downtown Miami's Jackson Memorial Hospital, a place that sees such carnage it often resembles a war zone.

Ryder is one of the busiest trauma centers in the nation, seeing an average of 11 trauma patients a day -- about as many as the biggest military hospital in Iraq.

Jackson Memorial serves some of the city's most crime-ridden sections, and patients arriving at the trauma center have been stabbed, injured in grisly auto accidents, wounded in shootouts with high-powered assault weapons, or hurt in falls and fights.

The Army sends 10 forward surgical teams a year through Ryder, which was selected six years ago because of the volume of bloodshed. It is the Army's only trauma training center. The Air Force has similar programs in Baltimore, St. Louis and Cincinnati; the Navy's trauma program is in Los Angeles.

This time, the professionals being trained are Ohio reservists with the Army's 848th Forward Surgical Team. In their civilian lives, some of them raise families, tend bar, go to college or work for the post office. The team leader is Col. Michael Oddi, a 59-year-old thoracic surgeon in Akron, Ohio.

"My practice consists of a lot of surgery, but we don't do a lot of trauma surgery. So a program like this, to prepare us for acute, multiple casualties, really helped us on our last deployment, and it will help us again," Oddi said. "It is extremely busy here."[75]

Miami's Black population and "Black culture" provide excellent training for the Army doctors and surgeons, who prepare for the grisly horrors of war by repairing the bullet-ridden bodies of Black people and sewing up knife victims from the combat zone of The

---

[75] http://www.usatoday.com/news/nation/2007-10-25-270679764_x.htm

Capital of Latin America.

Because of budget cuts, the military must use Black Undertow cities in America to prepare trauma surgeons and emergency personnel, since "Black culture" provides, free of charge, an endless 'war-like environment' in which to train, such as the so-called "inner city" of St. Louis:

> The partnership between the Air Force and the hospital came about because of, in part, the downsizing of the military medical system that began more than a decade ago. The cuts closed military hospitals. As a result, most Air Force medical personnel now tend to work in smaller clinics and treat few serious injuries.
>
> "They typically don't get to see gunshot and stab wounds," said Capt. Scott Fallin, administrator of the St. Louis program. "Being here in the inner city prepares them for some of the blunt-trauma injuries they will see."[76]

Another once-great city, Philadelphia, is the fastest growing Black Undertow city in America, as the retreating white population, heading for the calmer waters of the suburbs, leaves the eroding remains of "white culture" in its wake. With this erosion comes Climate Change, as this story of trauma centers illustrates:

> Dr. Mike Reihart did his residency at Albert Einstein Medical Center in the Logan section of Philadelphia, a city where doctors see some 30 percent of all shooting victims in Pennsylvania.
>
> Compared to that, Lancaster is a picnic.
>
> But Reihart, attending emergency physician at Lancaster General Hospital, said Lancaster is less of a picnic these days, particularly on weekends. "Some nights are starting to feel a

---

[76] http://www.stltoday.com/news/local/metro/article_91465b40-8d81-526c-870e-cdf123dc8eee.html

little like Philly," he said.

Statistically, the two cities can't compare. There have been 30 shootings in Lancaster in the past eight months. In Philadelphia, gunfire has claimed more than 135 lives in less than six months.

But emergency physicians at Lancaster General say the frequency with which they see gunshot victims has definitely increased. The director of the emergency department, William Adams, told the Philadelphia Inquirer last week that over the past 10 years, the hospital had seen "about a fourfold increase" in the number of gunshot victims it treats. "Where we used to see one or two a month, now we see one or two a week," said Adams.

Reihart, who sees many of those patients, said the increase is disconcerting. But it's nothing he and other medical staff at LGH can't handle.

In fact, he said, gunshots are actually easier to treat than blunt trauma, the type sustained in car accidents. Penetrating trauma, like gunshot wounds, "are a little easier; you know there's a hole here, and a hole there," he said. Blunt trauma, by contrast, often involves broken bones and significant internal injuries.

If someone is shot in the abdomen, said Reihart, they go immediately into surgery. "The science of gunshot wounds is changing," he said. "There are so many gunshot wounds in big cities" physicians in places like Los Angeles have figured out how to triage patients without surgery.[77]

Some people like to cite statistics that show crime is dropping in America. The problem with this approach is that statistics are often

---

[77] http://lancasteronline.com/news/lgh-doctor-served-in-philadelphia-war-zone/article_65bbae7c-0d08-561f-a17f-a8a25a9f00eb.html

misleading, taken out of context, or manipulated. Therefore, we at SBPDL prefer to deal with *facts*. And the fact remains than 1 million Black males are in jail, removing from the streets a significant portion of the criminal element of this nation (at only 5 percent of the United States population, Black males are significantly represented in the criminal class of America, and having committed more than 50 percent of the murders in 2010, those trends aren't slowing down).

More so, advances in medical technology and surgery techniques (thanks to the endless supply of gunshot victims the Black Undertow provides) have greatly increased the odds of an individual surviving a bullet or knife wound. And thanks to the Black Undertow providing so many instances of trauma and medical emergencies in "inner cities" throughout America, our military can successively prepare doctors and emergency teams for the horrors of war they will encounter overseas.

All courtesy of "Black culture."

Now do you see why Whitopias are necessary? Now do you see what those who escape The Nothing (horrible reference to *The Neverending Story*) that follows the Black Undertows are evading?

I would love to read stories and accounts of dealing with the Black Undertow at trauma centers in Birmingham, Atlanta, Memphis, New Orleans, Dallas, Kansas City,Washington D.C., Milwaukee, Chicago, New York City, Los Angeles, Detroit, Cleveland, and other cities with a large Black population.

It's hard to believe that the United States offers so many cities that would be excellent stand-ins for battle zones where military doctors and emergency personnel could so readily train and prepare for the horrors of war.

Such is the horror of the Black Undertow.

"Baltimore City, You're Breaking My Heart": Tracey Halvorsen, Being White in Baltimore, and Fear of Black Crime in a Majority Black City

Only in an era dominated by the state-mandated worship of blacks (via public indoctrination of blacks and their obvious moral superiority) would a show like *The Wire* come to epitomize all that is great about television.

An attempt to sanitize Baltimore's black population (which has driven away not only whites, but any racial group hoping to find peace and stability in the same streets Edgar Allen Poe once roamed) by branding them as the "oppressed" – rather than the "oppressor" - David Simon's HBO show is proof-positive why this insane era of Black worship must come to an end.

In one episode of *The Wire*, a black drug dealer makes this tongue-in-cheek observation to one of his black bodyguards: "Do you know what the most dangerous thing in America is? A n--ger with a library card."

This, of course, lacks credulity. The most dangerous thing in America is not a black who can read. It's the person who excuses black dysfunction as anything less than the fault of the individual n--ger engaging in it, as we see on a daily basis in Baltimore.

This is a city where witness intimidation (remember the Dawson family?), jury nullification (remember Joel Lee, a Korean, who was killed by a black dude in Baltimore, only to have a nearly all-black jury find his accused black murderer not guilty?) and the idea of black political supremacy (racial payback: "now the shoe is on the other foot") is standard operating procedure.

A few years back, when a white Johns Hopkins University student, John Pontolillo, killed a black career criminal (49-year-old Donald

Rice, who had been arrested more than two dozen times for burglary, breaking-and-entering and auto theft) with a samurai sword, the *Baltimore Sun* editorialized against those celebrating his demise. [No Cause For Cheers: Our View: The Gleeful Reaction To The Killing Of A Burglar By A Hopkins Student With A Samurai Sword Is Unseemly And Ignores The Tragedy That Has Engulfed Two Lives, 9-17-2009]:

> The burglar, Donald D. Rice, wouldn't ordinarily deserve much sympathy. He was a career criminal with a long record of thefts. He had just gotten out of prison the previous Saturday after serving six months for a conviction in Baltimore County. By all accounts he was neither an admirable character nor an innocent victim.

> But even burglars don't deserve to be killed with a razor-sharp sword. And Mr. Pontolillo - whose thinking may have been clouded by the adrenaline rush of fear, panic and anger - must now spend the rest of his life grappling with the anguish and remorse of having snuffed out another's life.

> This is certainly nothing to celebrate. The glorification of the incident online and around town belies the horror of the killing and its aftermath. Even if it ultimately is judged to have been legally justified, the question of whether the situation couldn't have been handled differently will remain.

> No amount of adulation as a modern-day ninja vigilante is likely to take away the pain Mr. Pontolillo is liable to feel in years to come as the awful reality of this gruesome episode sinks in.[78]

Pontolillo's samurai sword heroics were later celebrated in a fake SGA campaign at Johns Hopkins, with undergrad students of that elite institution knowing black criminals prey upon them, and

---

[78] http://articles.baltimoresun.com/2009-09-17/news/0909160119_1_burglar-samurai-sword-pontolillo

realizing their own lives are at risk .[79]

Like Stephen Pitcairn, a white undergraduate who was about to enroll in medical school and assisted with breast cancer research. Two black people murdered him back in 2010.[Hopkins researcher's promising life cut short in robbery: Two arrested in connection with crime robbery charges against suspect were dropped in May, Baltimore Sun, 7-27-2010]:

> Dropped off at Penn Station after a weekend trip to New York to visit his sister, 23-year-old Stephen Pitcairn was talking to his mother on his iPhone at about 11 p.m. and walking north in the 2600 block of St. Paul St. when a man and woman demanded money.
>
> Police say he turned over his wallet, then took a knife to the chest.
>
> A resident was in his home ironing when he saw three people who appeared to be fighting, then heard a scream. He ran outside, saw Pitcairn lying on his stomach in the gutter and called 911.
>
> "I made it back and held his hand, and I told him that everything was going to be OK," said the man, who was shaken and did not want to give his name. "He said, 'Help me,' and then I held his hand until he expired. I didn't want him to be alone.
> "Nobody wants to die alone."
>
> Police said Pitcairn was officially pronounced dead at Maryland Shock Trauma center after midnight. He would have turned 24 Tuesday.
>
> Anthony Guglielmi, the Police Department's chief spokesman, said Pitcairn's mother heard the robbery over the phone.

---

[79] http://www.jhunewsletter.com/2009/10/01/samurai-incident-used-in-sga-campaign-70879/

Police arrested and charged two people in connection with the crime, each one with a predictable rap sheet. Lavelva Merritt, 24, has a long history of drug-related arrests and convictions. John Alexander Wagner, 34, has been charged in robberies and assaults, never receiving anything more than what amounted to time served, even after violating his probation repeatedly, court records show.

In charging documents, police said they were told by witnesses that Merritt and Wagner were overheard saying that they had "robbed and 'hurt' a 'white boy.'" Detectives recovered a brown wallet, Pitcairn's iPhone, several folding and fixed blade knives — and shoes containing what appeared to be blood.[80]

"White boys" are merely walking ATMs in Baltimore.

Right?

Or if you're a Korean merchant hoping to do business in the war-torn Baltimore (like Joel Lee's parents), you have to take the extraordinary precaution of putting their entire store behind Plexiglas to protect both employee and inventory from the predatory black population. [Korean businessmen want out of inner city, The Free Lance Star, 11-11-1992]

> Baltimore (AP) - In the back of Chung's Grocery the police emergency number stands out in bold black letters on a crudely made cardboard sign next to the telephone.

> When night falls in the poor, mostly black, inner-city neighborhood, the Chungs retreat behind a plexiglass shield to protect themselves from armed visitors, even before the metal grating is pulled across the tiny storefront.

---

[80] http://articles.baltimoresun.com/2010-07-27/news/bs-ci-md-homicides-stabbing-2-20100726_1_robbery-drug-related-arrests-and-convictions-detectives

Despite the presence of often elaborate security systems, at least three Korean-American grocers have been killed over the past two years. Many others, like the Chungs, were robbed.

Police say it is not because of who they are, but where their stores are located, that Korean immigrants have been the targets of crime. But that's consolation for the more than 250 Korean families who put in 70-to 90-hour work weeks at their "Mom and Pop" stores, most of which are located in the inner city.

Suk Bum Chung - no relation to the Chungs - worked 12 hours a day, six and seven days a week, for six years before he was gunned down during a holdup at his small grocery store last November. He had hoped to bring his wife and six children to the country once his business was thriving.

Once he wrote home to say, "I understand the problems of crime here. But I don't know what to do about it. It is very dangerous here and maybe I should come back to Korea," his son recalled after the shooting. [81]

Baltimore.

Problems of crime.

Almost exclusively crime committed by black people.

Which brings us to a web site, Medium.com, and a post by Tracey Halvorsen that has gone completely viral. Titled "Baltimore City, You're Breaking My Heart: This is Why People Leave," Halvorsen writes:

Life takes you places, you follow a course that isn't completely

---

[81] Korean businessmen want out of inner city, The Free Lance Star, 11-11-1992

of your own making. One day you wake up, and it's really all up to you. So where do you want to live? I happen to live in a city. Baltimore, to be specific.

And I'm growing to absolutely hate it here.

I'm tired of hearing about 12 year old girls being held up at gun-point while they walk to school.[82]

I'm tired of saying "Oh Baltimore's great! It's just got some crime problems."[83]

I'm tired of living in a major crime zone while paying the highest property taxes in the state.[84]

I'm tired of hearing the police helicopter circling overhead every night, and seeing the spotlight shine in my window.

I'm tired of reading about juveniles arrested for violent crimes who are let go because if it's not a "murder" case, there's no time to worry about it, or resources to deal with it.

I'm tired of checking in on neighbor and Baltimore Sun editor Jon Fogg's Go Fund Me page to see if his family has met their goal to raise funds to help him recover from the brutal attack he suffered as he went from his car to his front door after work.

---

[82]

http://www.baltimoresun.com/news/maryland/crime/blog/bs -md-ci-12-year-old-girl-robbed-20140206,0,5595591.story

[83] *http://baltimorecrime.blogspot.com/*

[84] *http://www.foxnews.com/politics/2013/02/06/city- baltimore-is-on-path-to-financial-ruin-report-says/*

I'm tired of hearing city leaders delude themselves that people will move to, or visit, Baltimore—with visions of the Inner Harbor and the National Aquarium in their minds.

I'm tired of being surrounded by drug addicts.[85]

I'm tired of answering the question, "Is Baltimore really like The Wire?" Answer: "Yeah it's a complete shit-hole war zone depending on what street you turn down".

I'm tired of looking at 11 year olds as potential thieves, muggers and murderers on my walk home from the office.

I'm tired of living next to a beautiful park that I'm scared to walk into at any time of day, thanks to regular stories of day-time muggings, drug dealing and gang violence.

I'm tired of doing the mental checklist of what I will do if I hear someone break into my house.

I'm tired of watching the murder count go up and up like a lottery pool. [86]

I'm tired of thinking about neighbor Zach Sowers, beat to death by a pack of kids outside his Canton home several years ago, completely unprovoked.[87]

I'm tired of thinking about the horrifying final moments for 51 year old neighbor, Kim Leto, stabbed to death in her own home by two teenagers.[88]

---

[85] *http://welcometobaltimorehon.com/a-bleak-narrative-behind-the-title-heroin-capital*

[86] *http://data.baltimoresun.com/bing-maps/homicides/*

[87] *http://www.zachsowers.com/news.php*

[88]
http://www.baltimoresun.com/news/maryland/crime/blog/bs

I'm tired of hearing people talk about how coveted the internships are at Johns Hopkins because you get "battle zone" experience.

I'm tired of wondering why city leaders haven't said shit about recent horrific murders committed by children in supposedly "safe" neighborhoods. And city officials ignore the fact that neighborhoods like Canton and Butcher's Hill (supposedly appealing neighborhoods for young professionals, students and families seeking an urban living experience) have seen robberies up 35 percent and violent crime up 30 percent.[89]

Not once does Tracey mention 'blacks' as being the root of the problems causing Baltimore City to break her heart.

It's why grocery store owners put their entire stores behind Plexiglas; it's why Johns Hopkins students made a samurai-sword-wielding undergraduate a hero; it's where the destructive motto "no snitching" was born; it's why jury nullification and witness intimidation is the name of the game in the city.

R-A-C-E.

It's that simple: race.

Blacks.

Crime isn't the "elephant in the room" of Baltimore; nor is "inequality," as WYPR producer Lawrence Lanahan claimed in a

---

-md-highlandtown-murder-arrrests-20140202,0,6009593.story

---

[89] https://medium.com/p/1873a505ce2a

response to Tracey's piece titled "Whose Heart is Baltimore Breaking, Really?" (attempting to rationalize black crime as a response to oppressive 'white privilege'); no, it's simply an out-of-control black population that Norplant in the Baltimore Public Schools once tried to end.[90]

Being white in Baltimore is exactly like being white in Philadelphia; eventually, the dwindling white population of America will realize the experiences of whites in these two eastern seaboard cities was a harbinger of the future.[91]

It's race, stupid.

They Just Aren't Like Us: The Story of the 2002 Murder of the Dawson Family in Baltimore, What was Dubbed the City's "Alamo"

When reading about Baltimore and its 63.5 percent black population, no story typifies the insanity of the majority demographic better than the 2002 murder of the Dawson family. The black practice of "no

---

[90] http://micpenpick.wordpress.com/2014/02/07/whose-heart-is-baltimore-breaking-really/

[91] http://www.vdare.com/articles/philadelphia-freedom-not-available-for-anyone-white-in-philly-who-tells-the-truth-about-cri

snitching" took on a new meaning when the home of Angela and Carnell Dawson was set ablaze Oct. 16, 2002, in retaliation for the Dawson's "breaking ranks" and reporting nearby drug dealing activity to police. Angela and the couple's five children perished in the blaze and Carnell died a week later in the hospital.

The family was black, fighting to stay in the city of Baltimore while their fellow black citizens were doing their level best to make the city uninhabitable for any ethnic group (even calling police 109 times between 2000-2002 to report drug dealing).

Then again, this is a city where a 1992 report found that 56 percent of the black male population of Baltimore between the ages of 18 and 35 years-old was in some form of trouble with the 'racist' judiciary system [Legal system betrays young black men, Baltimore Sun, 9-1-1992]:

> The National Center on Institutions and Alternatives is reporting today that well over half of the young black men in this city are entangled in the criminal justice system on any given day.

> NCIA's study found that 56 percent of Baltimore's black men between 18 and 35 years old were either incarcerated, on probation or parole, awaiting trial or sentencing, or being sought on an arrest warrant.

> The one thing the NCIA study does not show is that an increasing percentage of the decision-makers at every level of the criminal justice system are black, as are an increasing percentage of the lawmakers on both the state and local level.

> The black community had hoped that putting black law enforcement officials in decision-making positions would make a difference, that they would set different priorities, find different solutions.

> But for the most part, blacks are making the same decisions

that their white counterparts made.

And they are making the same excuse.[92]

The report said 34,025 of the 60,715 young black men in Baltimore, or 56 percent, were "under criminal justice supervision on any given day in 1991," yet this wasn't nearly enough to keep Darrell Brooks from taking a can of gasoline to the Dawson home and setting it ablaze... all because this family dared try and make the city a better place. Though he was on probation, Brooks was one of those local thugs the *New York Times* mentioned as not taking kindly to Angela reporting black drug dealers to the police.[93]

For their efforts to make Baltimore a better place, her entire family paid with their lives. [In Baltimore, Slogan Collides With Reality, New York Times, 9-2-2003]:

> Darrell Brooks stood at the front of a courtroom, tears streaming down his cheeks, and choked out an apology.
>
> He had killed seven people, five of them children, and now he said he felt sorry.
> "I will never, ever, as long as there is breath in my lungs, ever forgive myself," he said last Wednesday. "I knew those kids. I loved them. I swear I didn't mean it, I swear."
>
> The lanky Mr. Brooks was off to prison for life for burning down a house full of people last October, a crime that seared the heart of this city and blasted a signal that things in Baltimore were still out of control.
>
> Mr. Brooks, a drug dealer, did not Believe. He had not gotten the message, stamped all over the city, on garbage cans, squad cars, T-shirts, skyscrapers, even thumping

---

[92] http://articles.baltimoresun.com/1992-09-01/news/1992245165_1_criminal-justice-system-evil-young-black-men

[93] http://www.nytimes.com/2002/10/17/us/fire-kills-mother-and-children-at-home.html

basketballs.

Believe. One word, printed in black and white, as if things were that clear. It began as a high-concept public relations campaign, begun by the mayor, Martin O'Malley, to tackle Baltimore's most infamous problem, drug crime. For years, the city had been at or near the top of the list of per-capita misery statistics: most murders, most addicts, most high school dropouts, most cases of H.I.V. and syphilis.

Believe was a way to address those ills, not through programs, but through commercials, banners and bumper stickers. Few cities had ever tried anything so abstract.

"It's spiritual warfare," Mr. O'Malley said.

But just as the mayor's new religion was taking off, Mr. Brooks reached for the gasoline.[94]

Witness intimidation, Baltimore-style.

It's an impolite, publicly-unmentionable fact that it's the black population of Baltimore ensuring the city leads the nation in per-capita misery statistics, with Johnnie Cochran Jr. even suing the city for $14 million (it would later be dismissed). The "grounds" for such a frivolous suit? Apparently, the city's "Believe" campaign encouraged black residents to report black dealers, making the city negligent for failing to providing police protection/witness protection for those who put themselves in danger. [Mayor derides Cochran's claims: Lawyer's blaming city for arson that killed 7 is labeled `pretrial hype', Baltimore Sun, 1-9-2003]:

> In addition to the Believe campaign, Cochran has blamed the deaths on the criminal justice system's failure to lock up Brooks for having violated his probation, which is a state

---

[94] http://www.nytimes.com/2003/09/02/us/in-baltimore-slogan-collides-with-reality.html?src=pm

responsibility.

A lawyer with Cochran's firm said Tuesday that the city's Believe campaign, which encourages residents to report dealers, was "reckless" because it urged people such as the Dawsons to put themselves in danger without providing effective witness protection.[95]

Quality of life can truly be measured by the percentage of the black population found in a city: the higher the percentage, the closer you'll be to the situation in Baltimore, where citizens hide behind locked doors and those who dare to snitch are barbecued; the lower the percentage, the greater the odds of hearing children's voices on Halloween night as they trick-or-treat through safe neighborhoods without adult supervision.

At the time of the horrific Molotov cocktail firebombing of the Dawson house, the white mayor of Baltimore, Martin O'Malley, would later recall, "The hardest moment of this administration was going to March Funeral Home and filing by five tiny caskets. But the Dawson loss just strengthened my resolve. The tragedy was our Alamo, it was not our Waterloo."[96]

Unfortunately, Baltimore's Waterloo came long ago, when blacks rioted in the aftermath of the Martin Luther King assassination. It took 5,500 National Guardsmen, 400 state troopers, and 1,200 city cops to occupy Baltimore and bring order to a lawless black population in 1968; it's doubtful those same numbers could accomplish the same feat today.

It's difficult to determine if law and order ever really returned to Baltimore, with white flight transforming the city into just another majority black, urban disaster. [100 Years: The Riots of 1968: Part of

95 http://articles.baltimoresun.com/2003-01-09/news/0301090075_1_dawson-family-cochran-lawyer

96 http://articles.baltimoresun.com/2003-09-11/news/0309110127_1_omalley-drug-treatment-pressure/2

our "100 Years: The Twelve Events That Shaped Baltimore" series, *Baltimore* magazine, May 2007]:

> And yet, nearly 40 years after the riots, Ruby Glover still laments that "so much in the city today almost brings back those memories—with the gangs, and the way that police have to work on streets where I grew up, where I laughed and entertained. There's still great fear, but it's coming not just from whites to blacks—now it's blacks to blacks."[97]

Eventually, the Dawson house would be rebuilt, re-branded as a sanctuary from the violence of black Baltimoreans. Though if you try hard enough, you can still detect the lingering smell of gasoline, a mark of witness intimidation even the Italian mobs would never employ.

More than $1 million was spent to erect the Dawson Family Safe Haven Center in East Baltimore, on the exact spot where the destroyed home once stood. In assessing the state of the neighborhood 10 years after the tragedy, one resident observed they felt more at home in American-military-occupied Iraq than in black-occupied Baltimore [10 years after Dawson killings, uneven results in Oliver: Family was killed in fire after complaining about drug dealers, Baltimore Sun, 10-13-2012]:

> Wanda Brewer, 52, who operated heavy machinery for Halliburton at Camp Anaconda in Iraq, returned to the neighborhood to look after her ailing grandmother. She looks back bleakly on the last decade.
>
> "Nothing changed," said Brewer, who lives on East Oliver Street. "We just got poorer — a lot of us went to jail."
>
> After returning, she found that she was "more at war here than I was in Iraq."

---

[97] http://www.baltimoremagazine.net/features/2007/05/100-years-the-riots-of-1968

Still, there is evidence of positive change. Crews are at work renovating some of the neighborhood's vacant houses — there are nearly 1,000.

Scriber said the streets were never as clean 10 years ago as they are today.

His department spends $270,000 a year to run the Dawson community center and is proud of the investment. The program is intended to help children with their studies while keeping them away from the temptations of the streets.[98]

A friend of the Dawson family would concur with Brewer's bleak assessment of the city (courtesy of the black population). [Home Where Family Died Is Now Safe Haven, New York Times, 4-8-2007]:

Aaron Anderson, 15, who lives nearby and knew the Dawson children, added: "It's sad. I'd rather not be here and them still alive, but the center will play a big role in keeping kids off the streets."

"The streets are terrible," Aaron added. "Anything can happen on any given day. You can get shot, killed, everything. Maybe it might save somebody's life and make them realize they should come in here and do their homework. It's easier." [99]

But why are the streets so terrible?

Why would a nation under the heel of U.S. Military occupation be considered a safer place for a black woman than the streets of her

98 http://articles.baltimoresun.com/2012-10-13/news/bs-md-ci-dawson-murder-ten-year-20121013_1_darrell-l-brooks-oliver-neighborhood-drug-dealers

99http://www.nytimes.com/2007/04/08/us/08baltimore.html?_r=0

own (black) hometown?

In a city utterly purged of white privilege, shouldn't "Black Utopia" magically appear in its place any day now?

No. That's why programs like Safe Streets are necessary. [Street cred used to disrupt the norm in some of Baltimore's most violent areas, ABC2news.com, 11-21-2013]:

> Baltimore is infected.
>
> If violent crime is a disease, then after years of steady remission, a rise in homicide totals and non-fatal shootings shows it is starting to relapse.
>
> But, deep inside some of this city's most important arteries, much like a vaccine, old pathogens of violence are working to inoculate the very disease they once helped create.
>
> ABC2 spent a night with the Safe Streets operation in Park Heights.
>
> It is one of four chapters around the city run by the Baltimore City Health Department; others include McElderry Park, Mondawmin and Cherry Hill.
>
> In short, Safe Streets is a public health model aimed at curing violence as if it is a disease.
>
> ABC2 News is the very first media organization trusted to go inside this program at the street level with television cameras, spending hours on a typical canvass, walking the streets with the men who once ruled them.
>
> Reformed now as outreach workers and so-called violence interrupters, the employees of Safe Streets spread a different message to the high risk youth following their old path.
>
> What makes them listen?

"I come from these streets. I grew up here. This is where I am from... I am stopping another black brother from getting hurt, another black brother from going to jail. There are so many ways to throw your life away out here. Just trying to stop that, just trying to show them there is a different way," said an outreach worker known on the streets as Porky.

They are showing them a different way from the normal the incredibly tough streets have taught them. Walking through their small part of Lower Park Heights on a Thursday night, it didn't take long to see.

On the corner of a crowded McDonald's parking lot, two young men began a back and forth that was immediately interrupted by Safe Streets violence interrupter Aaron.

We have agreed not to publish or broadcast specifics, but Aaron put an end to it by simply telling both men there is a different way to resolve this and each should walk away.

Both men did walk away peacefully, and Aaron will later write up the mediation to revisit it later. It seems like an obvious lesson, but the code of these streets is altogether different.

Safe Streets data shows 96 percent of their mediations in Park Heights are "likely or very likely to result in gun violence." Had the mediation not happened at the brush-up we witnessed, Aaron explained, a violent incident was likely to ensue.[100]

"Baltimore is infected." Just what is the source of this infection, good reporter at ABC's affiliate?

Cancer?

---

[100]http://www.abc2news.com/dpp/news/local_news/investigations/street-cred-used-to-disrupt-the-norm-in-some-of-baltimores-most-violent-areas#ixzz2saVCJ1p7

AIDS?

Is it incurable, inoperable at this point?

In 1991, fifty-six percent of Baltimore's black males between the ages of 18 and 35 were under criminal justice supervision "on any given day"; what do you want to bet that number is approaching 75 percent today?[101]

When reflecting on the negative impact of their 63.5-percent-black population, Baltimore's beleaguered residents should never forget the horrific deaths of the Dawsons.

This black family dared to make their community - and by extension, the entire city - a safer place.

As repayment for their good citizenship, *one of their own* murdered the entire family.

Despite the sporadic efforts of good families like the late Dawson's, Baltimore's black population continues to murder citizens and destroy civilization.

They just aren't like us.

America Doesn't Need Gun Control, it Needs Black Control: New Study Confirms Enormous Financial Burden on Hospitals of Black Gun crime

What can we infer from a new paper , titled "Hospitalizations Due to

---

[101] http://articles.baltimoresun.com/1992-09-03/news/1992247140_1_young-black-men-black-man-hoelter

Firearm Injuries in Children and Adolescents ", that could help us craft a sensible policy regarding gun control in America?[102]

How about you read the findings of this report, published in the journal *Pediatrics*, and then come up with some ideas? [Guns sent 20 children to U.S. hospitals every single day, study finds, Los Angeles Times, 1-27-14]:

> Twenty children or adolescents were hospitalized for firearm-related injuries every day in 2009, and 453 died of their wounds, a new report says.
>
> The study provides one of the most comprehensive recent efforts to tally the number of children hurt nationally in gun-related incidents. It was published Monday in the journal Pediatrics.
>
> A national database of patients younger than 20 who were admitted to hospitals in 2009 shows that boys represented nearly 90% of the total, and that the rate of gunshot-related hospitalizations for African American males was 10 times that of white males.
>
> Blacks ages 15 to 19 were 13 times more likely than their white peers to be injured by gunfire.
>
> And 70% of all black children hospitalized for gun injury (compared with 32% of all white children injured by firearms) were classified as victims of assault. Latino children and adolescents were three times likelier than white children to be hospitalized with a firearm-related injury.
>
> Hospital care for youths injured by gunfire cost $147 million in 2009, according to the report, but that is a fraction of the overall cost of the injuries. It doesn't include physician-related services, rehabilitation and ongoing care and rehospitalization, and does not take into account many

---

[102]http://pediatrics.aappublications.org/content/early/2014/01/22/peds.2013-1809.abstract

victims' loss of future productivity. (Past research has found that almost half of children hospitalized for gun-related injury are discharged with a disability.)

Among Latino youths, firearm-related injuries were three times higher than among white children, the data show. And African American girls were more than six times as likely as their white counterparts to be injured by gunfire.[103]

Got any ideas yet?

The only benefit of a true zero-tolerance gun control policy among the black population (this paper makes it clear which demographic is responsible for the incredible financial burden on hospital care for treating those children of gunfire wounds) is we can train our trauma surgeons employed by the military on life-saving techniques before they go into a war zone.

For the killing fields of Baltimore, Cincinnati, and Philadelphia provide hourly opportunities for new techniques to be developed that will save the life of a black person shot by another black individual (one of the truly unexplored reasons why homicides have declined so significantly in places like Chicago and New York City: heightened proficiency of emergency room surgeons/care courtesy of an almost endless supply of black bodies to experiment new techniques upon). [104]

Consider this: a study conducted by Dr. David Livingstone, Wesley J. Howe Professor and chief of trauma surgery at Rutgers-New Jersey Medical School and director of the New Jersey Trauma Center, reviewed all the interpersonal gunshot cases at the hospital between 2000 and 2011, using the data from the trauma registry, emergency

---

[103] http://www.latimes.com/science/sciencenow/la-sci-sn-guns-toll-children-20140127,0,2247874.story#ixzz2rjR08bfk

[104] http://online.wsj.com/news/articles/SB10001424127887324712504578131360684277812

department billing and hospital finance records.

Only four percent of his patients were white (odds on what percentage of blacks were behind these shootings?) [Degree of Gunshot Violence Takes Turn for the Worse, Study Suggests, AnesthesiologyNews.com, 1-3-2014]:

> Of the 6,322 patients who presented with firearm injuries, 92% were male. They were young, with a mean age of 27 years (±9 years). In fact, they were very young: 29% of all gunshot victims were between the ages of 20 and 24, and nearly 20% were teenagers aged 15 to 19.
>
> In keeping with other studies, the research confirmed that gunshot violence disproportionately affects blacks and Hispanics. Eighty-six percent of gunshot patients who presented at the Level 1 trauma center were black, and 9% were Hispanic. Whites and Asians represented 4% and 1% of all gunshot patients, respectively.[105]

What does the average person treated at the University of Maryland Shock Trauma Center (serving Baltimore's majority-black population) look like?

Funny you should ask...

> Violence is the leading cause of death for young adults in Baltimore and is a widely recognized public health concern.
>
> VIP Background Dr. Carnell Cooper started the Violence Intervention Program (VIP) in 1998 after seeing victims of traumatic violent injury being treated, released, and readmitted months later due to another, often more serious, violent injury.
>
> Dr. Cooper recognized that this "revolving door phenomenon" occurred repeatedly, with patients being discharged without

---

[105]http://www.anesthesiologynews.com/ViewArticle.aspx?d=Web+Excl usives&d_id=175&i=December+2013&i_id=1020&a_id=24685

any form of counseling or intervention to the same streets where they had sustained their injuries. Seeing this caused Dr. Cooper to ask a simple scientific question: "How can we reduce the number of repeat victims of intentional violent injury coming through the doors of Shock Trauma every day?"

To answer this question, Dr. Cooper, Dr. Paul Stolley, and other colleagues completed a comprehensive case-control study (Archives of Surgery, Vol. 135, No. 7, July 2000) that identified the risk factors for repeat victims of violence. The study identified the following risk factors:

- African-American male

- Median age 31 Unemployed

- No health insurance

- Income less than $10,000 yearly

- Current drug user

- Past or present drug dealer

- Positive test for psychoactive substances upon admission

- Additionally, eighty-six percent (86%) of the victims felt that disrespect was involved with their injury, and a majority of the victims had a history of involvement with the criminal justice system.[106]

How about a more in-depth look at the societal cost (in terms of wasted man-hours and tax dollars trying to save criminals' lives) of black people on trauma centers in Baltimore? (A gun is just a tool; a person must make a conscious decision to use this tool as a weapon.)

---

[106] http://umm.edu/programs/shock-trauma/services/injury-prevention/violence/components/vip

[The trauma of gun violence: Dr. Edward E. Cornwell III, trauma chief at Johns Hopkins Hospital, describes gunshot wounds as "more and more a juvenile disease.", Baltimore Sun, 3-12-2000]:

So what happens when the human body meets the gun industry's deadliest creations? It's not pretty. Ask Dr. "Eddie" Cornwell, the trauma chief at Johns Hopkins Hospital. During the 16 years he has been a trauma surgeon, Cornwell has saved his share of gunshot-wound victims, and he has watched many others go to the medical examiner for autopsies.

Edward E. Cornwell III, 43, realizes that only a quirk of fate separates him from the African-American youths he is trying to save. He says his parents made the difference.

Cornwell has strong opinions about gun violence. Recently, he shared his thoughts with Perspective Editor Mike Adams.

M.A. *How many gunshot wounds does Hopkins treat annually?*

E.C. It's been slowly increasing. We had about 365 in 1997, about 380-some in 1998 and 390 last year. Baltimore actually stands out a bit, apart from the national trend.

From the early to the late 1990s, in Boston, New York Los Angeles, Miami, Washington, the numbers of penetrating trauma, gunshot wounds and stabbings, have gone down. Baltimore is different, and I don't have a complete explanation for it. But, in the neighborhood around Hopkins, about 80 percent of the crime is centered around trying to obtain or sell illegal drugs.

How would you describe the typical gunshot wound victim treated here at Hopkins based on age, race and economic background?

Simply put, young black males. The typical patient would be in his late teens or early 20s, someone from the surrounding neighborhood. As I said before, in 1999, we had about 390 gunshot cases, and those patients from the narrow age of 15 to 20 years old represent close to 60 percent of our gunshot wounds and close to two-thirds of all of our deaths.

What's the societal cost of these gunshot cases? Who's paying the bill?

You and I are paying the bill. The taxpayers are paying the bill. That's the sad truth throughout the country. To be a Level 1 Trauma Center as we are, we need to be open, ready and available 24 hours a day. That means the lights are on, the CAT scan is ready, the operating room is ready to go, the blood bank is available, people are in-house who are specialists in certain areas and prepared to take care of these patients whether they show up or not. And then, when the patients show up, they may or may not be able to pay. Many of my patients are Male X, Male Y, Male P, for hours before we even know a name.[107]

A sensible gun policy for America?

Make it illegal for black people to own a gun.

Those black people found possessing a gun?

Throw them in jail immediately.

Those found using a gun in a crime?

Execute immediately.

America doesn't need gun control; it needs black control.

---

[107] http://articles.baltimoresun.com/2000-03-12/topic/0003140350_1_gunshot-wounds-cornwell-johns-hopkins

Two Black Males (one the son of a police dispatcher) Murder White Female Bartender in her Baltimore Home: Just another "Robbery Gone Wrong"

Not too long ago, I received an email from a lawyer representing the family of a murdered white male, in a city long known to be hostile to the dwindling white minority living there.

He requested a picture of the deceased be removed from the site, since the victim counted black individuals as his friends when he was still capable of breathing.

Black people were responsible for this white male's murder, meaning his "counting black individuals among his peer-group" didn't persuade (or dissuade) those same individuals from taking his life.

I agreed to honor the family's request, under one simple condition: that he please tell the family the man is still dead, and that even though he had black friends, it didn't protect him from being senselessly slaughtered by black people.

Which brings me to the story of a white female in Baltimore, Kimberly Leto. The 51-year-old bartender was murdered in her home by two black males in a "robbery gone wrong" (according to the *Baltimore Sun*).[108]

Even more unsettling is that one of the black suspects has a mother employed as a dispatcher with the Baltimore Police Department (a

---

[108] http://articles.baltimoresun.com/2014-02-02/news/bs-md-highlandtown-murder-arrrests-20140202_1_two-teenagers-highlandtown-police-headquarters

civilian employee).

Oddly, none of the articles on this story mention that Leto was a white female, a productive member of society murdered inside her home in America's Monrovia, Baltimore. . [Police arrest teenagers in Ellwood Avenue homicide: Kimberly Leto found dead inside Patterson Park home, WBALTV.com, 2-3-14]:

> Baltimore City police have arrested two teenagers in connection with the killing of a woman in her Patterson Park home, while neighbors say they're shocked and saddened at the loss of such a good person.
>
> Baltimore police on Sunday arrested Allen Pinkney, 15, and Alonzo Gorham-Ramos, 14, on murder, first-degree conspiracy to commit murder, first-degree burglary and dangerous weapon with intent to injure charges.
>
> Around 7:30 a.m. Friday, officers found 51-year-old Kimberly Leto dead inside her home in the 400 block of South Ellwood Avenue. Police said Leto suffered from trauma to her body. The manner of Leto's death is still pending from the State's Medical Examiner.
>
> Leto worked at O'Donnell's Pub on Potomac Street in nearby Canton. Regulars at the bar and friends of the victim, who called her Kimmie, said they're shocked and saddened by what happened to her.
>
> "She was just a wonderful person. When she walked in she just had a certain glow about herself," said friend Kevin Carrick.
>
> "She was always so full of life. You never saw her with a sad look on her face. She was always smiling and laughing," said friend Stephanie Stickline.
>
> Police said Ramos faced charges of breaking into Leto's house in August, and they believe the motive Friday was burglary, too. Officials said Ramos' prior arrest is what led them to him

so quickly in Leto's slaying.

"This is a heartbreaking tragedy on so many levels. Our purpose today is not to claim victory with this arrest but to lament that such a tragedy occurred in the first place," said Police Commissioner Anthony Batts.

Despite the arrests, people who live and work in the Patterson Park neighborhood were left with even more questions.

"For a 14- and 15-year-old to do this, why couldn't they just -- if they had to take something, why not just take it and go? Why did they have to kill her?" questioned Carrick.

Police also confirmed that Ramos' mother is a dispatcher, a civilian employee, with the Police Department.[109]

Here's how the *Baltimore Sun* remembered Leto.[Police arrest two teenagers in killing of Highlandtown woman, Baltimore Sun, 2-2-14]:

Kimberly Leto, of the 400 block of S. Ellwood Ave., was found dead inside her home overlooking Patterson Park early Friday with what police described as "upper body trauma." A neighbor said she was told by police the home had been broken into from the rear, and a chair could be observed pushed under the rear kitchen window, which was half-open.

Police said they believe that Gorham-Ramos and Pinkney killed Leto in a robbery gone wrong. Change, electronics and small personal items were taken from the house, police said.

Batts called the killing "unconscionable" and expressed regret that the crime will result in three lives being thrown away — not only Leto's, but also those of the two teenagers.

---

[109] http://www.wbaltv.com/news/maryland/baltimore-city/city-police-find-dead-woman-in-home/-/10131532/24224314/-/w982bo/-/index.html#ixzz2sHEfFDA6

"It is unacceptable to see family after family ripped apart by such petty behavior," he said. "This is a heartbreaking tragedy on so many levels."

Investigators said they were able to quickly identify Gorham-Ramos and Pinkney as suspects because Gorham-Ramos had been charged with burglarizing Leto's house before.

Police confirmed Pinkney's mother works for the department as a dispatcher.Leto was well-known to patrons as a bartender at O'Donnell's Pub in Canton. Another bartender working there Sunday before the Super Bowl said the staff at O'Donnell's was still trying to cope with news of their colleague's death."It's still tender," she said.

City Councilman James B. Kraft, who represents Highlandtown, said he had requested additional officers, including on foot patrol, in the neighborhood before Christmas and again this year.

He said the mayor's administration and police commanders told him the department is too understaffed for the requests to be fulfilled.

"I don't have a gun. I don't have a badge," he said. "I can't stand on every corner. All I can do is try to get [police officers] where they could be and try to get more of them."[110]

What does my conversation with a white victim's lawyer in the beginning of the chapter have to do with the murder of Leto?

Because the mere mention of a "racial angle" of this killing will upset Leto's family and friends. They will take to mainstream and social media with claims that she had black friends and displayed a "Coexist" bumper sticker on her car.

---

[110] http://articles.baltimoresun.com/2014-02-02/news/bs-md-highlandtown-murder-arrrests-20140202_1_two-teenagers-highlandtown-police-headquarters

It doesn't matter.

She's dead.

All she saw in those last terrifying moments of her life: two black males in what police labeled as merely a "robbery gone wrong."

Sounds more like "murder gone right"...

Violence Prevention Ideas Discussed in Emergency Planning Meeting in Baltimore City Hall; 20 Years Ago, Norplant was the Solution to Future Violence Baltimore

White-on-white violence (be it homicide, robbery, assault, etc.) in a metropolitan area never seems to be significant enough to warrant government interventions or community marches.

More to the point, no one protects members of the white community who engage in crime, inflict damage on property, or are wanted in homicide investigations.

You see, those white people who engage in homicide are usually suffering from severe mental illness or other psychological damage; thus, they pose no threat to the greater community at large.

However, preventative measures ARE needed in the *black* community, where criminal, anti-life pathologies are so prevalent a call for a "march to end violence" is an annual event; and where police cajoling the black community to cooperate with a homicide investigation is a daily chore.

This is certainly the case for 65-percent-black Baltimore. [Violence prevention ideas aired at City Hall meeting: Bloody start to 2014 spurred emergency planning session, Baltimore Sun, 1-25-14]:

> The founder of last year's 300 Men March and two Baltimore City Council members held an emergency planning meeting Friday evening at City Hall, saying the bloody start to the new year spurred them to develop a violence prevention strategy sooner than they had originally anticipated.
>
> The city recorded 16 homicides in the first 12 days of the year. January's toll stood at 18 as of Friday night. Last year, there were 235 homicides in Baltimore, an 8 percent increase over 2012 and a four-year high.
>
> "A murder a day wasn't something we could just sit on," said Munir Bahar, who founded the march movement last year to galvanize residents, particularly men, to combat violence. "We were kind of hoping the wintertime would calm things down a little and we would have more time for planning."

Also Friday, it emerged that a 24-year-old man killed this month was the nephew of City Council President Bernard C. "Jack" Young. Tavon Antonio Young, who was sentenced in 2009 to five years in prison for his role in a high-profile drug distribution conspiracy, was found fatally shot Jan. 17 in an alley in the Harwood neighborhood.

The funeral was Friday, and Young was unavailable for comment. His spokesman, Lester Davis, said the councilman was "spending his time supporting his sister and their extended family during this period of grief."

Last May, a 20-year-old cousin of Mayor Stephanie Rawlings-Blake was fatally shot, the victim of a suspected home invasion robbery.

Friday's meeting was called by Bahar and Councilmen Brandon Scott and Nick Mosby. "We wanted to get a plan together and get people mobilized, so when spring hits we can be ready to deploy into the neighborhoods," said Scott, who represents Northeast Baltimore and is vice chairman of the council's Public Safety Committee.

A standing-room-only crowd of about 100, including community group leaders and Police Department representatives, packed a meeting room at City Hall as Bahar, a fitness trainer, delivered a high-energy presentation.

"This is the charge: How do we do more?" he said. "How do we increase our presence on the streets?"

Among the ideas he outlined were the creation of a "mobilized street force" of at least 100 people and a citywide communications network of 1,000 residents to alert their neighbors to incidents in "real time."

The 300 Men March took place July 5, cutting east across the city along North Avenue. Promoted largely through social media and word of mouth, the nearly 10-mile trek drew more than 600 people, according to participants, among them

Rawlings-Blake and Baltimore police Commissioner Anthony W. Batts.

A number of smaller marches were held later in the summer, including one in which about 60 men walked through East Baltimore, speaking to people they met and handing out fliers detailing a "code of honor" for peacefully resolving conflicts.

Bahar said before the meeting that last year's higher homicide total did not make him feel those efforts had been in vain. He said he knew that lasting change takes years.

"What's disheartening is the lack of participation from the community," he said. "We can only round up 30 to 40 men to come out on the streets at night and do this anti-violence work. That's the discouraging part."[111]

When government leaders have members of their own family involved in criminal activity, you know that city is beyond repair.

Furthermore, any violence prevention ideas discussed that doesn't mention the violence has a biological source - black people - is an exercise in futility.

Strange that only one score and two years ago, America was on the verge of becoming a sane place.

And Baltimore was the city on the cutting edge of a tomorrow where "violence prevention meeting" at city hall would have been the subject of a dystopian future, instead of one free of the burden of a people fucking their way to the ruin of a entire civilization (strangely, the byproduct of this "union" being completely subsidized from cradle-to-grave by productive members of society). Even conservative hack George Will praised Baltimore for the measure they enacted, writing [Baltimore's Fledgling Norplant Program Seems Careful, Consensual

---

[111] http://articles.baltimoresun.com/2014-01-24/news/bs-md-300-men-meeting-20140124_1_300-men-march-munir-bahar-youth-violence

- And Needed, Philly.com, 3-18-1993]:

> And those black activists who profess to see Norplant as a "genocidal" attack on black fertility should answer this:

> What is more dangerous to the flourishing of black America, Norplant for teenagers or a growing number of black adolescents headed for a life in poverty because they were born into poverty to a single mother whose life chances were blighted by a pregnancy at age 15?[112]

Norplant. A way to decrease pregnancy among black Baltimore teenagers.[113]

A plan to try and save the future of Baltimore, by waging a war against destructive decisions; makes sense, right?

A way to make Baltimore safer for not just white people, but all people in a manner of a generation by terminating pregnancies among a demographic completely unprepared to care for the black children they'd unleash upon the world. [Norplant Is Getting Few Takers At School, New York Times, 6-3-1994]:

> Providing Norplant to Paquin's students was seen as an example of the struggle being waged by officials in Baltimore and other cities to reduce the rising number of out-of-wedlock births, a phenomenon that is held responsible for many of today's social ills, including poverty, welfare dependency and high crime rates.

> But so far, officials say only 36 of 700 students at Paquin have turned to Norplant in the nearly 15 months it has been available.

---

[112] http://articles.philly.com/1993-03-18/news/25951495_1_norplant-program-contraceptive-implant-teenage-pregnancy-rates

[113] http://articles.baltimoresun.com/1992-11-03/features/1992308221_1_norplant-progesterone-egg

Earlier this year, health officials here extended the Norplant option to 2 more of the 21 high schools in the city. But Bernice Rosenthal, director of school-based clinics for the health department, said only two students have had the device inserted by staff members in those clinics.

Shunned by School Boards

Officials of Advocates for Youth, a Washington-based group that promotes sex education and birth control for adolescents, say school boards around the country have shied away from offering the contraceptive in school-based health clinics. About 1 percent of 105 such clinics that responded to a survey provide Norplant in their clinics, the organization said.

Baltimore health officials say many young women have shunned Norplant because of misinformation about its side effects and because of accusations by some blacks that making Norplant available in predominantly black schools like Paquin was "genocide."

"I know anecdotally from patients that it's still being talked about on the street," said Dr. Peter Beilenson, Baltimore's Commissioner of Health. "There are rumors about Norplant that are just not true."[114]

Just who was spreading these rumors Norplant wasn't safe?

Not George Will.

He approved of the idea (the Republican Party had not been completely hijacked by the civilization-destroying Pro-Life movement yet).

Long regarded as one of the top conservative thinkers, Will wrote this about the Norplant controversy in the intellectually freer climate of 1993. [Blighted by Pregnancy, Baltimore Sun, 3-18-1993]:

---

[114] http://www.nytimes.com/1994/05/03/us/norplant-is-getting-few-takers-at-school.html

Begin here: In 1990 nearly 10 percent of Baltimore girls aged 15 to 17, almost all unmarried, gave birth. That is why in 1993 the city is embarking on a program to make Norplant, a long-term (five-year) contraceptive implant, available to teenage girls at school clinics and elsewhere.

The case against the program can be put concisely: By substituting chemical protection for moral restraint, it sends a message of resignation regarding behavior once considered deviant and reprehensible but now redefined, in the name of "realism," as normal.

Norplant has been embroiled elsewhere in controversial welfare and criminal-justice policies raising questions of morally or legally dubious coercion. There have been proposals for monetary incentives or sanctions for unmarried welfare mothers to agree to implants. Judges have proposed implants in lieu of prison for women convicted of drug or child abuse.

But leaving aside the question of when it might be acceptable for society to encourage Norplant use, Baltimore's evolving program seems careful, consensual and needed. And those black activists who profess to see Norplant as a "genocidal" attack on black fertility should answer this:

What is more dangerous to the flourishing of black America, Norplant for teen-agers or a growing number of black adolescents headed for a life in poverty because they were born into poverty to a single mother whose life chances were blighted by a pregnancy at age 15?[115]

No.

It was the Nation of Islam, who'd rather black people (primarily males) have the right to play predator to the entire Baltimore community once they grew up, instead of never have been born in the first place. [150 protesters object to Norplant in schools Nation of

---

[115] http://articles.baltimoresun.com/1993-03-18/news/1993077033_1_norplant-rebecca-pregnancy

Islam members call it 'genocide' BALTIMORE CITY, Baltimore Sun, 10-1-1993]:

> Carrying placards reading "Stop Norplant genocide" and "No Norplant experiments on our teens," more than 150 people jammed the Baltimore school board meeting last night to protest the city's plan to let schools offer the contraceptive.
>
> The protesters, most of them members of the Nation of Islam, the black Muslim group led by the controversial Louis Farrakhan, called on the board to forbid school clinics to offer Norplant.
>
> They denounced the contraceptive as "social engineering" designed to reduce the black population. They claimed it has not been adequately tested and said it encourages teen-age sex instead of abstinence.
>
> "I would urge you to not use our girls as guinea pigs in this social experiment," said Debra H. Freeman, a spokeswoman representing Mr. Farrakhan's organization.
>
> The protest came a month after Mayor Kurt L. Schmoke decided to let five high schools decide for themselves whether to offer Norplant to teen-agers in school clinics. Mayor Schmoke was out of town last night and could not be reached for comment.[116]

An attempt to end the "cycle of dependency" and reliance on long-term welfare was what this Norplant program in Baltimore was attempting to do. After all, a 1994 article noted, "In Baltimore, the city dedicates an entire school, with grades six through 12, to helping pregnant girls keep their lives on track."[117]

---

[116] http://articles.baltimoresun.com/1993-10-01/news/1993274047_1_norplant-school-clinics-baltimore-school

[117] http://articles.philly.com/1994-01-31/news/25822525_1_welfare-within-five-years-welfare-reform-long-term-welfare

It was - if we are to believe the "poverty creates violence" canard - a way to stop future criminals from ever being born in the first place (consider it the "Kill Jamal Conner" plan from a black-theme *Terminator* movie).

But poverty doesn't create violence; black people create violence, which turns an entire area into one brimming with poverty.

That's Baltimore in 2014.

It's why the black community marches against violence (all black in origin) on a yearly basis.

It's why the black community demands answers to the violence (all black in origin) at City Hall meetings on a yearly basis.

It's why businesses flee Baltimore and those remaining behind barricade their employees in Plexiglas.

America was on the verge of sanity in 1992.

Instead, America went the route of Ralph Reed.

Salvation isn't coming, though.

What IS coming, you may ask? A swarm of feral, thuggish "Jamal Conners" , courtesy of HUD, on a mission to to infiltrate every peaceful white enclave in the country -- an effort to spread black pathologies as official state policy to those white communities in need of "vibrancy".

In need of a little Baltimore...

The United States had a shot at salvation in 1992.

Today, we are on the verge of another Democrat win in 2016, facing the appointment of leaders like Bill de Blasio to executive-level positions. Perhaps Andrew Cuomo, too.

George Will was a moderate Republican, whose approval of Norplant in 1993 was drowned out in the *March for Life*.

Fitting that this march helps ensure Baltimore continues to be nothing more than a city of yesteryear, the blight a reminder of all that was; the crime and horrendous school system a reminder of all that will be.

What Is Life Like for the White Minority in South Africa? Exactly what life is like for the White Minority in Baltimore

What would it be like to live as a white person in South Africa, a nation your ancestors created and yet has now been democratically taken away from you by black people... black people who have created the conditions that have directly led to that country's complete demise?

A country where the dispossession of whites is nearly complete.

Well, if you're one of the few remaining members of the white population of Baltimore, you are experiencing what life is like for whites in post-Apartheid South Africa, where the numeric majority of blacks voted themselves into power and enjoy the daily spoils of their conquest.

Much like the black-on-white violence in South Africa, the murder of a 51-year-old white bartender, Kimberly Leto, by two blacks males (16-year-old Allen Pinkney and 14-year-old Alonzo Gorham-Ramos, the latter already a father) is sending shockwaves through Baltimore's diminished white population. [Woman's death in burglary leaves Southeast Baltimore reeling: Residents putting pressure on police to step up patrols after Kimberly Leto's death, Baltimore Sun, 2-4-14]:

> Residents in Southeast Baltimore have been unnerved by the notion that a resident would be killed by apparent strangers in the security of her home overlooking Patterson Park.
>
> City Councilman James B. Kraft, who represents the area, has said he is increasingly frustrated that the city has not heeded his calls for more officers on foot patrol
>
> Mike Beczkowski, who leads neighborhood crime awareness walks in Canton, said he doesn't understand why the mayor's office or police haven't responded to Kraft's requests.
>
> He said neighborhoods in Southeast Baltimore are "the wealthiest in the city" and "prone to more criminal attacks like this."
>
> "Despite repeated requests, the mayor says we can't have them and has sent them elsewhere," Beczkowski said. "We

plan on flooding her office with calls and emails until we do."

He has advised residents to take their own safety precautions. "Our advice is for everyone to get a burglary system to help prevent break-ins," Beczkowski said.

"Our safety requires ongoing vigilance."[118]

"Ongoing vigilance."

That is the necessary requirement for Baltimore's white population, especially when the city posted 27 homicides in January of 2014 [City Records 27 Murders In January; Victim Identified,WBAL.com, 2-1-2014][119]

No white suspects, almost all black victims. Then again, this a city that, back in 2000, considered fewer than 300 murders to be cause for celebration, hoping it was a sign that civilization was making a comeback. [Fewer than 300 homicides at last - Crime: For the first time in more than a decade, Baltimore's toll for a year breaks a barrier that it had seemed impossible to breach only months ago., Baltimore Sun, 1-1-2001][120]

The overwhelming number of black people in Baltimore necessitates police-state measures to maintain some semblance of order: Police consultant William Bratton observed that Baltimore has one of the highest police officers per capita in the nation (46 officer per 100,000), yet even this isn't enough to lower crime. Bratton, a respected police expert, says the priority of any police department is to maintain positive relations with the African American community, since that's

---

[118] http://www.baltimoresun.com/news/maryland/crime/blog/bs-md-ci-teen-murders-20140203,0,5392417.story#ixzz2sOJCS6P7

[119] http://www.wbal.com/article/105186/2/city-records-27-murders-in-january-victim-identified

[120] http://articles.baltimoresun.com/2001-01-01/news/0101010157_1_homicides-baltimore-norris

the primary community they'll deal with. [Bill Bratton hired to review Baltimore Police Department:'Respect crime' fuels most violence in city, Bratton says, WBALTV, 7-25-13]:

> One of the country's top policing experts now hired in Baltimore to reshape the city's Police Department is speaking out about what he calls "respect crime" -- the reason Baltimore has seen such a surge in violence.[121]

Though no community leader has the courage to support white minority interests (Baltimore is 63.5 percent black and 28.2 percent white), or demand justice for white victims like Kimberly Leto , those black people united in keeping power in their hands will protect their own interests by supporting race-based organizations such as the Vanguard Justice Society - a black-only police union - and the Vulcan Blazers, a black-only firefighter association in Baltimore.

In his book *Firefighter*, Herman Williams (the first black fire chief in Baltimore as well as America) reveals that members of the Vulcan Blazers were mad with him that he didn't immediately engage in ethnic cleansing and fire all whites once he was appointed head of the department:

> To my surprise and disappointment, my old colleagues in the Vulcan Blazers, the African-American firefighters' organization I helped found, started criticizing me in the community and with the NAACP. Some of the anger came from unrealistic expectations, because there were some black guys who really expected me to do some "ethnic cleansing" in the department, throw out the whites, and appoint only blacks. I could brush that off as just nonsense. No city official in Baltimore history had done more for black empowerment in city government than I had at Public Works, Transportation, and now the fire department, where frankly just about every day I as playing footloose with the

[121] http://www.wbaltv.com/news/maryland/baltimore-city/bill-bratton-hired-to-review-baltimore-police-department/-/10131532/21151124/-/lkd160z/-/index.html

regulations to get what I wanted. (p. 249, Williams)

Translation: *we are in charge now, so we must demand payback from white people who remain in our city for what their ancestors did to us.*

Black racial solidarity was evident back in 1999 when the majority black city elected a white mayor (Martin O'Malley), mainly because no law-abiding black candidate could be found. A black pastor, Rev. Frank M. Reid, endorsed O'Malley and was promptly uninvited from a black Baptist Convention as a result of his "betrayal." [Ministers withdraw invitation to Reid: Baptist group notes pastor's endorsement of O'Malley for mayor, Baltimore Sun, 9-21-1999][122]

Oh, but it gets better. Some black "power brokers" also threw their endorsements to O'Malley, ostensibly because of his history of "empowering African Americans" (a more likely reason: O'Malley was the only Democrat on the ticket without a police record). [A Divisive Mayoral Race in Baltimore, NY Times, 8-8-1999]:

> After weeks of political chaos featuring 27 declared mayoral candidates, six of them with arrest records, a campaign showdown loomed noisy as summer thunder here this week in a rowdy scene outside City Hall.
>
> "Man, you're stabbing us in the back," one black politician shouted at another as demonstrators disrupted a news conference, called to endorse a mayoral candidate, and drove their rivals across the street.
>
> But the demonstrators' target, Howard P. Rawlings, the State General Assembly delegate, was determined to go forward with his role as a political kingmaker. He called on this gritty city's black majority to support the leading white mayoral contender, Martin O'Malley, a city councilman.

---

[122] http://articles.baltimoresun.com/1999-09-21/news/9909210182_1_baptist-ministers-conference-ministers-conference-memorial-baptist-church

"O'Malley is a new generation of white political leadership,"
Mr. Rawlings, who is black, declared after he retreated from
the hooting and hollering demonstrators, bused to City Hall
on Thursday by the rival campaign of Lawrence A. Bell 3d,
the City Council president and the leading black candidate.

'O'Malley has a track record of empowering black Americans,"
Mr. Rawlings said in front of the television cameras.

Mr. Bell, who had been increasingly upset at the rise of Mr.
O'Malley from the status of also-ran to possible unity
candidate, was nowhere in sight on Thursday. But his
political lieutenants directed the disruptive rally and
denounced the potentially decisive endorsements of Mr.
O'Malley as treachery by "so-called pseudo-Negro political
leaders."[123]

Only white candidates that agree to play ball with the black
community can be elected; prominent blacks ("so-called pseudo-Negro
political leaders") who dare side with a white person will be deemed
an enemy of the people.

A black majority in any neighborhood/community/school/city/nation
will always translate into demands for "blacks to be in charge".
Baltimore's White Shadow, CBS News, 8-13-2001]:

"We should have an African-American mayor," says Rev.
Gregory Perkins, a civil rights activist who has been active for
decades. Perkins argues that whites usually vote along racial
lines and therefore so should blacks.

Asked whether his first choice will always be the black
candidate, Perkins says, "Most definitely." But isn't that what
people fought against in the 1960s – viewing things purely in
term of race?

"In America, it's a reality," says Perkins. "And I'm convinced

---

[123] http://www.nytimes.com/1999/08/08/us/a-divisive-mayoral-race-in-
baltimore.html

no one can represent me like me."[124]

Brown University political-science professor Marion Orr was quite vocal about his desire for a black mayor: it's our city, and a black mayor is symbolic of our victory over white racism. It's our "prize". [MAYORAL RACE: Seeking the City's Top Job Becomes a Study in Black and White, City Paper, 8-11-1999]:

> The election of a white mayor at this stage would likely leave a bitter taste with many African-American leaders and cause friction, Orr says: His or her ability to bring people together would be hampered by a sense among African-Americans that they "lost the prize."

> Many agree with Orr that Baltimore, a 60-plus-percent-black city facing mammoth social and economic challenges, should elect an African-American mayor. Miles reckons a white mayor could accomplish what he or she wants from a management standpoint; given Baltimore's strong-mayor form of government, any chief executive has considerable leverage to shape the budget and round up City Council votes for pet bills. But in terms of human dynamics, Miles says, "it would be a city managed under a great deal of tension."

> "If O'Malley wins, the big problem is going to be when he tries to govern the city," Hopkins' Crenson says. "People are going to be watching him for the slightest hint of favoritism toward whites, the slightest bit of racism. The symbolic political quotient is going to get very high."[125]

What happens if the elected black officials show the slightest hint of favoritism toward blacks? Does that qualify as the slightest bit of racism?

"The prize" was always about racial control of a city (or country). That's the reason South African blacks fought to end Apartheid;

---

[124] http://www.cbsnews.com/news/baltimores-white-shadow/

[125] http://www2.citypaper.com/news/story.asp?id=8582

similarly, that's why black people want to maintain control of Baltimore.

To be fair, O'Malley did try to enact a few positive changes once in office, like ape Bratton's zero-tolerance police policies from New York City. Unfortunately, such an "extreme" policing strategy, while very effective, would "unfairly affect blacks" in Baltimore, since blacks in the city are virtually the only demographic committing crime. [Black officials raise zero-tolerance fears: O'Malley tells group that enforcement will not be race-based, Baltimore Sun, 12-21-1999]:

> Concerned that zero-tolerance policing could increase racial profiling by police, about 20 African-American elected officials met yesterday with Mayor Martin O'Malley to ensure that officers do not target suspects because of their race.
>
> State Del. Howard P. Rawlings, who organized yesterday's meeting, said it was the first in which African-American City Council members and state legislators met with the mayor "to discuss an issue of such significance."[126]

Baltimore's black community isn't as concerned about crime as it is with maintaining control of the city and ensuring that police policy doesn't remove too many registered voters from streets. This certainly seems to be the case, since black jury nullification is the hallmark of justice[127] in majority black Baltimore. [Baltimore mayor may count on sympathetic jurors, Fox News, 1-15-2009]:

> If Mayor Sheila Dixon goes to trial before a Baltimore jury, it might include some of the best friends she could hope to find.
>
> The city's jurors -- often poor, uneducated and distrustful of police and prosecutors -- have historically been sympathetic to

---

[126] http://articles.baltimoresun.com/1999-12-21/news/9912210181_1_zero-tolerance-mayor-martin-o-malley-police-department

[127] http://articles.baltimoresun.com/2008-08-21/news/0808200122_1_jessamy-jury-nullification-jury-system

defendants, most of whom are black.

"Jurors in Baltimore city, typical jurors, they render verdicts from the gut," said Warren A. Brown, a city defense attorney for more than 20 years. "To hell with the law, to hell with the facts, they will render a verdict that they think is fair, is right."

And while Dixon isn't your typical defendant -- among other things, the city's first black female mayor is accused of stealing gift cards meant for needy families and treating herself to fur coats and pricey hotel stays on her developer-boyfriend's tab -- her attorneys are already playing to potential jurors by portraying the case as a witch hunt by the state prosecutor.

Her attorney, Arnold M. Weiner, ridiculed State Prosecutor Robert A. Rohrbaugh, a gubernatorial appointee who investigates public corruption, for his relentless pursuit of Dixon and his failure to indict her on a more serious charge, like bribery.

"The state prosecutor went on a journey that was nothing but a big circle," Weiner said.

A study released in fall 2008 by the Abell Foundation, a nonpartisan think tank that examines poverty in Baltimore, found juries in the city less likely to convict defendants than those in the surrounding suburban counties. The study cited both socio-economic factors --the Baltimore jury pool is poorer and less educated than in the suburbs -- and race-- the city is two-thirds black and 92 percent of defendants were nonwhite.[128]

That's Baltimore's definition of "justice": protecting the people, *the black people* from the "racist" judicial system. This is the same city

---

[128]

http://www.foxnews.com/printer_friendly_wires/2009Jan15/0,4675,Ba ltimoreMayorJuries,00.html that gave birth to the 'stop-snitching' movement,[129] and witness intimidation[130] is championed on the streets. The police strategy of 'keep talking' was greeted with laughter, while rappers keep celebrating their "stop snitching" motto as unwritten law. [131]

And control of City Hall means a repudiation of the crime-fighting techniques introduced by the white mayor. [Rawlings-Blake says city won't return to days of 'mass arrests' under O'Malley: O'Malley's police department arrested one out of six Baltimore residents some years, Baltimore Sun, 9-20-2013]:

> Baltimore Mayor Stephanie Rawlings-Blake released a statement this afternoon, saying her police department would not return to the days of "mass arrests" under Gov. Martin O'Malley's tenure as mayor.
>
> "Returning to the days of mass arrests for any and every minor offense might be a good talking point but it has been proven to be a far less effective strategy for actually reducing crime," Rawlings-Blake said in a statement.
>
> Recently, the governor has argued for increased arrests in Baltimore as a way to combat violent crime. O'Malley, who advocated zero-tolerance policing policies while mayor, says he is concerned that Baltimore has stalled in its crime-fighting efforts, emphasizing that arrests are only half of what they were during his time as mayor.[132]

---

[129] http://articles.baltimoresun.com/2004-12-08/news/0412080180_1_stop-snitching-bethea-denver-nuggets

[130] http://articles.baltimoresun.com/2004-12-29/news/0412290396_1_bethea-video-dvd

[131] http://www.baltimoresun.com/bal-te.md.dvd11may11,0,7017704.story

[132] http://www.baltimoresun.com/news/maryland/politics/blog/bal-rawlingsblake-says-city-wont-return-to-days-of-mass-arrests-under-

Crime is increasing. Homicides are increasing.

Kimberly Leto, a white 51-year-old bartender is dead, courtesy of two black males who grew up believing that Baltimore belongs to them; that it's okay to promote *their* racial interests above all others; that protecting black criminals is their duty; and that "the prize" is maintaining black hegemony over the ~~city that reads~~ *City that Bleeds*.

If you want to know what being white in South Africa is like, take a trip to Baltimore.

"America's Monrovia": Will the Last White Person Out of Baltimore Please Turn Out the Lights?

Baltimore: a 63 percent black city.

Arguably, this is one of America's most dangerous places, where "everyday citizens" (everyday *black* citizens), in utter disregard for

omalley-20130920,0,169982.story

the white man's law, are transforming the city into the USA's version of Monrovia, Liberia.

Although HBO's *The Wire* tried to humanize the downtrodden black population, it's blacks who are engaging in "everyday" malice toward Baltimore's viability. Blaming "gangs" for the criminal behavior isn't going to work anymore, either: last year alone, police determined that only 3 of its 224 homicides were drug-related. [Batts: Crime Dropped for "Everyday Citizens" in 2013", Baltimore Sun, 1-2-14]:

> With murders, non-fatal shootings and street robberies up in 2013, Police Commissioner Anthony W. Batts emphasized in television interviews Monday that crime affecting "everyday citizens" was moving in the right direction.
>
> "It's not throughout the city as a whole," Batts told WBAL-TV of the violence. "It's very localized and unfortunately, it's with African American men who are involved in the drug trade and 80 to 85 percent of the victims are involved in the drug trade going back and forth."
>
> "For everyday citizens, we are seeing those areas I mention drop. Burglaries are down, rapes are down, breaking into cars are down. All those categories are down," Batts said.
>
> Though retaliatory killings, stick-up boys, [and] warring drug crews are behind many cases that get publicized, murders and shootings also affect everyday people. Police dispatcher Alva Porter, whose son was brazenly gunned down in a barber shop as bystanders appeared unfazed, is but one example from 2013.[133]
>
> Another example: Mayor Stephanie Rawlings-Blake's 20-year-old cousin was killed in May.

---

[133] http://articles.baltimoresun.com/2013-11-15/news/bal-video-masked-gloved-gunman-bursts-into-baltimore-barbershop-20131115_1_barber-shop-gunman-gun-jams

Batts also said that "80 to 85 percent" of victims of violence were African-American men involved in the drug trade. But overall, only 84 percent of city homicide victims are black men.

And according to the homicide unit's analysis of this year, police determined a drug motive in just 3 of 224 cases (as of Dec. 17). "Argument" was the motive behind 18 cases, robbery was behind 13 cases, nine were domestic (official department Comstat data lists 13 domestic homicides this year, up 86 percent), and three were general "neighborhood" disputes.[134]

A lack of impulse control.

Poor future-time orientation.

Low IQ.

An inability to maintain the civilization white people left behind when they fled the blackening city limits of Baltimore.

But, hey, it's 'everyday people' that gun violence is affecting! [NAACP: Baltimore gun violence affects 'everyday people' too, Baltimore Sun, 1-2-14]:

> Asked for reaction, Tessa Hill-Aston, the president of Baltimore's chapter of the National Association for the Advancement of Colored People, said "all deaths are a serious issue because each one of those people are someone's loved one."
>
> "Most of it is drug-related, but there's a lot more to all that," she said. She said "everyday people" affected by gun violence include the mothers, wives, siblings and children of gun violence victims.
>
> She extended the scope of those affected to include those

---

[134] Batts: Crime Dropped for "Everyday Citizens" in 2013", Baltimore Sun, 1-2-14

impacted when someone whose relative is murdered doesn't show up to work the next day. "Everybody has a family member that works somewhere that impacts the community," she said.

Marvin "Doc" Cheatham, the past NAACP president and a West Baltimore resident, said he has a "great deal of confidence" in Batts. But he said the violence on the west side affected more than just those who were hit by bullets.

"We need more coverage, we need more foot soldiers, we need more patrol people on the ground," Cheatham said, noting that the Western District saw the most homicides in the city.[135]

The foot soldiers of the civil rights movement already cleared out white people for you to take democratic control of the city, Mr. Cheatham (one vote, one race, one rule). Certainly the newest fire chief of Baltimore (a total affirmative-action flunky) is the perfect example of "racial democracy", his first order of business - straight from the black mayor – being to "increase diversity" immediately and efficiently.[136]

Most of the violence/murder/gun crime in Baltimore isn't gang-related, it's black-related. As was the violence in 2012 during the St. Patrick's Day festivities in the city, which the police kept under wraps for nearly two months [St. Patrick's Day violence exceeded initial reports, police dispatch tapes show: Records describe teens fighting all over downtown and the Inner Harbor, Baltimore Sun, 5-12-14]:

As an unseasonably warm St. Patrick's Day drew to a close in Baltimore, teens by the hundreds swarmed downtown, keeping one step ahead of police while battling from corner to corner, mostly with fists, sometimes with knives.

---

[135]http://www.baltimoresun.com/news/maryland/crime/blog/bal-naacp-baltimore-gun-violence-affects-every-day-people-too-20140102,0,6856560.story#ixzz2pJ5F7BJs

[136] http://articles.baltimoresun.com/2013-12-30/news/bs-md-ci-fire-follow-20131230_1_fire-chief-chief-herman-williams-jr-james-clack

As authorities watched from a helicopter and on video from surveillance cameras, youths marched seemingly at will through the Inner Harbor and streets north and west, frequently clashing that Saturday night. Dozens of officers called in from across the city scrambled to keep up with the attacks, shutting key intersections and trying to push the youths away from the center of tourism.

"I need somebody to go to Pratt and Light [streets] for the male who was assaulted, Charles and Pratt for the assault, Pratt and Light again for the juveniles," a police dispatcher urgently called out in a single breath amid the melee. "I need somebody to go to Pratt and Light, a medic is trying to get through. Somebody has stomped a male in the crowd. The [ambulance] just passed a large group of kids assaulting the male with one child on the ground."

The full scope of the March 17 disturbance has not previously come to light. Recordings from more than three hours of dispatch tapes obtained by The Baltimore Sun through the state's Public Information Act reveal a far more violent landscape than police initially described — as well as several incidents, including a reported knifing at a Harborplace pavilion, that were not disclosed.

A police commander and the department's chief spokesman defended how the agency confronted the youths, making 10 arrests, saying that at no time did events spiral out of control.

"It's never the idea to make mass arrests," said Maj. Dennis Smith, commander of the Central District. "The idea is to ensure everybody's safety. If you find the aggressor, you go after him. ... We had over 500 people come from different sides of town. But they didn't take over."[137]

Of course these (race undisclosed) *youths* took over. [Delegate warns of 'black youth mobs': McDonough urges 'no-travel zone' at Inner

---

[137] http://articles.baltimoresun.com/2012-05-12/news/bs-md-ci-violence-downtown-police-20120420_1_pratt-and-light-youths-police-commander

Harbor, Baltimore Sun, 5-17-12]:

> A Baltimore County delegate said Wednesday that the governor should send in the Maryland State Police to control "roving mobs of black youths" at Baltimore's Inner Harbor, prompting a colleague to label the message "race-baiting."
>
> Del. Patrick L. McDonough, a Republican whose district includes part of Harford County, distributed a news release with the headline: "Black Youth Mobs Terrorize Baltimore on Holidays." In it, McDonough said he had sent a letter to Gov. Martin O'Malley urging him to use the state police to help prevent attacks and to declare the Inner Harbor area a "no-travel zone" until safety can be guaranteed.
>
> McDonough refused to back down, saying he had heard from police that the crowds involved in several recent incidents were all black. Failing to mention the race of the participants, he said, would be "political correctness on steroids."
>
> McDonough said his statement was prompted by several recent problems, including a St. Patrick's Day disturbance and a recent incident in which he and his wife witnessed a fight involving about 100 youths at Pratt and Calvert streets.
>
> The lawmaker said that his statement has brought attention from out-of-town news media and that he planned to give national television interviews warning visitors against traveling to the Inner Harbor. He charged that Mayor Stephanie Rawlings-Blake and city police haven't taken sufficient action and have been covering up the extent of the problem.
>
> "A no-travel zone is an action that needs to be taken to protect lives," he said.[138]

A "no-travel zone" for the entire 63-percent-black city is probably necessary, Mr. McDonough.

Will the last white person out of Baltimore not only turn out the light,

---

[138] http://articles.baltimoresun.com/2012-05-17/news/bs-md-mcdonough-race-20120516_1_youth-mobs-baltimore-mayor-mayoral-spokesman-ryan-o-doherty

but be sure to spray-paint a name change on the 'city limits' sign?

"Welcome to ~~Baltimore~~ Monrovia."

Portlandia vs. The Wire: In all of 2013, Portland (72% white) had 16 homicides; In January 2014, Baltimore (64% black) already has 22 homicides

Portland, Oregon is 72 percent white. A city of more than 603,000 people, blacks represent just 6.3 percent of the population. In fact, Portland is one of America's whitest "big" cities. [Census ranks Seattle among whitest big cities, Seattle Times, 4-23-11][139]

~~Bodymore, Murderland~~ Baltimore, Maryland, is 28.2 percent white. At 621,000 people, the size of its population is comparable to Portland; however, Baltimore is 63.6 percent black.

The two cities are best represented in pop culture via the television programs *Portlandia* and *The Wire*; both are expressions of the type of community a majority white or a majority black population will create.

Did you know that in 2013, the city of Portland registered only 16 homicides? [Portland's 16 homicides in 2013 are fewest in more than 40 years, The Oregonian, 1-03-2014][140]

139

http://seattletimes.com/html/localnews/2014859409_censusrace24m.html

[140]http://www.oregonlive.com/portland/index.ssf/2014/01/portlands_16

Or that, during the same year, the city of Baltimore registered 235 homicides? [Batts: Crime Dropped for "Everyday Citizens" in 2013", Baltimore Sun, 1-2-14][141]

The cities are roughly the same size demographically, and both tend to vote overwhelmingly for Democrats. Yet if New York City had Baltimore's murder rate, 3,160 people (invariably, almost all black, since that's who is being murdered in Baltimore... by other black people) would have been killed last year.[142]

Furthermore, did you know that, as of January 28, 2014, twenty-two people (almost all black) were murdered in Baltimore? [Baltimore shooting marks deadliest start to year since '07: Homicide detectives investigating double shooting near Pimlico Race Course, Baltimore Sun, 1-29-14][143]

Translation: an average month (well, less than a month) in 63-percent-black Baltimore is deadlier than a whole year in 72-percent-white Portland.

So while the *American Thinker* continues to publish stories with ridiculous titles like "Guns Don't Kill People, Democrats Kill People",[144] in reality it should read, "Guns Don't Kill People, Dangerous Minorities Do." The black police commissioner of Baltimore, Anthony W. Batts, admitted as much (though he was lying

_____

_homicides_in_2013.html

[141]http://www.baltimoresun.com/news/maryland/crime/blog/bal-batts-crime-dropped-for-every-day-citizens-in-2013-20131231,0,3144312.story

[142] http://www.baltimorebrew.com/2014/01/02/baltimores-jump-in-homicides-in-2013-defies-national-trends/

[143] http://www.baltimoresun.com/news/maryland/baltimore-city/bs-md-ci-pimlico-double-shooting-20140128,0,3884746.story

[144]http://www.americanthinker.com/2014/01/guns_dont_kill_people_democrats_kill_people.html

about "motive"). [Batts: Crime dropped for 'everyday citizens' in 2013, Baltimore Sun, 12-31-13]:

> "It's not throughout the city as a whole," Batts told WBAL-TV of the violence. "It's very localized and unfortunately, it's with African American men who are involved in the drug trade and 80 to 85 percent of the victims are involved in the drug trade going back and forth."[145]

In Portland, crime is always relatively low.

In Baltimore, 90 percent of registered voters identify as Democrats. Portland votes heavily Democrat as well; indeed, it's one of the most left-leaning populations in America. But with only 6 percent of its population being black, as opposed to Baltimore's 63 percent, the corresponding social problems are noticeably absent.[146]

In Portland, HIV/AIDS is hardly a crisis (save for the black population)[147]; meanwhile, in 63 percent black Baltimore, efforts are under way for the city government to distribute more free needles to drug users in an attempt to stem the rising tide of HIV/AIDS [Baltimore wants to give out thousands more needles to drug users: Effort to curb HIV is one of mayor's top bills in General Assembly this year, Baltimore Sun, 1-14-14][148]

---

[145] http://www.wbaltv.com/news/maryland/baltimore-city/mayor-police-commissioner-spell-out-crime-plan-for-2014/-/10131532/23702028/-/23vt7dz/-/index.html

[146] http://www.nytimes.com/1999/09/15/us/baltimore-democrats-pick-white-councilman-in-mayoral-primary.html

[147]http://www.oregonlive.com/living/index.ssf/2012/08/hivaids_in_portland_a_crisis_b.html

[148] http://articles.baltimoresun.com/2014-01-17/news/bs-md-srb-legislative-agenda-20140117_1_clean-syringes-baltimore-county-addicts

And while many of those homicide suspects in Portland had little in common with the majority population of the city, almost every murder suspect in Baltimore in 2013 was either a black male or female.

In Baltimore, blaming the drug trade on murder and crime has become a national pastime (a way to deflect from the obvious dysfunction and poor impulse-control found in the majority black population), but how does that explain the fact that many people in Portland (home to many liberal ideologies) also consume vast amounts of marijuana as well as other street drugs?.

In other words, if Baltimore is besieged by 'drug' violence, why is the city of Portland free of similar 'drug' violence?

In fact, recent statistics suggest that Baltimore is relatively free of drug-related violence; instead, *black* violence permeates the rotting corridors of the city [Motive known in few city homicides, police data shows, Baltimore Sun, 1-4-14]:

> Just three of Baltimore's 235 homicides in 2013 have a known drug motive, and police say 30 of the victims were verified gang members, year-end statistics show.
>
> As the year came to a close with an increase in homicides and shootings, Police Commissioner Anthony W. Batts said in television interviews that up to 85 percent of the victims of the city's gun violence were black men involved in the drug trade.
> He was not available for further comment.
>
> Black males made up 84 percent of the city's homicide victims in 2013. And while officials say that drugs and gangs fuel much of the violence in Baltimore, detectives investigating the deaths verified drug motives in just three of the cases, according to police records. The motive is listed as unknown in 164 cases, the records show.
>
> The refrain about drug ties is drawn from the criminal records of the victims. Police Department data indicates that

74 percent of the homicide victims last year had a drug arrest on their record and 86.4 percent had been arrested for some crime.

Among homicide suspects, 86 percent had criminal records and 72.5 percent had drug arrests.

Gang ties, not tracked by the department before 2013, were determined in 66 cases, and 30 of the victims were listed as gang members.[149]

The "unknown" motive is very well-known: it's called being "disrespected." [The trauma of gun violence: Dr. Edward E. Cornwell III, trauma chief at Johns Hopkins Hospital, describes gunshot wounds as "more and more a juvenile disease." Baltimore Sun, 3-12-2000][150]

In 63 percent black Baltimore, it's an annual tradition for the black mayor to appeal to his constituents to stop the violence and make the community safer. [Mayor calls on citizens to do their part to fight violence: Rawlings-Blake says 'all-hands-on-deck' effort is needed, Baltimore Sun, 1-8-14][151]

In 72 percent white Portland, it's a daily tradition to enjoy safe streets, clean parks, spotless public transportation, and a thriving downtown nightlife.

Blaming Democrats for gun violence is the default position for those still enamored with the idea of racial equality, hoping the ghost of Martin Luther King will deliver black people from the "liberal plantation" and safely guide them to the Republican Country Club.

---

[149] http://www.baltimoresun.com/news/maryland/sun-investigates/bs-md-sun-investigates-crime-stats-0105-20140104,0,1458193.story

[150] http://articles.baltimoresun.com/2000-03-12/topic/0003140350_1_gunshot-wounds-cornwell-johns-hopkins

[151] http://www.baltimoresun.com/news/maryland/politics/bs-md-ci-mayor-police-community-20140108,0,570262.story#ixzz2rpJwwepT

But the earth isn't flat. The earth isn't the center of the universe. Race is real.

The contrasting conditions of Portland and Baltimore prove this.

Two cities, almost exactly the same size in population.

Only difference: one is more than 70 percent white, the other is almost 70 percent black.

... Suddenly there came a tapping, As of someone gently rapping, rapping at my chamber door

"If we don't act now, we may not have much of an America left to defend." - Secretary of Defense Albert Nimzick in "Independence Day"

In many parts of this nation, there is no United States of America. When college kids can no longer play an innocent game of 'zombie apocalypse' without being threatened by black gang-members [Zombie game at Kentucky's Transylvania University leads to possible gang threat,

Kansas City Star, 4-30-13], you begin to see how much of our country has already been ceded -- how the rule of law has been subverted, and the monopoly on violence, traditionally belonging to the state, now belongs to the gang-bangers. [152]

Two stories illustrating the plight of emergency workers/nurses trying to provide healthcare to the black communities of Baltimore and Chicago should once again provide insight into the conditions this government (that you pay tax dollars to fund) allows to continue in our formerly productive, safe major cities.

Unlike the alien invaders from the 1996 film "Independence Day," who traveled millions of light-years to wage war on our major cities, it's our fellow countrymen who are destroying the viability of Baltimore and Chicago one street, one neighborhood, one community at a time. [Aberdeen EMS crews locks itself in ambulance during fight, Baltimore Sun, 5-1-13]:

> An Aberdeen EMS crew locked itself in its ambulance Tuesday night when it arrived at a call in Perryman and encountered a large fight.
>
> The ambulance was responding for a call of a sick woman in the 400 block of Daugherty Lane around 9:30 p.m. Tuesday, according to Richard Gardiner of the Harford County Volunteer Fire & EMS Association and Edward Hopkins, spokesman for the Harford County Sheriff's Office.
>
> When they arrived, the EMS crew reported people were fighting in the road and they "locked themselves in the unit for their own safety," Gardiner said.
>
> After taking shelter in the ambulance, the EMS crew called

---

[152] http://www.kansascity.com/2013/04/30/4210194/zombie-game-at-kentuckys-transylvania.html

911 to report the situation, making note that items, possibly rocks, were being thrown at the ambulance.

More than 30 people were fighting outside the medic unit, according to Gardiner, and the unit was "basically surrounded with people fighting and throwing things at each other and was not safe to leave."

So many people were in the area, he wrote in a message, the ambulance couldn't get out safety through the crowd without possibly hitting someone.

"So they stayed out, called the police and locked themselves in the unit," Gardiner wrote.

Sheriff's deputies responded and saw no one near the ambulance, Hopkins said. The patient for whom the ambulance had been dispatched was uncooperative and would not speak to police.

Deputies spoke to EMS personnel, who then reported nothing had been thrown at the ambulance and that they locked themselves into the vehicle out of fear of the crowd and fight.

It is unclear whether things were thrown and didn't hit the ambulance, or if the ambulance was targeted by the things being thrown, Hopkins said. Deputies checked the surrounding area and could not find anyone who was involved in the incident, he said.

No report was written because there was no damage, Hopkins said.

The woman was taken to a local hospital, Gardiner said.[153]

Similarly, life as a Chicago home health nurse requires a security

[153] http://www.baltimoresun.com/news/maryland/harford/aberdeen-havre-de-grace/ph-ag-aberdeen-ems-calls-911-0503-20130501,0,1636797.story#ixzz2S9M2TNcR

guard to accompany each caregiver as they go about their
duties [Nurses dodge bullets to provide care, CNN, 3-2-13]:

Atundra Horne walks along the battered cement pathway to
her patient's home with a set jaw and a solemn face.

A computer with patient records is slung over her shoulder; a
backpack stuffed with gauze, bandages and other medical
equipment rolls behind her. Horne is a home health nurse,
and her patients live in some of the roughest areas in
Chicago.

On this day she is working in Auburn Gresham, a
neighborhood on the South Side. Horne's workplace is far
from water coolers and cubicles; instead, she says, it involves
drugs, prostitution and the occasional clap of gunfire.

"There is a lot of crime," said Horne, who has been a nurse for
14 years. "It is a danger you face every day that you're out
here." The threat of danger is so acute that trailing a few
steps behind Horne is a security officer toting a loaded gun. A

year and a half ago it became standard protocol for Horne and
her colleagues at Advocate Health Care to travel with armed
security officers, who offer protection while the nurses treat
patients. There are people hanging out on street corners,
there are drug dealers congregating," nurse Beth Kairis said,
describing the rough areas where she works.

"You see different crime scenes and makeshift memorials for
people who were shot the night before." Kairis recalled a
recent visit to care for a baby who was quite ill. As she and
the security officer pulled up to the house, they found out
there had just been a shooting less than a block away.

Mobs of people filled the street; the situation was dangerous.
Leaving the baby without care was not an option, but neither
was entering the home under unsafe circumstances. Kairis
said she ended up being ushered in and out of the home by a
group of police officers. My View: How we talk about guns in
my Chicago classroom "Sometimes it's unnerving just to get

out of the car," said Kairis.

"Sometimes (after a visit) I get back in the car and think, 'I know nine out of 10 people would not have gone into that house. Am I crazy?" For her own peace of mind, Kairis recently devised a plan for avoiding problems.

The night before she does home visits, Kairis studies her patient roster and the neighborhoods where patients live. She tries to cluster her calls for efficiency and safety. "We hit the worst areas earlier in the day, then not-so-bad areas later in the day," said Kairis, who has been a nurse for six years.

"Occasionally when something is going on in an area, we might have to change course a little bit and revisit that area later." At each home, the security officer, usually a retired or off-duty Chicago cop, often will enter a residence to ensure it is safe and then keep watch outside.

"We keep an eye on all this stuff so that the clinician can do what she needs to do without fearing for her safety," said Tom Flanagan, a retired police officer and president of Accord Detective Agency, a company that provides security for Advocate's nurses.[154]

If our major cities were destroyed by outside enemy forces, we could rebuild.

But as our major cities are destroyed from within, by a *population beyond criticism* (protected by their blackness), we witness the continued decline of not only urban areas, but large areas of the United States, courtesy of a hostile population no longer subject to the jurisdiction of federal law.

Samuel Francis dubbed the situation "Anarchy-Tyranny"; we at SBPDL call it just another example of life under Black-Run America

---

[154] http://www.cnn.com/2013/03/02/health/nurses-gunfire-chicago/index.html

(BRA).

Future historians will have no words to explain this epoch, since no foreign power conquered cities like Detroit, Birmingham, Baltimore, Chicago or Milwaukee -- it was a population (who as individuals can be assets, but as a group represent the greatest liability to the peace and stability of a community) whose growth was almost exclusively funded by the law abiding tax payers of that former nation.

Year-Around Curfew Centers Needed in Baltimore to stop Black "Juvenile Delinquents" from Committing Crime: Francis Scott Key, The Star-Spangled Banner, and Starship Troopers Collide

Francis Scott Key, watching the American flag soar high above Fort McHenry on September 14, 1814, despite constant bombardment by British forces, was so moved by the experience in Baltimore, he penned the 'Star-Spangled Banner', a song that would become our national anthem.

Not two hundred years later, that same American flag soaring above Baltimore has been unable to withstand catastrophic levels of white flight - due to unsustainable rates of black crime - which enabled black political hegemony to protect an intifada of black violence (Johns Hopkins University reports that 90 percent of the 8,000 juveniles arrested in Baltimore in 2007 were black males).[155]

The city, where our national anthem was penned, is dead.

Dead.

Conservatives have no answer (just embrace Martin Luther King's "Dream"!) and liberal answers are even more preposterous ("if we don't mention race when discussing crime, we can't be called racists!").

However, both parties are quick to blame a lack of a father-figure in the lives of underprivileged children (raised solely by welfare addicted mothers or grandparents) as the source of black dysfunction, without first asking why these underprivileged black women are having kids at all?

Roughly 22 years ago, a study confirmed that more than half of black men in Baltimore (56 percent) were under criminal supervision on any given day in 1991. [Officials question study of city's young black men, Baltimore Sun, 9-3-1992]:

> Despite a report showing that 56 percent of young black men in Baltimore were in trouble with the law, the city's top law enforcement official said yesterday that "there are more good ones than bad ones."
> State's Attorney Stuart O. Simms said the report by the National Center on Institutions and Alternatives (NCIA) included so many minor offenses and charges that it unintentionally supported "the bad stereotype of African-American males ages 18 to 35 today."
>
> Del. Elijah E. Cummings, chairman of the Governor's Commission on Black Males, said the report -- which made front-page news Tuesday -- told black male students "on the very day they began school that you're probably not going to make it. That's a hell of a message to send out."
>
> But both officials said they agreed with the report's conclusion that American society was dealing with young black men mainly by punishing them and not by developing

---

[155] http://www.jhu.edu/jhumag/0608web/sowers.html

programs that could help prevent them from getting into trouble.

"The criminal justice system is the forced solution to too many problems," Mr. Simms said. "The real solution lies at the front end --through prevention, education, job training, new housing."

Mr. Cummings said that "if all you see is black men being arrested, there's an assumption when a black man walks down the street that he will do harm. I feel it even as an elected official and a Phi Beta Kappa. I feel as a black man that I'm being watched."

The report said 34,025 of the 60,715 young black men in Baltimore, or 56 percent, were "under criminal justice supervision on any given day in 1991."

Herbert J. Hoelter, director of NCIA, said the report was intended to show how young black men are disproportionately targeted by the criminal justice system -- often for petty offenses -- not to further negative stereotypes of young black men.

About one-fourth of the young black men cited in the study as being in trouble with the law in 1991 were in state prison or on parole.

The great majority -- more than two-thirds -- were on probation, awaiting trial or had outstanding arrest warrants against them.[156]

The majority of these criminal black males fathered bastard black children in Baltimore (raised by *blameless* mothers) that have gone on to engage in the same type of behavior as their fathers.

With much of the city unsafe for law-abiding citizens (when a park is no longer a welcome place for people to exercise, enjoy fresh air, or take their kids, you know your city is dead), inattentive black parent(s) have forced their black leaders in Baltimore to enact some

---

[156] http://articles.baltimoresun.com/1992-09-03/news/1992247140_1_young-black-men-black-man-hoelter

sort of control mechanism.[157]

Nothing drives people away from public parks more than the plague of stray bullets.

Baltimore is plagued with stray-bullet killings, with black people in the heat of some meaningless argument firing their weapons and missing their target. Collateral damage. Examples include a public park shooting 1995[158]; a wounded six-year-old in 2008[159]; another in 2012[160]; and a 10-year-old death in 2013.[161] A four-old-black boy was shot in 2007, prompting a fiery response from the police chief of the city. [Boy, 4, hit by stray bullet: City police official expresses anger at 'mindless' shooting, Baltimore Sun, 1-3-2007]:

> All they heard were the gunshots, and the first thing that Chanel Lee and her husband Donte Bond tried to do was protect their children.
>
> The family had just returned home from shopping, and Bond hurriedly tried to unlock the front door to his Northeast Baltimore house. Lee stood behind him with their 4-year-old son and 2-year-old daughter.
>
> When they finally made it inside yesterday, Bond told Lee, "Check the kids." They took off one of their son's shoes and saw blood - and a bullet hole near his heel.

157

http://www.abc2news.com/dpp/news/crime_checker/baltimore_city_crime/10-arrests-as-teens-use-social-media-to-mob-downtown-baltimore

158 http://articles.baltimoresun.com/1995-11-20/news/1995324034_1_hardy-stray-bullet-body

159 http://articles.baltimoresun.com/2008-08-24/news/0808230238_1_moses-stray-bullet-northeast-baltimore

160 http://articles.baltimoresun.com/2012-01-10/news/bs-md-ci-shooting-woman-20120110_1_stray-bullet-gunshot-wounds-gunfire

161 http://articles.baltimoresun.com/2013-01-03/news/bs-md-cecil-county-shooting-20130103_1_ajs-court-stray-bullet-celebratory

"He just started crying," Lee, 24, said of her injured son, Donte. "I thought he was crying because we were trying to push him inside."

The bullet was one of several fired from a gun used by a man who police said might have intervened in an argument between two female neighbors.

Last night, police issued a warrant charging Torino Truitt, 31, of the 700 block of Appleton St. with attempted second-degree murder, first- and second-degree assault, a handgun violation and reckless endangerment.

The dispute began with name-calling and ended with bullets flying through the neighborhood - a seemingly senseless escalation of violence.

"This is exactly what's happening in the city, all over the place," said Deputy Commissioner Frederick H. Bealefeld III. "Just mindless, crazy shooting incidents that are occurring right now."
Bealefeld said the shooting was the latest example of people using guns to end arguments.

"These are minor disputes that are being resolved by armed individuals," Bealefeld said.

"The ability of the Police Department to mediate every slight, every insult, every bad name ... is beyond any police department's capabilities," he said.[162]

With parents, *black* parents, no longer teaching basic rules governing civil behavior, the plague of nonfatal shootings, black-on-black homicides, and stray bullets injuring/killing citizens will continue.

Curfew Centers (started in 2010)[163], paid for by the dwindling white tax-base of Baltimore (remember, 40 percent of the city budget of

---

[162]Boy, 4, hit by stray bullet: City police official expresses anger at `mindless' shooting, Baltimore Sun, 1-3-2007

[163]http://www.abc2news.com/dpp/news/region/baltimore_city/baltimore%27s-juvenile-curfew-center-opens

Baltimore is paid for by the state of Maryland), are the latest solution to the city's plague of unsupervised black children. [Baltimore Opens City Curfew Center, CBS Baltimore, 6-14-2011]:

> Baltimore City officials are collaborating to keep teens off the streets and out of trouble this summer.
> Jessica Kartalija reports they're announcing the opening of the City's Curfew Center.
>
> The center will stay open through the night and teens will be given something to eat while they wait for their parents. Counselors will be on-hand to talk with families.
> "I don't think kids should be outside at night. There's no telling what could happen to them," said Kayla Ivy.
>
> Now the city of Baltimore is imposing a curfew, hoping situations like that one don't happen again.
>
> "Children under the age of 17 are not allowed out without an adult after midnight on weekends and after 11 p.m. on weeknights," said Mayor Stephanie Rawlings-Blake.
>
> City schools, law enforcement and juvenile justice departments are all on board.
> Teens caught violating the law will come to the Curfew Center on North Avenue.
> "Last summer, over 1,000 were brought to the Curfew Center. Seventeen percent were under the age of 13," Rawlings-Blake said.
>
> The center aims to end violence, make parents accountable for their children and provide supervision.
>
> "You guys have to step up in your community and step up for yourself and take advantage of the opportunities the mayor has laid out for you," said Police Commissioner Fred Bealefeld.[164]

Not enough.

Children as young - wait, *black* children - as young eight are running around Baltimore's streets. Parents? They don't care what their children do (just look what they've done to the city!).[City officials

---

[164] http://baltimore.cbslocal.com/2011/06/14/baltimore-opens-city-curfew-center/

consider earlier youth curfew: Councilman Scott pushes legislation to require children, teens to be off the streets, Baltimore Sun, 9-9-2013]:

> Top city leaders are supporting an effort to tighten Baltimore's curfew law that could require children younger than 14 to be off the street as early as 9 p.m.
> Councilman Brandon M. Scott introduced legislation Monday that would abolish the city's midnight curfew for children and teens and instead set a staggered deadline for youths to be indoors based on their age and whether school's in session.
>
> Scott called the current curfew — established nearly 20 years ago — absurd for failing to distinguish between an infant or teenager, and for allowing youths to stay outdoors so late.
>
> "If their parent was out there with them, OK. But they're 8-year-olds, and there is no adult anywhere in sight," Scott said at 10:30 p.m. on a recent night as he watched a group of boys playing football in a street in Belair-Edison. The Northeast Baltimore neighborhood was a scene of violence this summer.[165]

Curfews are not enough. Black violence is reaching epidemic proportions (the few white areas trapped within the city limits a favorite target of black crime),[166] meaning the black political establishment must respond. Besides setting up new enforcement zones,[167] those curfew centers will now serve as year-round detention facilities to house unsupervised black children. [Mayor proposes year-round curfew centers: Rawlings-Blake unveils anti-crime initiatives during State of the City address, Baltimore Sun, 2-10-14]:

> Baltimore will open several year-round, 24-hour centers to enforce the city's curfew for children and teens and connect troubled youths to services under a plan Mayor Stephanie Rawlings-Blake unveiled Monday in her State of the City address.

---

[165] http://articles.baltimoresun.com/2013-09-09/news/bs-md-ci-curfew-20130909_1_curfew-law-school-nights-northeast-baltimore

[166] http://www.baltimoresun.com/news/maryland/crime/blog/bs-md-ci-southeastern-crime-20140212,0,3461887.story

[167] http://www.baltimoresun.com/news/maryland/baltimore-city/bs-md-ci-new-crime-zones-20140211,0,2731742.story

Youth Connection Centers, modeled after similar programs in Washington and Miami, will replace the city's curfew center in the Barclay neighborhood that operates from June to August.

The first center is expected to open in the northwest or southeast section of the city by this summer, the mayor said. City officials could not provide an estimated cost, but said it would be funded both with general fund dollars and grants.

"We know when our young people are on the streets at night that they are more likely to either become victims of violent crime or the perpetrators of it," Rawlings-Blake said in her 36-minute speech to an audience that included Lt. Gov. Anthony G. Brown and schools interim CEO Tisha Edwards.

The mayor spent nearly half her address discussing her administration's strategy for combating violence, including increasing the number of geographic zones patrolled by officers from four to 17 and adding a staff commander for the CitiWatch surveillance program to better respond to crime in real time.[168]

Year-round curfew centers.

Because black parent(s) in Baltimore are incapable of providing responsible parenting to their - odds are good - bastard black children.

Think about this for a second.

Year-round curfew centers are needed in 63.5 percent black Baltimore, because black parent(s) have little regard for supervising their children.

Even those as young as eight-years-old...

The British were unable to subdue America during the War of 1812,

---

[168] http://www.baltimoresun.com/news/maryland/politics/bs-md-ci-mayor-city-address-20140210,0,1496964.story#ixzz2tEOXFoDD

memorialized in the "Star-Spangled Banner" (... *but the flag was still there)*; yet in 2014 Baltimore, the black population has done far more damage than the British Army could ever hope to inflict.

Do you remember your class lecture from Robert Heinlein's *Starship Troopers*?

Called "History and Moral Philosophy", it was a class taught by fictional character Jean DuBois.

You remember it, right?

Set well into the future, Dubois lectures on the collapse of democracy and the chaos that engulfed America in the late-20th century.

"Law-abiding people," Dubois had told us, "hardly dared go into a public park at night. To do so was to risk attack by wolf packs of children, armed with chains, knives, homemade guns, bludgeons . . . to be hurt at least, robbed most certainly, injured for life probably — or even killed. ... Murder, drug addiction, larceny, assault, and vandalism were commonplace. Nor were parks the only places — these things happened also on the streets in daylight, on school grounds, even inside school buildings. But parks were so notoriously unsafe that honest people stayed clear of them after dark."

Dubois continues:

> "These juvenile criminals hit a low level. Born with only the instinct for survival, the highest morality they achieved was a shaky loyalty to a peer group, a street gang. But the do-gooders attempted to 'appeal to their better natures,' to 'reach them,' to 'spark their moral sense.' *Tosh!* They *had* no 'better natures'; experience taught them that what they were doing was the way to survive. The puppy never got his spanking; therefore what he did with pleasure and success must be 'moral.'

> "The basis of all morality is duty, a concept with the same relation to group that self-interest has to individual. Nobody preached duty to these kids in a way they could understand — that is, with a spanking. But the society they were in told them endlessly about their 'rights.'

"The results should have been predictable, since a human being has *no natural rights of any nature.* ...

Mr. Dubois then turned to me. "I told you that 'juvenile delinquent' is a contradiction in terms. 'Delinquent' means 'failing in duty.' But *duty* is an *adult* virtue — indeed a juvenile becomes an adult when, and only when, he acquires a knowledge of duty and embraces it as dearer than the self-love he was born with. There never was, there cannot *be*, a 'juvenile delinquent.' But for every juvenile criminal there are always one or more adult delinquents — people of mature years who either do not know their duty, or who, knowing it, fail.

"And *that* was the soft spot which destroyed what was in many ways an admirable culture. The junior hoodlums who roamed their streets were symptoms of a greater sickness; their citizens (all of them counted as such) glorified their mythology of 'rights' . . . and lost track of their duties. No nation, so constituted, can endure."

Ladies and gentlemen, the circumstances that Mr. Heinlein predicted would destroy democracy (in a book *published back in 1959*) has come true. Welcome to Baltimore.

Curfew Centers... needed year-round in Baltimore to keep black juvenile delinquents from terrorizing the city, its public parks, and the Inner Harbor.[169]

Baltimore is no longer the land of the free and the home of the brave; it's the home of an eternally-protected class of black criminals, which popular culture (*The Wire*) re-brands as a bunch of perpetually victimized angels.

A group of white residents from Baltimore's southeast side packed a forum addressing crime in the city, with Mayor Stephanie Rawlings-Blake, Police Commissioner Anthony W. Batts, City Council members and state lawmakers in attendance.

It became obvious that Rawlings-Blake's main priority is ensuring

---

[169]

http://www.abc2news.com/dpp/news/crime_checker/baltimore_city_cri me/delegate-warns-of-black-youth-mobs-in-baltimores-inner-harbor white tax-payers continue to foot the bill for those year-round curfew centers [Southeast on edge over crime as neighbors call for measured debate: Some worry area complaints minimize struggles of poorer neighborhoods, Baltimore Sun, 2-12-14]:

> Crime can be a concern in any neighborhood, but this year the issue has taken on new urgency in neighborhoods like Canton and Highlandtown. Many are calling on the city to shift law enforcement resources into the area, but others say that perspective minimizes the plight of poorer parts of the city that have struggled with violence for years.
> The event was organized by Del. Luke Clippinger, who said the area's problems reflect broader issues in a city with a climbing homicide rate.
>
> Rawlings-Blake has called on residents to offer solutions in the debate over crime, and in response to one blog post voicing a litany of frustrations, pointed out that no area of town is entitled to more resources than another.
>
> The mayor disputed the notion that "when crime happens in an area where the income taxes and property taxes are higher, we're supposed to care more."
>
> "I am focused ... on action and finding partners who are doing more than complain, that are willing to do more than write a check for their property tax," Rawlings-Blake said.
>
> But some residents said they have had enough of crime in the city. Brian March, who lives about two blocks from where a man was robbed and beaten with a brick last month in Canton, said it doesn't seem as if law enforcement cares enough.
>
> "I've already considered moving. Crime's been bad for a while," March said. "I haven't seen a cop walk through my area in 13 years."[170]

The 'History and Moral Philosophy' class from *Starship Troopers* has proven to be prophetic; that this futuristic fictional work, written over half a century ago, became reality in the birthplace of our national anthem is one of the great ironies of our time.

Freedom has failed.

---

[170] http://www.baltimoresun.com/news/maryland/crime/blog/bs-md-ci-southeastern-crime-20140212,0,3461887.story#ixzz2tEZrO6vA

Democracy has died.

The rotting carcass of our "country" is on full display in a city like Baltimore, where the black politicians are more concerned for the *rights* of its poor black communities than protecting the integrity and civility of its productive ones.

Control: The Ultimate Goal of the Civil Rights Movement Seen through the Lens of Black Political Control in Baltimore

Control.

One word.

Two syllables.

That's all life is about.

Be in control of your finances; your relationship; your work/life balance.

Control.

It's a simple concept at the heart of the civil rights movement; usurp control from white America to...blacks.

Control of not just a city, but the fire department, the accounting department, the police department, the allocation of city contracts with vendors, the school board, the city council, and – most importantly – the "narrative."

How else could a city like Baltimore -where blacks are 63.5 percent of the population - still assert that a $900,000 grant from the U.S. Department of Commerce's Minority Business Development Agency (MBDA) is necessary to promote minority job creation and business competitiveness? [Baltimore wins $900,000 grant to boost minority business competitiveness, Baltimore Business Journal, 9-16-13][171]

When a loan from the MBDA is justified on the basis of promoting "minority business interests" in a black majority city, you can be sure that every "truth" held by the establishment concerning racial differences in intelligence is 100 percent wrong.

Nonetheless, the black mayor of Baltimore, Stephanie Rawlings-Blake, considered this "loan" cause for celebration in her State of the City address. Noting Baltimore "won" the grant to build a minority business development center, the irony of a majority black city needing such an infusion of tax-dollars in the first place was lost on the celebrants. [Mayor Rawlings-Blake Speaks On Crime, Education, Entrepreneurship in State of City Address, Afro.com, 2-12-14].[172]

But control is all that matters.

Black control of the city, regardless of how bad things get, also profit from the "narrative" demanding that all black failure be forever blamed on white people (sadly, many whites accept this version of reality). Black revisionist history, wherein the past is never dead, asserts that contemporary whites still enjoy the privilege of their ancestors' racism. Despite efforts like the 25-member Mayor's Council on Minority and Women-Owned Business Enterprises in 2012 (which would set goals for awarding city contracts to... you guessed it... minority and women-owned businesses), the narrative dictates a white person always be blamed. [Rawlings-Blake creates minority

---

[171] https://www.blogger.com/Baltimore wins $900,000 grant to boost minority business competitiveness

[172]http://www.afro.com/sections/news/baltimore/story.htm?storyid=81472

business advisory council, Baltimore Sun, 7-18-2012][173]

With many people, primarily whites, believing "judging by content of character" is the most noble, laudatory goal, the city of Baltimore – controlled by blacks – believes otherwise. For instance, from their perspective, too many white people (and too few black people) hold jobs in the fire department.

Therefore, Baltimore appointed a government official assigned to specifically recruit non-whites. [Fire department to cut diversity-minded recruitment division: Current division chief says mission to attract African-Americans remains vital, Baltimore Sun, 4-22-13]:

> The move has caused concerns among African-American leaders in the department. Lloyd Carter, the deputy chief for recruitment, who would be reassigned under Mayor Stephanie Rawlings-Blake's budget for the next fiscal year, said he believes his position and the small division built around it should be saved.
>
> "They wanted to improve diversity in the department, and now there's no funding for it?" Carter said in an interview. "The department is no more diverse than it was."
>
> Officials said the Fire Department is currently 32 percent black, a level it has maintained since at least 2011. The city population is 65 percent African-American.
>
> The special division and two positions — created in 2011 as part of efforts to boost minority outreach — would be cut under the plan, and recruitment duties would be absorbed into other divisions, including the training academy, according to department officials.
>
> Henry Burris, president of the Vulcan Blazers, an organization that advocates for black firefighters, said he is

[173] http://articles.baltimoresun.com/2012-07-18/news/bs-bz-mayor-council-minority-women-businesses-20120718_1_women-owned-businesses-advisory-council-ceo-of-bithgroup-technologies

"strongly against" the plan. The organization had called —
unsuccessfully — for a U.S. Department of Justice
investigation into what it described as "systemic
discrimination in hiring, discipline and recruitment" in the
department.

"If there is a cutback, it should not be in recruitment, because
there is a lack of minorities in the Baltimore City Fire
Department," he said. "The only way you will get that is if you
have a dedicated crew out there recruiting city residents."

In 2004, the department faced criticism and outrage for hiring
an all-white class of recruits. As a result, hiring methods
changed and the department promised progress.

But by 2011, allegations of racism persisted, and Rawlings-
Blake announced the National Association for the
Advancement of Colored People and the Urban League would
work with department leaders to increase minority
outreach.[174]

Control.

It's our city now.

How dare you believe such public jobs as a firefighter could go to
white people?

Whites have no organization advocating on their behalf because of
their naïve assumptions that everyone "judges by content of
character." Blacks... they only judge by one rule: *are blacks in
control?* If not, racism is the only culprit, and we must overcome such
an idea!

---

[174] http://articles.baltimoresun.com/2013-04-22/news/bs-md-ci-fire-
recruitment-cut-20130422_1_all-white-class-vulcan-blazers-
recruitment

The new black fire chief, Niles Ford, has only one objective from City Hall: hire more non-whites.[175]

Control.

Though Clarence Burns –a 40-year Democrat operative - was technically the first black mayor of Baltimore (he was never elected), Kurt Schmoke was the first *elected* black mayor of the city. He made it clear who was in charge during his victorious speech on Election Day [Baltimore Mayor Loses to Younger Foe in Primary, New York Times, 9-17-1987]:

> "We're looking to the future now," a beaming Mr. Schmoke told the wildly cheering crowd at the Fifth Regiment Armory early today. "We're not looking to the past. We're looking to the future."[176]

Control. [THE END: What Kurt Schmoke Did Right, and How He Went Wrong, Baltimore City Paper, 12-1-1999]:

> A month later, at the inauguration ceremony at the Baltimore Arena, the mood was "electric," recalls Bill Cunningham, a former City Council member and longtime friend of Schmoke. "It was a new-day-is-dawning thing."
>
> "It was generational, us vs. them," says Jody Landers, who was also on the council at the time. "It was like, 'It's our turn now.'"
>
> That sentiment was shared by many African-Americans across the city. "We were looking for someone to encompass our hopes for the future, someone who would validate our own journey," the Rev. Arnold Howard of Enon Baptist Church says.

---

[175] http://articles.baltimoresun.com/2013-12-30/news/bs-md-ci-fire-follow-20131230_1_fire-chief-chief-herman-williams-jr-james-clack

[176] http://www.nytimes.com/1987/09/17/us/baltimore-mayor-loses-to-younger-foe-in-primary.html

"He went into office with all that on him. He was the new savior. He was the one who would fulfill our dreams."[177]

That "dream" wasn't color-blind.

The "future" of Baltimore: black-political control, with the Ivy-League educated Schmoke the man to remake the city in a black-centric image. Only three years into his term, this future quickly came to pass. [City Council OKs Plan for 5 majority black districts, Baltimore Sun, 3-19-1991]:

> In a raucous, shoe-waving session, the Baltimore City Council threw out Mayor Kurt L. Schmoke's status quo redistricting plan last night and replaced it with one that would create five councilmanic districts with black majorities and leave only one -- East Baltimore's 1st District -- with a white majority.
>
> The plan, proposed by Councilman Carl Stokes, D-2nd, was given preliminary approval on a 10-7 vote, with two council members abstaining. A final vote on the Stokes plan could come as early as Thursday.
>
> Mr. Stokes said he proposed what amounted to wholesale revision of the mayor's plan for redrawing the lines of the city's six council districts because the Schmoke plan did not do enough to shake up the political machines that have kept the City Council predominantly white when Baltimore itself has a black majority.
>
> Opponents were incensed, however, saying that it "raped" their neighborhoods and had been proposed before community leaders could express their views.
>
> The argument was fierce and broke down largely along racial lines. At one point, Councilwoman Sheila Dixon, D-4th, took off her shoe and waved it in the faces of her white colleagues, saying, "You've been running things for the last 20 years -- now the shoe is on the other foot. See how you like it."

---

[177] http://www2.citypaper.com/news/story.asp?id=3650

Mayor Schmoke learned about the proposal with most other council members at a luncheon yesterday and was angered by the lack of public notice, according to his spokesman, Clinton R. Coleman.

However, supporters of the proposal said they had made their concerns about increasing black populations in predominantly white districts known for the past two months.

"I'm disappointed in what Mayor Schmoke said about the proposal," said Councilman Lawrence A. Bell, D-4th. "Here we have an African-American mayor who got into office on the backs of black constituents [and] who says this plan is unfair and bad politics. That's outrageous."

"If this amendment passes, it's a rape of our communities," said Councilman Martin E. "Mike" Curran, D-3rd, said of Mr. Stokes' plan. "I can't stand and let this go on. I made a commitment to put a black candidate on our ticket, but apparently that's not enough."

Councilwoman Vera P. Hall, D-5th, said Mr. Stokes' proposal had deeper goals. In supporting his plan, she said she hoped to empower black community groups and give them stronger voices for change.[178]

Control.

In regular politics, the winner gets the spoils; in *racial* politics, the racial winner gets to spoil democracy for the racial losers.

But political control in the hands of Baltimore's blacks didn't equate to success. [For Baltimore Mayor, A Shaky Incumbency, New York Times, 9-7-1995]:

But when Mr. Schmoke stopped by the Southwest Senior Center in a struggling, racially mixed neighborhood here last

---

[178] http://articles.baltimoresun.com/1991-03-19/news/1991078120_1_council-districts-council-members-city-council

week, few people greeted him with encouragement as he tries for a third term. Instead, they spoke up about filthy, crime-ravaged streets and abandoned buildings.

They were polite enough to Mr. Schmoke, who dutifully jotted their complaints in a notebook. But once the Mayor was out of earshot, some past supporters said they would not vote for him again -- and the primary is next week.

"All the money is leaving the city; what do we do?" asked Fannie Fitzgerald, 67, a retired nurse who said that as a black woman she was proud to support Mr. Schmoke four years ago but is too discouraged to vote at all this year.

"There's an empty house next to mine. The bricks are falling down. It rains in there. And the drug dealers have taken over. This has been five years. What do we do?"

Most striking about Mr. Schmoke's campaign is that support from white voters is so thin that for the first time he has geared his campaign to blacks. His bumper stickers are red, black and green, the colors of the black liberation movement, and his slogan is "Makes Us Proud." The unmistakable appeal to blacks has infuriated some whites and even some blacks, who accuse Mr. Schmoke of stoking racial tensions.

"I'm not apologetic at all," Mr. Schmoke said. "For the majority population of this city, those colors have traditionally been symbols of pride and empowerment, not division."[179]

The 1995 Democrat primary campaign (against a white woman, Mary Pat Clarke) was completely, 100 percent racially motivated,[180] with Schmoke adopting the black flag of liberation as his campaign colors.

---

[179] http://www.nytimes.com/1995/09/07/us/for-baltimore-mayor-a-shaky-incumbency.html?pagewanted=all&src=pm

[180] http://articles.baltimoresun.com/1995-09-14/news/1995257004_1_kurt-schmoke-kurt-l-wink

[Candidates' bumper stickers raise issue of racial politics CAMPAIGN 1996, Baltimore Sun, 3-30-1995].[181]

It was about control.

That same election year, the mayoral race in Baltimore was all about racial control as well. [Times owner says appeal to black pride not enough, Baltimore Sun, 8-13-1995]:

> On Sundays such as this, The Baltimore Times arrives. There are 32,000 copies printed each week, which are distributed through scores of the area's black churches, and through supermarkets and street boxes, and in this politically charged season its arrival tends to make the mayor of this city, Kurt L. Schmoke, duck for cover.
>
> Consider these words, from a recent front-page editorial written by the Rev. Peter Bramble, 49-year-old pastor at West Baltimore's St. Katherine's Episcopal Church who owns the Times and makes it a kind of political extension of his pulpit:
>
> "For the first time in his political life, Schmoke is wrapping himself in blackness -- African-American flag colors and symbols. He is even wearing kinte cloth ties! Now, is not that absolutely funny?
>
> "It seems as though Larry Gibson, Schmoke's campaign manager, knows that only 'pride' could help him and his candidate against a woman, Mary Pat Clarke, who has made it her duty to deliver the goods when blacks have asked her favors over the years. Gibson knows that no honest Baltimorean can deny that Mary Pat Clarke delivers the goods. You ask her to do something in the community and it is done. . . .
>
> No one, black or white, could take that record of service from her."

---

[181] http://articles.baltimoresun.com/1995-03-30/news/1995089095_1_bumper-stickers-schmoke-black-and-green

Consider these words, from another front-page editorial by
Bramble:

"If Schmoke had a record of helping blacks to advance, Larry
[Gibson] should have been using that record of success to
convince blacks that a third term would be good for Baltimore
in general and blacks in particular. Because there is no record
in this area, they resort to 'black pride.' Can we take that to
the bank?"

But Bramble's words are clearly provocative in a political
season in which many Baltimoreans feel they're being asked
to choose sides along racial lines. Consider:

* In the race for City Council president, the white candidate
Joe DiBlasi, competing with three black opponents, candidly
admits, not working hard in black districts because I'm not
going to win [there]. Some might call it racist; I call it
concession."

* In the race for mayor, representatives of 500 predominantly
black churches back the mayor -- and back Joan Pratt, the
black political novice who's running for comptroller against
veteran legislator Julian Lapides, who is white.

* The interracial Fraternal Order of Police endorses Clarke
for mayor, prompting the black Vanguard Justice Society not
merely to back Schmoke but to angrily declare the FOP
endorsement "an attempt to miseducate African-American
members of the Police Department and the community." The
mayor, attending the Vanguard press conference, says the
endorsement "speaks for itself."

"I'm very black," Bramble was saying last week. "I promote
everything black. But I have to be honest. This unity thing,
there ++ has to be more than that. I can't lie. I can't say a
white person who's been there has not been there.[182]

---

[182] http://articles.baltimoresun.com/1995-08-
13/news/1995225034_1_kurt-schmoke-black-pride-bramble

Control.

Who will do the most for "Us?" [Up in Schmoke, New Republic, 8-10-1998]:

> Schmoke ran for his third term in 1995 against City Council President Mary Pat Clarke, a facile white populist in the Schaefer mold. Schmoke used red, black, and green for his campaign colors and "Makes Us Proud" for his campaign slogan. The city's white establishment reared back in horror. "You didn't have to be a Rhodes Scholar to see he was making a racial appeal," says one white Baltimore politician in a typically biting remark. The Sun endorsed Clarke, calling Schmoke "a sad disappointment." But Schmoke's racial ploy worked, and he trounced Clarke by 20 points. Even though Clarke outpolled Schmoke nine-to-one in many white sections of the city, Schmoke outpolled her nine-to-one in most of the black neighborhoods. As Elijah Cummings, a black Baltimore politician who now serves in the U.S. House of Representatives, told The Washington Post: Black voters saw Schmoke "as a home-grown man... They saw him as their son... We just did not want to be a New York and lose David Dinkins."[183]

Control.

Racial control of a city.

A novice (another lucky black) won the race for comptroller, trouncing a white Democrat in the primaries and sweeping the polls on Election Day. [Schmoke re-elected in 20% turnout African-Americans hold top 3 offices, City Council majority, Baltimore Sun, 11-8-1995]:

> Yet, a historic shift in power was quietly ratified, as African-Americans captured all three of the top elected offices and a majority of council seats for the first time in Baltimore's history.

---

[183] http://www.newrepublic.com/article/politics/schmoke

City Councilman Lawrence A. Bell III, who made a name for himself with his aggressive anti-crime crusade, rose to the city's second-highest office by soundly defeating Republican Anthony D. Cobb to become council president.

Accountant Joan M. Pratt, a political novice who surprised many by beating a veteran state legislator in the primary race for comptroller, won over rival Republican accountant Christopher P. McShane.[184]

Control.

Racial control, translating to virtually unlimited funds from Washington D.C.'s white taxpayers (in the form of Urban Development Action Grants) to Baltimore's Empowerment Zones.

Color-blind?

Not in Baltimore.

This was the city that, in the first half of the 20th century, sued the state of Maryland, claiming a lack of money for education – per-pupil spending - was the reason for the dismal academic performances in the overwhelmingly black Baltimore City Public Schools (BCPS). The ACLU rallied behind the cause, crusading on behalf of the black-controlled city of Baltimore.

The powerbrokers in Annapolis (the capital of Maryland) went along with their request, and granted hundreds of millions of dollars to BCPS... in exchange for control of the system.

To blacks in Baltimore, that was not cool. Not cool at all.

Control means *complete* control.

Racial control.

---

[184] http://articles.baltimoresun.com/1995-11-08/news/1995312131_1_city-council-schmoke-races-for-city

What is this? A plantation? [Md., Baltimore Plan Overhaul Of City Schools; State's Move to Increase Funds, Control Criticized, Washington Post, 1-22-1996]:

In Baltimore, even some skeptics who are worried about the racial implications of a state takeover in a predominantly African American city seem willing to give it a try.

"Our schools are in serious trouble, and it doesn't make a great deal of difference to me under whose auspices we fix them," said Garland O. Williamson, an African American businessman who serves on the Greater Baltimore Committee, a regional business group.

But the proposal has triggered indignant responses from some Baltimoreans who suspect it would be underfunded and overly punitive, and from others who fear it would be overfunded and not tough enough.

"The city is looked at as a hole of poverty, and we're just throwing money down it.

It's obscene, the racial prejudice and stereotypes behind this," said the Rev. Roger J. Gench, of Brown Memorial Presbyterian Church and a co-chairman of Baltimoreans United in Leadership Development, a church-based social-action group.

City Council member Kiefer J. Mitchell Jr. asked: "If we're going to do this, why have a mayor and City Council? Why don't we all resign? Why have a City of Baltimore if the state's going to run everything?"[185]

---

[185] Md., Baltimore Plan Overhaul Of City Schools; State's Move to Increase Funds, Control Criticized, Washington Post, 1-22-1996

Control.

Racial control. [Clergy, educators blast state plan to takeover city schools, Baltimore Afro-American, 8-10-1996]:

> Baltimore ministers and educators criticized as "outrageous" proposed state legislation that would restructure city schools under state control. But the community leaders stopped short of saying exactly what they were going to do about it.
>
> At a Thursday press conference, Rev. John L. Wright, president of the United Baptist Missionary Convention of Maryland, refused to announce his group's position regarding the school system until Monday when clergy members convene.
>
> He did, however, restate opposition to using casino gambling revenue to fund schools - an idea introduced by Mayor Kurt Schmoke.
>
> "The people of this great state should know that the faith community will not sit idly by and watch as politicians make decisions that are not in the best interests of our children," he said. "This situation must be resolved before the beginning of the school year so that our children can begin the education process and our educators can begin to teach them."[186]

Control.

Racial control. Marion Orr's *Black Social Capital: The Politics of School Reform in Baltimore 1986- 1998*, makes it clear just how badly black Baltimore leaders did NOT want to lose control of BCPS:

> Schmoke was also influenced by local politics. The most vocal opposition to the city-state partnership was from members of

---

[186] Clergy, educators blast state plan to takeover city schools, Baltimore Afro-American, 8-10-1996

Baltimore's powerful black clergy... These ministers jealously guarded black administrative control of the BCPS. The church community considered the proposal an "outrageous" state "takeover," threatening the long tradition of black control of the BCPS. According to the Reverend Roger Gench... "racial prejudice and stereotypes [were] behind" the agreement."

Black community leaders, parent groups, and black ministers from Baltimore were perhaps the loudest critics of the proposal, arguing that the African-American community was giving up its rights to influence school operations. Many of these community leaders opposed sharing power with white state officials.[187]

Control.

Though you may help us out financially (no matter how poorly we do the job), we still want absolute control.[188]

When white candidate Martin O'Malley won a surprise victory in the 1999 mayoral race, his black foes came out publicly to broadcast that he was the wrong choice. [Can Mayor O'Malley Save Ailing Baltimore?, City Journal, Winter 2001]:

In a city in which Schmoke won his final term by appealing to racial pride, O'Malley's race quickly became controversial. "Racism," screamed some of the city's black preachers. "An O'Malley victory is the worst thing that could happen to the city, it would tear the city apart," thundered Reverend Doug Miles. But both Bell and Stokes ran race-baiting campaigns so over the top that the two candidates self-destructed. [Lawrence] Bell's supporters sent out white-hate fliers

---

[187] Orr, Marion. *Black social capital: the politics of school reform in Baltimore, 1986-1998*. Lawrence: University Press of Kansas, 1999, p. 180-182

[188] http://articles.baltimoresun.com/1997-03-26/news/1997085087_1_baltimore-city-city-council-state-aid

endorsing O'Malley—fliers that many thought the Bell campaign itself had produced. The candidate, surrounding himself with menacing Nation of Islam bodyguards, called for black voters to "vote for someone who looks like you." In the campaign's waning days, he even brought in those old warhorses of urban disaster, Marion and Cora Barry, to rally support. [Carl] Stokes played the race card too, though not quite so crudely. He came across as the same kind of well-meaning but ineffectual politician as Schmoke, insisting that New York's policing success was "nonsense"—"a license to hunt minorities." "I don't need to go to New York for new ideas," he exclaimed to campaign crowds.[189]

Control.

Racial control.

This was the real impetus of the civil rights movement, the usurpation of white political control and the ability to dictate the future in cities like Baltimore. In winning control, they also inherited control of the "narrative."

And since cities like Detroit, Birmingham, Gary, Newark, Camden and Baltimore have collapsed into third world status under black rule, the blame, as the narrative dictates, will always fall on the shoulders of whites.

Always.

That's the beauty of control.

But one thing is obvious: the collapse of Baltimore cannot be described in 'color-blind' terminology.

It's a byproduct of black control.

---

[189] http://www.city-journal.org/html/11_1_can_mayor_omalley.html

Louis Farrakhan Calls for "Our Own Courts" (black-controlled courts); The Stories of Joel Lee and Zach Sowers Show Blacks Already have them in Baltimore

Separation is good.

It is a peaceful solution.

Co-existence, on the other hand, has proven futile.

And costly.

At the conclusion of World War II, the Allied and Axis Powers in Europe and Japan were able to rebuild their cities quickly and efficiently. Even Hiroshima and Nagasaki, devastated by atomic bombs, were able to recover and grow to world-class cities.

But American cities?

Not a single shot was fired on United States soil during the Second World War, but looking at Baltimore, Detroit, Gary, Camden, and Newark, you'd have thought the sinister forces of Germany and Japan had unleashed a fury not even time could heal.

Which is why a speech given by Louis Farrakhan in Detroit (at the Nation of Islam convention) should not be so easily dismissed as just more ravings of a madman, but admirable acceptance to the conclusion of a grand experiment that has failed in every conceivable metric. [Louis Farrakhan: African Americans deserve own courts after failings of U.S. Justice System, USA Today, 2-24-14]:

> In a fiery speech delivered to 18,000 at Joe Louis Arena, Minister Louis Farrakhan blasted the U.S. judicial system as being biased against African Americans, calling upon the community to set up its own courts.
> "We want equal justice under the law," Farrakhan said on the last day of the Nation of Islam's annual convention, held in Detroit this year.

"Our people can't take much more. We have to have our own courts. You failed us."

With U.S. Rep. John Conyers, a Detroit Democrat, and Detroit City Council President BrendaJones sitting behind him, Farrakhan spoke for nearly three hours.

He urged unity among Muslim and Christian leaders, saying that "Jesus and Mohammed would be arm in arm," and he reiterated the Nation of Islam's view that the U.S. is a land headed for destruction unless it starts to obey the word of God.

The crowd often clapped and roared in approval during his talk, which included a discussion of African-American civil rights leaders over the past century. Farrakhan suggested that African Americans rely on the Quran and Bible to help set up their own legal system that would be more fair to African Americans.

"Has America been just to us?" he asked the crowd.

"No," the crowd responded.

"So ... if we retaliate, you can bring out your soldiers. We got some, too."[190]

Wait.

Notice he didn't say anything about "true" separation; you see, separation means self-reliance.

Black people can barely keep their houses and businesses in order *with* the power of the U.S. Federal Government propping them up through a massive transfusion of white wealth. How many days do you think an independent black nation would last without a source of white tax dollars from which the government can syphon wealth to support its black middle class?

What Mr. Farrakhan fails to appreciate is that the American judicial system is working quite nicely for black people, especially in a city completely controlled by black political power like Baltimore.

But these pesky things called "facts" don't deter people like

---

[190]http://www.freep.com/article/20140223/NEWS01/302230146/farrak han-nation-islam-Joe-Louis-visit

Farrakhan from relying on pure, unadulterated emotion (namely, black hatred of all things white) to rile up their unwitting base.

For instance, names like Joel Lee and Zach Sowers don't have quite the sex appeal as Jordan Davis, a black male who was gunned downed by a very white Michael Dunn.

Dunn will spend 75 years in jail for his crime. What about the murderers of Lee and Sowers?

For the former, none; for the latter, some of the attackers face a few years behind bars, others escaped punishment.

Both Lee and Sowers were murdered in Baltimore by black males. However, in a city where "racial consciousness" is comparable to that of Nazi (but without the correspondingly high social capital of the Germans), the judicial system is already separate and very unequal. [U.S. ends rights probe in Lee death Evidence in slaying considered too weak for federal indictment, Baltimore Sun, 1-16-1997]:

> An 18-month federal probe into one of Baltimore's most racially sensitive homicide cases ended yesterday when prosecutors decided not to pursue a civil rights indictment against an African-American man acquitted of killing Korean-American student Joel J. Lee.
> The decision disappointed Lee's father and Asian-American leaders, who were outraged in 1995 when a nearly all-black jury acquitted Davon Neverdon. Neverdon was found not guilty despite testimony from four witnesses who said they saw him shoot Lee in the face during a $20 mugging in Northeast Baltimore.

According to court testimony, Neverdon and three friends were walking together on Sept. 2, 1993, when Neverdon broke off and approached Joel Lee in the parking lot at Dutch Village Apartments in the 7000 block of McLean Blvd.

Lee, who was looking for a friend's apartment to borrow a book, was shot just below the right eye because he didn't turn over his wallet fast enough, according to testimony.

Neverdon's three friends and a woman watching from her apartment window testified against Neverdon. Two other men testified that Neverdon admitted to them that he killed Lee;

one testified that Neverdon gave him the .25-caliber handgun used in the killing and asked him to dispose of it.

In the weeks after the verdict, 150 people, mostly Korean-Americans, protested outside Circuit Court, asking for reforms in the jury system and blaming racial tensions between blacks and Koreans for the not-guilty finding.

During the deliberations, a juror sent Judge Kenneth L. Johnson a note voicing concern that "race may be playing some part in the deliberations," Johnson said. After the verdict was read, the judge told the jurors, "I hope to God in heaven this was not based upon race."

In August 1995, Kenneth Lee asked federal authorities to investigate the slaying, saying that the civil rights investigation was "my last hope" for justice.[191]

No justice. No peace.

Black jury nullification: protecting one of their own from the long, white arm of the law.

Racially repelling justice.

Farrakhan probably never heard of Zach Sowers.

A white guy, murdered in 63 percent black Baltimore.

But before he died, Sowers spent 10 long months lingering in a coma; 10 agonizing months for his wife, Anna. [Man left in coma after June robbery ends fight for life: `A long and treacherous battle', Baltimore Sun, 3-27-2008]:

In the 10 months since teenagers set upon Zachary Sowers and pummeled him into a coma, he lingered in oblivion. While his swollen face gradually resumed its natural form, he fought off infections and seemed to react, almost imperceptibly, to sounds in his hospital room.

---

[191] Error! Hyperlink reference not valid., **Baltimore Sun**, 1-16-1997

But Sowers never recovered consciousness. He died Tuesday night at Johns Hopkins Bayview Medical Center "after a long and treacherous battle" against his injuries, a Web site set up in his name announced yesterday. He was 28.

His wife, Anna, to whom he had been married just nine months at the time of the attack, said in a brief interview that she was grateful that "we had so many supporters to help us get through all of this."

The apparently random attack on Sowers occurred on a June night as he walked home in Canton. His wallet, cell phone and watch were stolen. One of the teenagers was seen stomping on Sowers' head, and was later sentenced to 40 years in prison.

News of the Sowers case stirred an uproar over rampant criminality on Baltimore's streets, particularly in neighborhoods such as Canton that city officials had sought to paint as safe for up-and-coming professional couples like Sowers and his wife. None was more vocal than Anna Sowers herself, who called her husband's main attacker, 16-year-old Trayvon Ramos, "an evil person, completely soulless."

After hearing of Sowers' death, Mayor Sheila Dixon issued a statement saying she was saddened, and offered prayers for his family and friends.

"His loss is a tragedy for the entire city of Baltimore," Dixon said. "We must continue to work hard to ensure the safety of every citizen."

The attack resonated because he was an innocent victim in a city where most killings appear to revolve around drugs. Sowers and his wife were, in many ways, the faces of the new Baltimore, willing to live in neighborhoods that had struggled with blight but showed promise.

Sowers was attacked after spending a Friday evening with friends in a bar. Because his wallet was stolen, he remained unidentified at Johns Hopkins Hospital for more than a day. His wife, who was in Chicago at the time, began to worry that something had happened to him because he failed to return phone calls or text messages, and his friends in Baltimore couldn't track him down.

With the help of city police, Anna Sowers learned that there was an unidentified man at Hopkins who had been found unconscious in the street. When she arrived at the hospital - nearly a full day after the attack - her husband's face was so badly bruised and swollen that she had trouble identifying him.

Ten days after the attack in the 300 block of S. Robinson Street, four teenagers were arrested. Police discovered that the teenagers had used Sowers' credit card to rent two movies - D?j? Vu and Smokin' Aces - and reviewed surveillance camera footage from a gas station that showed the car they drove.

Arthur Jeter, 18; Wilburt Martin, 19; Eric L. Price, 17; and Ramos were charged with attempted first-degree murder, robbery and related offenses. In December, Price, Jeter and Martin pleaded guilty to two counts of robbery after agreeing to testify against Ramos, who was accused of beating Sowers while Price watched. The other two had observed from the car.

In exchange for their guilty pleas, Price, Jeter and Martin received 30-year prison terms with all but 15 years suspended. They stand to serve about eight.

Anna Sowers, who had nothing but praise for the city police detectives who worked on her husband's case, said after the court hearing that the sentences "disgusted" her. "I feel that today, justice was not served at all," she said. "I feel like I've got no rights."

Amid all the crimes last year in Baltimore, the brutal attack on Sowers struck a chord. Politicians promised to step up law enforcement.

Anna Sowers told a reporter that she wanted politicians to do something about crime. "It's people like me and Zach who will make Baltimore a better city," she said. "I should be able to walk two blocks to my car at night and feel safe."[192]

The Sowers true crime was in believing they could move into a city dominated by black political power (and bursting with a robust black citizenry that represented almost 7 out of every 10 people) and "make Baltimore a better city," without any consequences. [ANTI HERO: Anna Sowers Tried to Speak Out Against Violence in Baltimore But Ended Up Tuned Out, Baltimore City Paper, 12/17/08]:

The beating of Zach Sowers had already galvanized young professionals in Canton and Federal Hill, who attended neighborhood rallies as he lay in a coma at Johns Hopkins Bayview Medical Center. Anna had launched a recovery fund and a loosely organized campaign to shake up City Hall with calls for tougher prosecutions and penalties for violent offenders. She met with some of the most powerful people in Maryland, most of who praised her courage and conviction. At first, it did not hurt and probably helped that she and Zach represented an educated, privileged class of new Baltimore residents. People gravitated to the brave, grieving widow who spoke her mind. A media fixation developed and Anna Sowers soon commanded attention from print reporters, pundits, and radio personalities.

But Sowers was wading into troubled waters. As newspaper stories, columns, and broadcast news reports dramatized her husband's attack, and talk-radio hosts pounced on Zach's beating as a symbol of urban failure, many started to question why such a fuss does not accompany the deaths of the hundreds of African-Americans who die every year in Baltimore.

---

[192] http://articles.baltimoresun.com/2008-03-27/news/0803270217_1_sowers

Baltimore's Population by Decade: Broken Down by Race

Year	Total Population	White Population	White Total (%)	Black Population	Black Total (%)
1910	558,000	473,000	85%	85,000	15%
1920	733,826	625,130	85%	108,322	15%
1930	804,874	662,124	82%	142,106	18%
1940	859,100	692,705	81%	165,843	19%
1950	949,748	723,655	76%	225,099	24%
1960	939,024	610,608	65%	325,589	35%
1970	905,759	479,837	54%	420,210	46%
1980	786,775	346,692	45%	430,934	55%
1990	736,014	287,933	41%	435,619	59%
2000	651,154	205,982	31.60%	418,951	64.3%
2010	620,961	183,830	28%	395,781	63.6%

(Source: U.S. Census Bureau and *Black Social Capital: The Politics of School Reform in Baltimore*, 1986-1998, p. 65)

From 85 percent white in 1910 to 28 percent white in 2010... black political control spelled out in numbers...

Many local leaders evaded, obfuscated, or deflected issues Sowers raised. Some simply ignored or stopped returning her calls. Some say they did not understand what she wanted from them. Some say her approach was wrongheaded. Others concede they feared a negative reaction if they went too far in support of an Asian-American woman whose white husband had been attacked by black youths.[193]

You see, black criminals are the unpaid foot soldiers of black political power: black elected officials in formerly-majority-white cities (that are now crumbling and failing) will leverage fear of high profile black-on-white muggings/rapes/murders to discourage white investors and keep gentrification and urban renewal to a minimum.

Everyone knows that with a new white population comes Starbucks, Whole Foods, Apple Stores, and a rush to repair and develop "blighted", neglected property ruined by the black population (who drove away the majority of businesses unwilling to invest in Plexiglas to defend its employees); with white people, comes higher property values, which push lower-class blacks out.

---

[193] Anna Sowers Tried to Speak Out Against Violence in Baltimore But Ended Up Tuned Out, Baltimore City Paper, 12/17/08

Anna Sowers quest for justice in her husband's murder was profiled in Baltimore Magazine with the fitting title "When You're Going through Hell, Keep on Going." (March 2009, Baltimore Magazine); Unfortunately, Anna, hell hath no fury like modern Baltimore.[194]

In 1910, the white population of Baltimore was well aware of what the black population (then only 15 percent) could do if unleashed and allowed to live anywhere without restrictions.

What they've done is create modern Baltimore, where law and order mean keeping Baltimore firmly in the political hands of Black control. Writing for the Maryland Law Review, Garret Power laments that white people once dared defend their civilization through the legal system, knowing the deleterious effects a rising black population would have on Baltimore's future. [Apartheid Baltimore Style: the Residential Segregation Ordinances of 1910-1913, Volume 42 Issue 2, 10-9-2012]:

> Milton Dashiell was George W.F. McMechen's brother at the Maryland Bar. Dashiell had been born in Dorchester County, Mary- land in 1859; he attended St. John's College in Annapolis, read law, and was admitted to practice in 1882. For a time, he practiced in Kentucky before he returned to his home state." According to all reports, his career was undistinguished; he was a "briefless lawyer."
>
> Dashiell resided on the southern fringe of the 11th Ward at 1110 McCulloh Street. The neighborhood was all white, but it was located just a block away from the Biddle Alley district, the infamous "lung block."
>
> The "Negro invasion" of Eutaw Place inspired Dashiell to draft a law designed to prevent blacks from further encroaching on white neighborhoods. The bill was introduced into the City Council by Councilman Samuel L. West.
>
> The bill took a long and tedious course. Public hearings were held at which the primary spokesmen against the ordinance were Negroes. Both branches of the City Council finally passed the ordinance, by a strict party vote - all Democrats voted in favor and all Republicans voted against.

---

[194] http://www.baltimoremagazine.net/people/2009/03/when-youre-going-through-hell-keep-on-going

The Baltimore Sun summarized the ordinance's provisions as follows:

- That no negro can move into a block in which more than half of the residents are white.

- That no white person can move into a block in which more than half of the residents are colored.

- That a violator of the law is punishable by a fine of not more than $100 or imprisonment of from 30 days to 1 year, or both.

- That existing conditions shall not be disturbed.

- No white person will be compelled to move away from his house because the block in which he lives has more negroes than whites, and no negro can be forced to move from his house if his block has more whites than negroes.

- That no section of the city is exempted from the conditions of the ordinance. It applies to every house."

In addition, the ordinance prohibited Negroes from using residences on white blocks as a place of public assembly and vice versa.

On December 17, 1910, City Solicitor Edgar Allan Poe issued an opinion declaring the ordinance constitutional. He opined that the ordinance was within the state's police power "because of irrefutable facts, well-known conditions, inherent personal characteristics and in- eradicable traits of character perculiar [sic] to the races, close association on a footing of absolute equality is utterly impossible between them, wherever negroes exist in large numbers in a white community, and invariably leads to irritation, friction, disorder and strife."

He determined that this ordinance was permissible under the fourteenth amendment to the U.S. Constitution because "a State has the right under its police power to require the separation of the two races wherever the failure to so separate then [sic] injuriously affects the good order and welfare of the community."

Many Progressives thus agreed that poor blacks should be quarantined in isolated slums in order to reduce the incidents of civil disturbance, to prevent the spread of communicable disease into the nearby white neighborhoods, and to protect property values among the white majority.

Historian George M. Frederickson tied these strands together:

If blacks were a degenerating race with no future, the problem ceased to be one of how to prepare them for citizenship or even how to make them more productive and useful members of the community. The new prognosis pointed rather to the need to segregate or quarantine a race liable to be a source of contamination and social danger to the white community, as it sank even deeper into the slough of disease, vice and criminality.

In 1922 the National Association of Real Estate Brokers (NAREB), of which the Baltimore Board was a member, published a textbook entitled Principles of Real Estate Practice. The textbook emphasized that "the purchase of property by certain racial types is very likely to diminish the value of other property."'

It was deemed un- ethical to sell blacks property that was located in white neighborhoods. As recently as 1950 the NAREB's code of ethics provided:

The realtor should not be instrumental in introducing into a neighborhood a character of property or occupancy, members of any race or nationality or any individual whose presence will clearly be detrimental to property values in the neighborhood.[195]

Modern-day Baltimore has become the living nightmare feared by white Baltimoreans of the past. It is why the National Association of Real Estate Brokers fought so long to protect the integrity and property values of a community.

Because social capital isn't something a bank can lend you, or the department of Housing of Urban Development (HUD) can create (via the threat of a rifle butt or a Drone attack).

It's created by a people who have hope that, by investing time and money into something today, they will achieve security for their

---

[195] Apartheid Baltimore Style: the Residential Segregation Ordinances of 1910-1913, Volume 42 Issue 2, 10-9-2012

family and property tomorrow.

That's what civilization is. Yet a de facto "separate courts and separate legal system" that Louis Farrakhan and the Nation of Islam (strangely, most of the goals of his organization are reflected in the explicit actions of Eric "My People" Holder and Barack Obama) advocate for have already come true in Baltimore.

As Joel Lee's family and Anna Sowers found out, the city is firmly in the hands of black control.

No justice. No peace (remember: Jordan Davis white killer, Michael Dunn, is going away for 75 years).

Funny: with control, the civilization whites created (and once dared defend) was the first casualty.

A Letter by a White Baltimore Woman from 1917 vs. Spike Lee's Rant Against Gentrification

It was something Miss Alice J. Reilley wrote in 1917, in a letter addressed to the mayor of Baltimore.

In the wake of the Supreme Court decision *Buchanan v. Warley* (declaring racial segregation in residential areas unconstitutional), Miss Reilley would ask a penetrating question that, almost 100 years later, still goes unanswered. [Apartheid Baltimore Style: the Residential Segregation Ordinances of 1910-1913, Maryland Law Review: Volume 42 Issue 2, 10-9-2012]:

> Black Baltimoreans seized the opportunity to renew their movement into white neighborhoods. Two black families moved into the 1100 block of Bolton Street, one of the oldest middle-class residential sections of the city; another family moved into the 1200 block of McCulloh Street.' White Baltimoreans responded with petulance and frustration. Miss Alice J. Reilley asked, "What is the use of trying to beautify a city or put in any civic improvements if Negroes are to acquire all of the property?"[196]

A haunting query from 1917 (penned when the city had a population of 558,000 and was 85 percent white), one that, the longer it goes unanswered, proves its eternal truth: *"What is the use of trying to beautify a city or put in any civic improvements if Negroes are to acquire all of the property?"*

Today, Baltimore has a population of 620,961 people (28 percent

---

[196] Ibid.

white/63.6 percent black). After reaching a peak population of close to one million in 1950, the city has completely collapsed since Miss Reilley's question, and all its implications, was first asked. [Blighted Cities Prefer Razing to Rebuilding, New York Times, 11/12/13]:

> BALTIMORE — Shivihah Smith's East Baltimore neighborhood, where he lives with his mother and grandmother, is disappearing. The block one over is gone. A dozen rowhouses on an adjacent block were removed one afternoon last year. And on the corner a few weeks ago, a pair of houses that were damaged by fire collapsed.
>
> The city bulldozed those and two others, leaving scavengers to pick through the debris for bits of metal and copper wire.
>
> For the Smiths, the bulldozing of city blocks is a source of anguish. But for Baltimore, as for a number of American cities in the Northeast and Midwest that have lost big chunks of their population, it is increasingly regarded as a path to salvation.
>
> The result of this shrinkage, also called "ungrowth" and "right sizing," has been compressed tax bases, increased crime and unemployment, tight municipal budgets and abandoned neighborhoods. The question is what to do with the urban ghost towns unlikely to be repopulated because of continued suburbanization and deindustrialization.[197]

Today, nearly 100 years to the date Miss Reilley's letter was sent to the mayor of Baltimore, attempts to beautify the city and engage in civic improvements means tearing down the white past to accommodate the black, bleak future.

Those "city blocks" were filled with once-beautiful row houses, now made inhospitable by a race of people far different from the people who first built them.

---

[197] http://www.nytimes.com/2013/11/12/us/blighted-cities-prefer-razing-to-rebuilding.html?_r=0

Far different.

But upon the row houses' removal, Miss. Reilley's question finally receives an answer.

97 years later.

Which brings up Spike Lee, the reigning champion of black directors, who recently commented on the gentrification (settlement of "blighted" black real estate by whites, which instantly improves property values and restores social capital) of his beloved Brooklyn. [Spike Lee's Amazing Rant Against Gentrification: 'We Been Here!', New York Magazine, 2/25/14]:

> I mean, they just move in the neighborhood. You just can't
> come in the neighborhood. I'm for democracy and letting
> everybody live but you gotta have some respect. You can't just
> come in when people have a culture that's been laid down for
> generations and you come in and now shit gotta change
> because you're here? Get the fuck outta here. Can't do that![198]

Democracy only applies to using the law to screw over white people on behalf of blacks (and increasingly all non-whites). Spike Lee understands this fact. Why can't you Trader Joe's/Whole Foods-shopping, Apple-product-buying, granola-chewing, Crossfit-participating, white-bread motherfuc*kers understand that fact?

Baltimore once had a culture, cultivated by a people represented by Miss Reilley (a culture swiftly exterminated when Shivihah Smith's "culture" took over), whose 1917 letter poses a question to which no modern-day advocate of equality can reply.

Today, Baltimore's culture is a byproduct of its majority population, and the title loan, pawn, and liquor stores encased in Plexiglas a powerful answer to Miss Reilley's 1917 question.

---

[198] http://nymag.com/daily/intelligencer/2014/02/spike-lee-amazing-rant-against-gentrification.html

Powerful.

The ability for a community to create wealth, increase property values, and maintain both a healthy tax-base and thriving business district depends heavily on the amount of social capital within the community. This was the underlying premise Miss Reilley's 1917 letter to the mayor of Baltimore.

Wherever the white Diaspora of Baltimore was scattered [Rating the 'Burbs: Schools, safety, parks, pools, taxes, population, hospitals, incomes, home values, and much more!, *Baltimore Magazine*, May 2003], prosperity followed. What was left behind in Baltimore was the dismal, dangerous conditions Spike Lee lauded as the unique "culture" of his people; he then balked at the idea of this "culture" being uprooted by gentrification![199]

What else was left behind in Baltimore? Renowned liberal crime-fighter David M. Kennedy (director of the Center for Crime Prevention and Control and a professor of criminal justice at John Jay College) dubbed it "hell."

Hell.

In his book *Don't Shoot: One Man, A Street Fellowship, and the End of Violence in Inner-City America Paperback* (purported to be the Bible on how to combat black crime in urban America) writes of his efforts to lower crime:

> Baltimore was *hell*. The worst of it was on the streets, but the rest of it was pretty bad too.

> The result made your blood run cold: gangs and drug markets and homicides everywhere. When we looked at a year's worth of homicides, it was 303 victims and 210 suspects... Three quarters of victims and almost 90 percent of offenders had criminal records, the highest we'd ever seen, averaging 8.5 and 9.6 priors respectively. Nearly 60 percent of the killings happened in or near a street drug market. Despite the

---

[199] http://www.baltimoremagazine.net/features/2003/05/rating-the-burbs

superheated street drug scene, only about 20 percent of killings had to do with drug business; the usual beefs, vendettas, and respect killings were the order of the day. [200]

What was it Miss Reilley wrote back in 1917?

Oh: *"What is the use of trying to beautify a city or put in any civic improvements if Negroes are to acquire all of the property?"*

So almost 100 years to the day of Miss Reilley's letter to the mayor of Baltimore, American citizens have a lot of empirical evidence proving her fears were 100 percent correct.

Just as bad money drives away good money, bad citizens drive away good citizens.

It's not a crazy question to ask: What would property values be like in Baltimore were the city 85 percent white today (as it was around 1917, when Miss Reilley wrote her letter)?

It's not a crazy question to ask: What would the jails of Baltimore (housing the people who helped turn the city into "hell") look like if the city were 85 percent white today?

With an average daily jail population of 4,010 (in 2008), Baltimore City has the highest percentage of its population incarcerated for the top 20 largest jails in the United States. With .629% of the jurisdiction in jail (Shelby County, TN -home of Memphis - and Philadelphia City, PA, both close seconds), the astounding cost of policing the 63-percent-black city should be obvious.

Adding to that cost is a network of surveillance cameras throughout

---

[200] Kennedy, David M.. *Don't shoot: one man, a street fellowship, and the end of violence in inner-city America*. New York: Bloomsbury USA, 2011. p. 107-108

the city (at $10 million to install and $1.4 million per year to operate) working as a 24/7/365 deterrent to crime. And just who do you suppose the cameras would be capturing while committing these crimes?[201]

Surprise! Nine out of every 10 people in Baltimore's jail are black.

A Justice Policy Institute Report from June of 2010 [BALTIMORE BEHIND BARS: How to Reduce the Jail Population, Save Money and Improve Public Safety] points out:

> African Americans make up the largest percentage of the people in the jail.
>
> Despite making up only 64 percent of Baltimore residents, African Americans comprise 89 percent of the people held in the jail; currently more than 2,900 African American men are incarcerated in the jail. The reasons for the high number of African Americans in the jail are numerous, but studies show that it is not related to actual behavior differences.
>
> In cities and states around the country reasons for the disproportionate number of African Americans in jail can include policing practices and enforcement in certain communities, disproportionate allocation of resources, disparate treatment by the courts and lack of quality defense, amongst other reasons. The responsibility for alleviating these disparities falls not only on criminal justice agencies, but on society as a whole, and needs to be addressed appropriately through both policy and practice at all levels of government and the community.[202]

Actually, the high level of dysfunctional behavioral among blacks

---

[201] http://articles.baltimoresun.com/2012-07-21/news/bs-md-ci-private-cameras-20120721_1_security-cameras-crime-cameras-citiwatch-system

[202] http://www.justicepolicy.org/images/upload/10-06_rep_baltbehindbars_md-ps-ac-rd.pdf

accounts for the disproportionate number currently in jail (in not just Baltimore, but all across America).

- Low-impulse control
- An aversion to saving money for the future (poor future-time orientation)
- A toxic level of self-esteem (hence, the high frequency of respect killings
- Though certain black individuals can achieve the cultural standards set by whites, collectively, blacks have one-standard deviation lower IQ than whites

Evidence of these alarming behavioral differences in her community is what drove Miss Reilley to write a letter to the mayor of Baltimore in 1917, asking: *"What is the use of trying to beautify a city or put in any civic improvements if Negroes are to acquire all of the property?"*

When Kennedy came to Baltimore to implement his magical "Operation Safe Neighborhoods" plan, the *Baltimore Sun* published a story absolving the black citizens of all personal responsibility/accountability for the condition of the aptly named Langston Hughes neighborhood in the Northwest District of the city. [Police, residents team up for a safer Park Heights: Gun violence targeted initiative aims to establish 'new rules on the street', 3/6/2000]:

> As a mother of nine, Jean Yahudah worries about whether her children are safe in her Park Heights neighborhood.
>
> She has had windows shot out of her Woodland Avenue home, bullets fired through her van, and every one of her children, ages 8 to 31, knows a friend or acquaintance who was shot or murdered during the past few years.
>
> "There's just too much violence," she said. "I want to live in a normal, safe and healthy neighborhood."
>
> Yahudah offered her home yesterday as a gathering point for volunteers, who picked up fliers and spread the word that gun violence will no longer be tolerated in Park Heights in

Northwest Baltimore.

Yahudah was also one of dozens of people who went yesterday to Agape Fellowship Miracle Church for a service aimed at winning support for a crackdown on gun violence called Operation Safe Neighborhoods. The service was at Langston Hughes Elementary School in the 5000 block of Reisterstown Road.

The effort occurred two weeks after state and federal law enforcement officials took 27 convicted felons from Park Heights into the Baltimore City state's attorney's office to warn them that prosecutors and police are intensifying their focus on gun violence in the community.

State and federal officials chose Park Heights for the initiative because of recent gun violence, she said. In 1999, 13 homicides and 36 nonfatal shootings occurred in the area and 49 firearms were seized by police, according to statistics compiled by Operation Safe Neighborhoods.

"This is unprecedented in that we never warn people that we're watching them and go after them if they use guns," said Kimberly Bowen Morton, a prosecutor and gun violence coordinator for the Baltimore City state's attorney's office.[203]

You can't live in a normal, safe, and healthy neighborhood, because such a community requires social capital, created and maintained by whites.

It all boils down to Miss Alice J. Reilley's 1917 letter (fearing the negative effects of a majority black community), juxtaposed with Spike Lee's rant against gentrification (lamenting the positive effects of a majority white community).

"What is the use of trying to beautify a city or put in any civic

---

[203] http://articles.baltimoresun.com/2000-03-06/news/0003060156_1_gun-violence-park-heights-safe-neighborhoods

improvements if Negroes are to acquire all of the property?"

versus:

> I mean, they just move in the neighborhood. You just can't come in the neighborhood. I'm for democracy and letting everybody live but you gotta have some respect. You can't just come in when people have a culture that's been laid down for generations and you come in and now shit gotta change because you're here? Get the fuck outta here. Can't do that!

It is now the official policy of the United States of America to turn every neighborhood, community, city, and state into nothing more than a Baltimore.

Nearly a century ago, Alice J. Reilley saw how residential desegregation turns out; now, as then, Spike Lee knows how gentrification of "blighted" black communities turns out.

If she could be resurrected today and see the state of her beloved city, well, she'd nod her head knowingly.

Her letter from 1917 prophesied why private Baltimore business owners would one day need to install Plexiglas to protect their employees and merchandise; yet perhaps even she would never have predicted Spike Lee actually finding cause to celebrate the very conditions that Reilley feared as a harbinger of things to come.

Her letter from 1917 is directly related to why white flight from Baltimore took place, and why the city's complete collapse into its own footprint was inevitable once political power was enshrined by the black majority.

What was it they knew?

What was it they knew?[204]

What was it they knew would happen?

What was it they knew would happen and attempted to stop?
[Garrett Power, *Apartheid Baltimore Style: the Residential Segregation Ordinances of 1910-1913*, 42 Md. L. Rev. 289 (1983)]:

On May 15, 1911, Baltimore Mayor J. Barry Mahool, who was known as an earnest advocate of good government, women's suffrage, and social justice, signed into law "[a]in ordinance for preserving peace, preventing conflict and ill feeling between the white and colored races in Baltimore city, and promoting the general welfare of the city by providing, so far as practicable, for the use of separate blocks by white and colored people for residences, churches and schools."[205]

More than 100 years later, Baltimore stands as irrefutable proof that a peaceful, conflict-free multiracial society is an unattainable dream; it's also proof that such characteristics in a majority-black society are impossibilities as well, with every quality-of-life metric trending downward in *The City that Bleeds*.

A century ago, the city of Baltimore, as well as America's other great cities, was a reflection of white Europeans' accomplishments, lives, and vocations aggregated together to showcase their wondrous capabilities; Baltimore today is a manifestation of black political power enshrined by a black demographic majority, showcasing how legitimate business and social capital evaporates almost immediately.

---

[204] http://articles.baltimoresun.com/1995-02-05/news/1995036002_1_baltimore-black-ghetto-shot-tower

[205] Garrett Power, *Apartheid Baltimore Style: the Residential Segregation Ordinances of 1910-1913*, 42 Md. L. Rev. 289 (1983) p. 289

Immediately.

Civilization recedes to the mean.

Always.

Obviously the white leaders of Baltimore, circa 1910, had empirical evidence of what could be unleashed if mechanisms weren't put in place to safeguard the civilization they created. Returning to Garrett Power's 1983 essay, we learn:

> Between 1880 and 1900 Baltimore's black population increased 47% from 54,000 to 79,000. During this same period, the city's white population was increasing by 54%. Hence, while the black population was increasing by 25,000 people, the proportion of blacks in the population was on a slight decline.
>
> Negro newcomers with little money and limited job opportunities sought out the cheapest housing in town. They rented shanties and doubled up in small houses, resulting in Baltimore's first sizeable slums. The first slum to reach maturity was "Pigtown" in Southwest Baltimore. A contemporaneous account from 1892 describes it as follows:
>
> *Open drains, great lots filled with high weeds, ashes and garbage accumulated in the alleyways, cellars filled with filthy black water, houses that are total strangers to the touch of whitewash or scrubbing brush, human bodies that have been strangers for months to soap and water, villainous looking negroes who loiter and sleep around the street corners and never work; vile and vicious women, with but a smock to cover their black nakedness, lounging in the doorways or squatting upon the steps, hurling foul epithets at every passerby; foul streets, foul people, in foul tenements filled with foul air; that's "Pigtown."* [206]

Doesn't this 1892 description of a black Baltimore ghetto sound eerily similar to the modern "blight" and the rationale for "urban renewal" in 2014?

This is a city where "hung juries" are now the norm – because black

---

[206] Ibid. p. 290

members of juries don't want to convict black criminals[207]; as they see it, the defendants are merely victims of a *racist judicial system*. In a city where a 2010 D.A. election was reduced to a contest of open racial accusations by the black incumbent, alleging the white challenger was "too tough on (black) crime", it's obvious the "preservation of peace" is impossible. [Race for top prosecutor has racial backdrop: Each side plays to base, analysts say, Baltimore Sun, 8-21-2010][208]

"Conflict and ill will" is now the hallmark of racial relations in contemporary Baltimore, where the endless onslaught of black crime and homicide is excused.

With a clear black majority, Baltimore is now a city where civilization is fading into obscurity; with remnants of a once-thriving civilization just a shadow behind the rising tide of barbarism our white ancestors dared try to keep in check.

While sons of the generation that defended the integrity of white Baltimore went off to fight fascism in Europe and the Yellow Peril in Pacific, back home a force was unleashed on American soil more fatal than an atom bomb.

Edited by Elizabeth Fee, Linda Shopes and Linda Zeidman, the early 1980s *The Baltimore Book: New Views of Local History* offers one of the most depressing anecdotes of the unintended consequences of World War II... the long-term defeat of the United States as a superpower:

> But during and immediately following World War II, an expanding black population created explosive housing pressures. By the late 1940s and early 1950s, the demand for housing finally resulted in black settlement in adjacent white areas to the west of Fulton.

> Following a pattern long established in Baltimore race relations, when blacks moved in, whites rapidly moved out.

---

[207] http://articles.baltimoresun.com/2007-07-28/news/0707280361_1_hung-juries-davidoff

[208] http://articles.baltimoresun.com/2010-08-21/news/bs-md-hermann-prosecutor-race-20100821_1_jessamy-supporter-gregg-bernstein-top-prosecutor

One black resident of the area remembers this episode of white flight:

Black people started moving out of confined areas somewhere around 1947 or 1948, but what would happen was that whites would evacuate a block or two blocks, and black people would move in. The evacuation would take place first. I remember streets like Fulton Avenue, Monroe Street – they were once totally white, and they went through the transition and changed somewhere between 1946 and 1949 – that was the time I was in the service. When I went in, there were no black people and when I came out, they were black streets... But it wasn't integration... it was an evacuation.

While the movement of the color line brought new housing opportunities to some, the older section of black homes east of Fulton Avenue deteriorated in the post-World War II period. A 1944 *Baltimore Sun* reporter wrote: "Homes are very badly in need of repair and paint; dead rats lie in the street where they were crushed by automobiles; alleys are littered with debris and foul-smelling garbage; lots where homes formerly stood are covered with a thick layer of ashes."[209]

America's exceptionality was borne of its white population, whose ability to create social capital where civilization could then flourish is the primary reason other nations are helpless to prevent their citizens from converging upon the USA every year.

That's it.

What was it they knew?

What was it they dared try and keep from overwhelming civilization?

Homicide in the city has, for decades, been almost exclusively a black problem.[210] And with Baltimore firmly established in pop culture (via shows like *Homicide* and *The Wire)* as one of America's most violent

---

[209] McDougall, Harold A.. *Black Baltimore: a new theory of community.* Philadelphia: Temple University Press, 1993.p. 210 - 211

[210] http://articles.baltimoresun.com/1990-12-24/news/1990358017_1_homicide-city-murder-1990-murder

cities, it's no wonder that a year with less than 300 murders was celebrated as overcoming a "psychological hurdle" by members of the white business community. [Fewer than 300 homicides at last: Crime: For the first time in more than a decade, Baltimore's toll for a year breaks a barrier that it had seemed impossible to breach only months ago., Baltimore Sun, 1-1-2001]:

> You don't want people being murdered on your streets, regardless of the reason or cause," said Donald P. Hutchinson, president of the Greater Baltimore Committee, a consortium of business executives.
>
> The group has pumped $350,000 into various crime-fighting efforts, studies and the hiring of a prosecutor to target gun offenders, arguing that the high homicide rate and violent reputation has hurt Baltimore's standing in the business community.
>
> For the most part, homicides are concentrated in depressed areas of the city, away from downtown and many residential areas. But Hutchinson said he feels uneasy walking in parts of other cities, such as Atlanta and New Orleans, and imagines that visitors feel the same about Baltimore.
>
> The homicide rate, he said, "has a tremendous psychological impact outside the city."[211]

The homicide rate is a reflection of the aggregated experiences of black individuals, all proud members and representatives of the black community in Baltimore.[212]

Thus, Hutchinson's statement should read, "the black population has a tremendously negative psychological impact inside the city, reflected in pop culture's image as America's most violent city."

Do you understand what white people in 1946-1949 were evacuating from now?

---

[211] http://articles.baltimoresun.com/2001-01-01/news/0101010157_1_homicides-baltimore-norris

[212] http://articles.baltimoresun.com/2005-12-11/news/0512110024_1_culture-cornwell-medical-students

Do you understand what white people, in charge of Baltimore back in 1910, were trying to protect their white posterity from yet?

No?

How about this? [Grave Markers: Spray-painted wall and makeshift shrines remember the young black men lost to the street., Baltimore Sun, 6-7-2001]:

> The young man is tapping the name on the concrete wall of 2510 E. Biddle St., tapping it insistently, emphatically, as he makes his point. This name, spray-painted here and across the street and around the corner, these words, "1 Love Dre 1975-1999," were not left randomly to disrespect property and community.

> "Don't disrespect this by calling it graffiti," he says. "This is a piece of my heart right here."

> His name is Troy, and pieces of his heart are all around East Biddle Street and Milton Avenue: "RIP Dre The good die young. Last days."

> Tombstones cover one wall across the street: Dre, Knuckles, Shawn, Wayne, all of them gone, but not forgotten. Remembered by Troy and other young men in the one public way they feel they are allowed.

> "All We Got Is Us," they have painted on one wall.

> They all know one another. They grew up together, the dope dealers and gunslingers, friends and relatives, all of them running together in neighborhoods as close-knit and tight as any other. Only here the scourge of drugs and crime and urban decay has settled in for a long, long stay. Theirs is a world of boarded-up homes and burned out rowhouses and this question: "I wonder if heaven got a ghetto?"

> On some walls, the names overlap, fresh tags stark against older ones faded by rain and sun and time, reminders of the more than 3,000 people killed in Baltimore in the last 10 years. These young men live with that violence, locked as they are in an embrace of life and death and memory and respect.

> Dre's friends say they would never think of going to a graveyard, sitting down with a bouquet of flowers and weeping. That is not their way. A candlelight vigil? Be real, they say. Imagine a dozen young black men gathering in a rough part of town to remember a dead friend. The police cars

would be rolling up. So, none of that.

But this you can do, they say, paint a name on a wall, smoke some marijuana, drink a 40-ounce or two of malt liquor and pour one out for Dre, or Shawn, and stand on the spot where a bullet took his life.

Across town, the brothers at Edmondson and Fulton avenues are working the cell phones like mad. Everybody has one. They are constantly flipping them open, then closing them, flipping them open again for a 15-second conversation.

Not much to say. The walls say it all. "RIP Duncan 99; RIP T-Kelly 00; RIP Vic 01," each name penned on a separate brick.

A few feet away, Lil Tee-Tie has a tag. He's still alive. But gone. Most likely for the rest of his life. He's doing triple life plus 60 years.

They remember their own.

"10-15 Years From Now Yall Gonna Miss A Nigga Like Duncan." That's Shine's message to the world, his last word about his cousin.

At East Preston and Ensor streets, Mo, Gillette, Lou and the others have gone beyond the RIP theme. They already have a wall dedicated to "Lipton" and "T. J. Money" and "Wilcox." Now they are leaving empty liquor and beer bottles on the stoop of the boarded up house where Mo spent the first 23 years of his life.

The neighborhood people covered the stoop with empty bottles. Then, they say, the police took every one. The young men brought more. And so it went. There might be 100 now, empty Hennesseys and Remy Martins, Steel Reserve 211s and Coronas. Mo left a magnum of Heineken.

"I know if they look down they're smiling because we ain't forgot them," says Gillette. "Every drink we tip out, they get some."

Every drink poured out, remembering some hood rats' life in Baltimore (mowed down by some other black male), is another reminder the black undertow will always overwhelm civilization.

Always.

What was it they knew?

That race is real and civilization is fragile.

What was it they tried to keep from happening?

Those who are responsible for civilization "evacuating" from what and where their ancestors worked hard every day of their lives to create; now, those same streets serve as the macabre setting for... makeshift memorials to dead blacks, gunned-down members of their own community.

The American experiment has failed.

A 1907 Baltimore Sun Ad for Housing: "The NEIGHBORHOOD IS EXCELLENT, And no negroes are in the immediate vicinity"

Would you want to live in a city where a pack of cigarettes is more important to one of your fellow citizens than the life of one of their so-called friends? [Schmoke rides on city's violent side Shootings: Amid Baltimore's triumphs, the mayor gets a first-hand look at crime on the city's west side., Baltimore Sun, 7-1-1998]:

> Yesterday, Mayor Kurt L. Schmoke hailed a new retirement community for the deaf as a monument to all that is good about Baltimore. Monday night, he stood at a crowded West Baltimore corner and saw all that is bad.

On a ride-along with police, the city's chief executive sped to three shootings and at one point stood over a wounded young man lying face down on a street with four bullets in his back.

"A friend of his comes along and looks down," Schmoke recalled yesterday. "And he doesn't say to the police or to me, 'How's he doing?' He says, 'What are you all going to do with that boy's cigarettes?' That is showing no regard for human life."[213]

A pack of cigarettes.

It's a city where "Stop the Tears"[214] and "Stop the Violence" programs, initiated to counter acts of spontaneous blackness, ultimately failed.[215] Completely. [Children's tears point up our failures, Baltimore Sun, 1-18-1997]:

> The marchers were called together by the Rev. Willie Ray of the "Stop the Killing" campaign. Joining him were the Rev. Arnold Howard of Enon Baptist Church and the Rev. Dr. John Wright of the First Church of Guilford in Howard County. Only two city officeholders -- Comptroller Joan M. Pratt and 6th District Councilman Melvin L. Stukes -- attended the march and vigil.

> It's a sobering thought. Black children being cut down in the city, and only five black religious and political leaders find the time to come to a march and vigil to make some kind of statement about the grisly situation. There is a crisis here, one city leadership needs to address.[216]

---

[213] http://articles.baltimoresun.com/1998-07-01/news/1998182002_1_schmoke-fraternal-order-southwest-baltimore

[214] http://articles.baltimoresun.com/1991-01-22/news/1991022170_1_police-department-city-police-guns

[215] http://articles.baltimoresun.com/1999-01-03/topic/9904280932_1_baltimore-s-homicide-baltimore-city-time-baltimore/2

[216] http://articles.baltimoresun.com/1997-01-18/news/1997018038_1_erica-vigil-officeholders

Even though the population is dropping by huge percentage points each year, an annual vigil to mark the melancholy reality of crime, murder, and mayhem still reserves a spot on the civic calendar each year. It seems counter-intuitive that the number of homicides are such that a New Year's Eve vigil will be required each year...[Baltimore's 2012 homicide victims remembered at New Year's Eve vigil: Mayor, police commissioner join activists to remember 216 slain men, women and children, Baltimore Sun, 12-31-12]:

> For minutes on end New Year's Eve night, the names and ages of 216 men, women and children who were killed in Baltimore in 2012 were read out loud on the steps of the city's War Memorial — a somber recap of a violent year in which homicides rose. "In a city where so many people are immune to these senseless crimes, it is imperative that we remember the victims," said Victoria Kent, a member of the Baltimore Guardian Angels community watch group, as about 50 others stood by.
>
> The vigil, in its fourth year, was attended by Mayor Stephanie Rawlings-Blake, Baltimore Police Commissioner Anthony W. Batts, City Council President Bernard C. "Jack" Young, council members Brandon Scott and Carl Stokes, members of the clergy and various city activists.
> Many among the crowd spoke to the need for communities to come together and provide those involved in the cycle of violence — many of them young men, many African-American — better outlets.
>
> "Too many people in our city have lost respect for human life, and too many of us have stood by and watched," Rawlings-Blake said. "We have to have that voice and say that we deserve, that every child and family in the city deserves, more."[217]

Every child and family does deserve more, and it's important to remember that more than 100 years ago, the actual sons and daughters of those who built Baltimore were faced with a crisis far greater than that of the British burning the city during the War of 1812: the Great Migration of blacks from the South.

---

[217] http://articles.baltimoresun.com/2012-12-31/news/bs-md-mayor-vigil-20121231_1_homicide-victims-city-violence-young-men

All of the maladies currently plaguing Baltimore occurred *despite* the best efforts of its white majority to prevent them back in 1910. *In The Baltimore Rowhouse* by Marry Ellen Hayward and Charles Belfoure, we learn that our ancestors were well aware of the deleterious effect of blacks on social capital than our short-sighted policy of just trying to run-away from the problem today:

> As the black population in Baltimore increased from 54,000 in 1880 to 85,000 in 1910, many blacks tried to move out of crowded enclaves. Speculative builders, Gallagher included, felt threatened by this and feared the effect upon sales and prices. In 1909 the U.S. Supreme Court refused to review a case involving a restrictive covenant barring the sale of property to a black.

> The following year the city council passed a segregation ordinance, in response to a black family's purchase of a house on McCulloh Street, on black closer to the city's most fashionable neighborhood, Eutaw Place, than blacks had formerly been allowed to live. In essence the law said that no "Negro" could move onto a block in which more than half the residents were white and that no white could move into a block that was more than half black.

> A developer could not open a street without first declaring whether it was for white or black occupants.
> Builders of houses on "white" blocks were quick to cite "the safety" of their neighborhoods in advertisements. "Walbrook, 3000 block W. North Ave.," ran one ad of 1907, "Attractive Section, No Saloons, No Colored. Up-To-Date Three-Story Houses, Every Convenience." L. Irving German asked readers of the *Sun* to: "Look at these fine two-story houses recently built in the 2000 block West Fayette Street, and see us at once about terms. We can make them very attractive to reliable men of character with small means. They are well built, contain six rooms, bath and pantry, are beautifully finished. Have sanitary plumbing, attractive wall paper and all conveniences. The NEIGHBORHOOD IS EXCELLENT, And no Negroes are in the immediate vicinity."[218]

---

[218] Hayward, Mary Ellen, and Charles Belfoure. *The Baltimore*

Rowhouse. New York: Princeton Architectural Press, 2001. p.

A pack of cigarettes.

"Stop the Violence" programs.

"Stop the Tears" programs.

Only one hundred years after the city council of Baltimore passed laws attempting to maintain some semblance of residential integrity in the city, Baltimore holds the dubious distinction of America's most violent, blood-soaked streets.[219]

And it was all because of blacks.[220]

Not drugs.[221]

Not guns.

Blacks.

Just like that real estate ad from the early twentieth century, it's "men of character" that help make a great neighborhood, community, or city.

Men without character?

They make modern-day Baltimore, which those white citizens of a century past (remember, the city was roughly 86 percent white then) did their best to keep from happening.

125-126

[219] http://articles.baltimoresun.com/2009-06-03/news/0906020063_1_baltimore-decline-in-homicides-city-homicide-rate

[220] http://articles.baltimoresun.com/2010-01-03/news/bal-md.ci.yearend03jan03_1_homicide-gun-charges-victims

[221] http://articles.baltimoresun.com/2001-07-15/news/0107150290_1_east-baltimore-norris-copeland

They must attend "Stop the Violence" rallies and carry candles at vigils on New Year's Eve, for it was on *their* watch (and only their watch) that a world where "Stop the Tears" programs are needed.

Got a cigarette?

Will Black Baltimore Give Him a Ticker Tape Parade? Black Cop Killer (called 'Political Prisoner' in 2001) Released from Jail... Does that Make Whites War Criminals?

There will be no Constitutional Convention.

Sorry, Mark Levin.

There will be no grand reawakening of the American spirit with Dr. Ben Carson at the helm of the 2016 GOP ticket.

Sorry, Glenn Beck.

What Fox News, Rush Limbaugh, and Michael Savage are predicting as a Great Conservative Takeover is, well, just fantasy for the benefit of the devoted few who still say their prayers, take their vitamins and recite the Pledge of Allegiance.

Sam Donaldson was right when he said "guys, it's not your country anymore – it's our country."[222]

And with the victory comes the spoils.

The black community of Baltimore has long sympathized with black criminals, and now, with black elected (and self-appointed) political leaders in charge, they effectively use the clarion call of "racism" (past or present, real or imagined) to unite blacks in a single purpose: retain control of their political destiny.

Jury nullification is a huge problem in majority-black Baltimore, with the black citizens siding more and more with black defendants (after all, the law is nothing more than an extension of continued white supremacy).[223]

So, almost 13 years to the day, a majority-black city council passed a resolution to pardon a black cop killer,[224] he's now walking free; Largely out of fear that jury nullification would result in Anglo-Saxon law being usurped by the law of racial loyalty in Baltimore.

Fitting, then, that a 2001 black city council of Baltimore branded this murderer a "political prisoner" (of what, white America?). What's worse, this murderer is now the City Council President of Baltimore, meaning that white Americans are now nothing more than war criminals in Baltimore. [225]

---

[222] http://www.mediaite.com/tv/abcs-sam-donaldson-to-tea-party-its-not-your-country-anymore-its-our-country/

[223] http://stuffblackpeopledontlike.blogspot.com/2014/01/primal-anger-over-dubious-acts-of.html

[224] http://articles.baltimoresun.com/2001-04-04/news/0104040312_1_conway-sager-black-panther

[225] http://articles.baltimoresun.com/2001-03-

And all of America. [Black Panther leader, convicted of killing cop, released from prison, Baltimore Sun, 3-4-14]:

> Former Black Panther leader Marshall "Eddie" Conway walked free Tuesday after spending four decades behind bars for killing a Baltimore police officer — making his one of the highest-profile cases affected by a high court decision that has cut short prison sentences for dozens of felons in recent years.
>
> Conway, now 67, always said that he was innocent, alleging political motives in the prosecution of a 1970 shooting that killed Officer Donald Sager, 35, and injured another officer. Over the years many supporters, including prominent Baltimore politicians, have joined his cause.
>
> Police union officials and Sager's family said they still believe Conway was guilty. But prosecutors — faced with the prospect of retrying a more than 40-year-old case built on the testimony of a fellow police officer and a jailhouse interview — said they could not have convicted him again.
>
> Conway sought a new trial under a 2012 decision by the Maryland Court of Appeals, which said verdicts before 1980 were invalid because of faulty jury instructions. Under a deal with prosecutors, Conway agreed to abandon his court fight in exchange for his release on time served.
>
> Conway walked out of the courthouse about 3 p.m. and then went to a friend's house to eat a plate of vegetable lasagna with his two sons and other supporters, according to Dominique Stevenson, a longtime advocate who co-wrote a book with him. Conway declined to be interviewed.
>
> "He's just taking it all in," Stevenson said.
>
> Supporters have long believed that Conway was set up because of his role with the Black Panthers, and on Tuesday

29/news/0103290086_1_conway-pardon-black-panther

Paul Kersey

the Baltimore branch of the National Association for the Advancement of Colored People and others hailed his release, calling it a "monumental day" and "an important page turner in this tragic story."

But Sager's son, who was 7 at the time of his father's death, said he was devastated.

David Sager said he was warned of the outcome more than a month ago in a meeting with Baltimore State's Attorney Gregg L. Bernstein.

David Sager said he debated whether to attend Tuesday's hearing. He decided against it.

"My mother passed away two years ago, and in a way I'm glad that she's not around to see this," he said. "This is a very sad day. I think this is another tragedy on our justice system, one of a string of tragedies."

Police union officials said they were troubled by the release. Gene Ryan, vice president of the city's Fraternal Order of Police lodge, said it was "difficult" to learn that Conway would not serve out his life in prison.

He blamed the appellate courts for creating the circumstances that have led to Conway and others winning release.

Since the 2012 ruling by Maryland's highest court, dozens have fought their convictions and prosecutors have made deals to release many of them, opening old wounds for victims' families.

In Conway's case, Bernstein said that dealing with someone convicted of killing a police officer created "a different set of issues and concerns."

Bernstein did not believe prosecutors would have been able to convict Conway in a retrial after so many years. "It's about ... whether there's sufficient evidence to convince 12 people beyond a reasonable doubt that he committed this crime," he said.

In 2001, the Baltimore City Council, including now-President Bernard C. "Jack" Young, passed a resolution urging Gov. Parris N. Glendening to pardon Conway, calling him a political prisoner innocent of murder. Through a spokeswoman, Young declined to comment Tuesday night.

NAACP chapter President Tessa Hill-Aston said the organization does not discount the fact that a police officer lost his life in the 1970 shooting. But she said Conway's prosecution came during an era in which black leaders were targeted by government officials to silence them.

"There were lots of African-American men who were accused and had bad trials," she said.

Dr. Marvin L. "Doc" Cheatham Sr., a former Baltimore NAACP president who helped organize rallies on Conway's behalf, said Conway was convicted with no physical evidence and that the officer who identified Conway did not see him at the crime scene.

"I continue to keep the family of the deceased officer in prayer, but Eddie had said from day one that he hadn't done it and folks have to remember that this was when the COINTEL program was at its height," Cheatham said. "They did not have a witness who saw him there. They had no fingerprints or evidence there. They basically convicted him on the basis of what we now call an informant."[226]

Back in 2001, Baltimore's black political leadership had no idea the power they wielded by maintaining a racially united front in response to white flight from the city. [Council pardon resolution protested: Police union is upset by effort to help man convicted in officer's death, Shooting occurred in April 1970, Baltimore Sun, 3-29-2001]:

[226] http://www.baltimoresun.com/news/maryland/crime/blog/bs-md-ci-eddie-conway-black-panther-released-20140304,0,4610997.story#ixzz2v6edGbM0

A City Council resolution urging Gov. Parris N. Glendening to pardon a man convicted of killing a police officer is sparking complaints from the police union, whose president wants lawmakers to publicly apologize.

"I demand that the City Council take immediate action to rescind this resolution in order to avoid exposing the wounds of our Fallen Heroes," wrote Officer Gary McLhinney, the union president, in a letter to the bill's sponsor, Councilman Norman A. Handy Sr. "The actions of the City Council are so egregious."

Council members who voted last month to urge a pardon for former Black Panther member Marshall "Eddie" Conway say he is a political prisoner innocent of murder.

They call the case circumstantial and question the integrity of a jailhouse informant who testified that Conway described the shooting to him.

"The union is entitled to its opinion," Handy said. "I'm simply expressing mine. He was convicted on at best spurious evidence."[227]

Donald Sager is still dead.

To the blacks in charge, however, he was just a white cop trying to uphold "white racism" (law and order) in a demographically transformed city.

Spoils of war. [Supporters of a pardon think lie sent man to prison, Baltimore Sun, 4-8-2001]:

> "I think it's just ludicrous," Juanita Sager, Donald Sager's widow, said last week. "I'm totally opposed to even the thought of [a pardon]. He [Conway] not only took my husband's life, he took my life and my son's life. We still pay for that." Sager's son was 7 when his father was killed.

---

[227] http://articles.baltimoresun.com/2001-03-29/news/0103290086_1_conway-pardon-black-panther

Now there's something for Handy and the resolution's co-sponsors - Helen Holton, Paula Johnson Branch, Bernard "Jack" Young, Keiffer Mitchell, Agnes Welch, Bea Gaddy, Robert Curran, Cathy Pugh, Lisa Stancil and Kenneth Harris - to ponder: If Sager's widow and son are still suffering, if they're still paying, why shouldn't Conway continue to do the same?[228]

Will black Baltimore have a ticker-tape parade for their exonerated hero; a Black Panther *they believe* was framed for murder?

Do you not understand the significance of this decision yet?

If you are white, you are a nothing more than a war criminal in Baltimore, as well as all of America.

That's what the false doctrine of white privilege attempts to preach, alleging that all wealth, real estate, and stock holdings by whites are illegitimate.

Jury nullification is the black's way of demanding payback (even if it means absolving guilty criminals and letting them back on the streets) for Jim Crow, white supremacy, and segregation --- all ideas that tried to stop black political rule in Baltimore 2014 from ever happening in the first place. [Jury distrust, bitter verdict:

Fallout: Many blamed the jury when a Baltimore teen was acquitted of murder in the death of a police officer. But police made errors -- and some jurors suspected worse., Baltimore Sun, 3-11-2001]:

> Experts say that urban jurors, particularly African-Americans, have grown increasingly willing in recent years to acquit defendants they believe are guilty if they detect any abuse of police power.
>
> Prosecutors, who despair that their cases now must be flawless to win, increasingly find themselves facing jurors for

---

[228] http://articles.baltimoresun.com/2001-04-08/news/0104080336_1_reynolds-conway-black-panther

whom police misconduct is an all-too-common experience.

"In this day and age, a person of color is going to have mistrust of the police because these things happen," says juror Linda Hawkes, a 48-year-old health claims processor who says her son once missed a funeral after being detained by police without reason.

In Baltimore, a computer survey by The Sun of 300 Circuit Court verdicts over a two-year period found that juries threw out more than 40 percent of criminal cases that came before them.

Tom Munsterman of the National Center for State Courts, a nonprofit judicial think tank in Williamsburg, Va., says similar numbers are emerging in cities all over the country.

Paul Butler, a black former federal prosecutor and professor at George Washington University Law School, says African-Americans have become "extremely sensitive to certain patterns of testimony or to lapses in accepted police procedure."

"And they're far less likely to overlook it, or to give police the benefit of a doubt, especially if there's compound errors."[229]

White Americans in Baltimore, and the country at large, are nothing more than war criminals now.

Obama, the Department of Justice, and black political leaders across the country will now begin releasing black "political prisoners" from 'white' jails.

In *Homicide, A Year on the Killing Streets*, David Simon talks about racial jury nullification with uncharacteristic candor and without the obfuscation typical of the *Baltimore Sun*:

---

[229] http://articles.baltimoresun.com/2001-03-11/news/0103110274_1_stennett-verdict-jurors

"As with every other part of the criminal justice machine, racial issues permeate the jury system in Baltimore," Simon said. "Baltimore prosecutors take almost every case into court with the knowledge that the crime will be seen through the lens of the black community's historical suspicion of a white-controlled police department and court system."

"The effect of race on the judicial system is freely acknowledged by prosecutors and defense attorneys-black and white alike-although the issue is rarely raised directly in court."

"Race is instead a tacit presence that accompanies almost every panel of twelve into a Baltimore jury room. Once, in a rare display, a black defense attorney actually pointed to her own forearm while giving closing arguments to an all-black panel: "Brothers and sisters," she said, as two white detectives went out of their minds in the back row of the gallery, "I think we all know what this case is about."[230]

So keep peddling your Constitutional Convention, Mark Levin.

This is the reality of America today.

Whites are nothing more than war criminals in modern-day America, with black cop killers treated as 'political prisoners' (heroes) by black elected officials, black leaders, and black groups like the NAACP.

That group called this day "monumental."

Nothing more than war criminals.

Just ask Zach Sowers widow.

America's future is nothing more than racial retribution by non-whites against whites, payback for the one point in our history when white America worked to protect racial interests of their own.

---

[230] p.455

Lynchings in USA over an 86-year time-span vs. Homicides in Baltimore over a 7-year time-span (91.5 percent Black-on-Black)

Two lynchings.

Matthew Williams and George Armwood.

These two lynchings united an entire community against what they perceived (white supremacy) was holding them down.

Today, this liberated community runs the show, united by black pride and galvanized by black political power.

Yet the conditions of this city are a stark reminder of the great fear whites once had of seeing their power supplanted, usurped by *something* else.

That *something* continually brings up the names of Williams and Armwood as justification for the continued guilt trip (a 21st Century Bataan Death March for whites) they force the grandchildren – and great-grandchildren - of Baltimore's whites to endure. [Breaking The Silence: A University of Maryland law professor writes a book on the last two recorded lynchings in the state - and the culture that let the crimes go unpunished, Baltimore Sun, 2-25-2007]:

I originally thought I was going to write this encyclopedic book of lynching," says Sherrilyn Ifill, a professor at the University of Maryland School of Law in Baltimore.

Instead, her research took a narrative turn as she focused on the tragic deaths of Matthew Williams and George Armwood, two black men murdered by white mobs on the Eastern Shore in the 1930s - the last two recorded lynchings in Maryland. Ifill wound up devoting five years to writing On the Courthouse Lawn ($25.95, Beacon Press).

Some 5,000 lynchings have been documented in the United States. Yet no one has ever been convicted of a lynching crime. Reverberations from that era of violence are still being felt in American society, Ifill contends. For that reason she is a proponent of racial-healing efforts modeled after the South African government's Truth and Reconciliation Commission.

"There is unfinished business in communities throughout this country," she notes in the introduction to her book, "where the reality of lynching and racial pogroms has never been fully confronted." Is there a definition per se of lynching?[231]

"Unfinished business?"

A South African-style "Truth and Reconciliation Commission," run by blacks, to make whites pay for their past (actions that dared stop the conditions of Cape Town 2014 from coming to nightmarish fruition in Baltimore...) is 'unfinished business.'

Whites must always pay.

Always.

---

[231] http://articles.baltimoresun.com/2007-02-25/news/0702230086_1_lynching-sherrilyn-ifill-university-of-maryland

Never mind what's happening now, we must always look to the past for evidence of the continued oppression of whites today.

The truth of lynching.

Though Oprah Winfrey, who donated $13 million to the building of the National Museum of African American History and Culture (NMAAHC, set to open in 2015 on the National Mall in Washington D.C. and costing a cool $500 million), claimed "millions of black people were lynched,"[232] it turns out only 3,446 blacks were lynched between 1882 and 1968:

> From 1882-1968, 4,743 lynchings occurred in the United States. Of these people that were lynched 3,446 were black. The blacks lynched accounted for 72.7% of the people lynched.
>
> Out of the 4,743 people lynched only 1,297 white people were lynched. That is only 27.3%. Many of the whites lynched were lynched for helping the black or being anti lynching and even for domestic crimes.[233]

So, over a span 86 years, 3,446 black people were lynched (many were lynched for actual crimes, mind you); that's roughly 40/lynchings per year.[234]

But here's the real fact you won't find at the NMAAHC, or will Sherrilyn Ifill even consider: From 2007 through 2013 in Baltimore, 1,629 lives were lost to homicides in Baltimore. Over a seven-year time period, 1492 of these homicides were black people, meaning 91.5 percent of the homicide victims in this 63.5 percent black city were black. [Patterns persist in city killings: Victims, suspects usually

---

[232] http://www.thegatewaypundit.com/2013/07/oprahs-millions-of-lynchings-turns-out-to-be-4743-one-of-four-victims-were-white/

[233] http://www.chesnuttarchive.org/classroom/lynchingstat.html

[234] http://law2.umkc.edu/faculty/projects/ftrials/shipp/lynchingsstate.html

black men with long criminal histories rate is among highest in U.S., Baltimore Sun, 1-1-2007]:

> Despite a seeming revitalization of several city neighborhoods, Baltimore's homicide rate remains among the highest in the country. A driving force behind this dubious distinction is that people such as Whitfield - young black men with lengthy criminal histories - continue to be killed in large numbers by others with similar backgrounds, according to police homicide figures reviewed by The Sun.
>
> Whitfield was gunned down on Hanover Street in South Baltimore about 1 a.m. Dec. 15. As of last night, 274 people had died by homicide in Baltimore - five more than the 269 victims in 2005.
>
> In 2005, 236 of the 269 homicide victims were black. Through mid-December of 2006, 236 of 256 victims were black.
>
> In 2005, 243 victims were men and 26 were women. In 2006, through mid-December, 231 men and 25 women were killed.[235]

But never mind those victims... let's keep talking about two black males lynched in the 1930s. White people may have lynched Williams and Armwood (they were criminals), but these actions were done to protect the integrity of the city and ensure Baltimore was a safe place live for law-abiding citizens. Today, Baltimore is the poster child for civic dysfunction and lawlessness.

Almost all of the violence in Baltimore is black-on-black, prompting former black drug dealers to launch a cottage industry as "reformers" hoping to better the black community. [On a mission to halt epidemic of killings: A graveyard visit helps a crusader drive home his point: Young men can change their lives and reduce homicides, Baltimore

---

[235] http://articles.baltimoresun.com/2007-01-01/news/0701010109_1_whitfield-criminal-histories-homicide

Sun, 12-12-2005][236]

Baltimore's reputation as an "unsafe city" wasn't made by white lynch mobs roaming the streets; it's due to the justifiable fear of dangerous black males turning large parts of the city into a sprawling, uninhabitable warzone. [Two men convicted in murder of 12-year-old Baltimore boy: Gang members fired randomly into group of teens to send a message, prosecutors say, Baltimore Sun, 3-17-14]:

> Two men were convicted Friday of randomly firing into a group of young people, killing a 12-year-old boy and wounding three others in an attempt to "send a message" to their East Baltimore neighbors.
>
> In May 2011, prosecutors said, Danyae Robinson, 31, and Derrick Brown, 20, fired at least 15 shots, seeking to avenge the shooting earlier that night of a fellow gang member — even though their victims had nothing to do with their gang's rivals or the earlier shooting.
>
> "This was a deplorable, unconscionable act of violence that hurt many and took the life of one of our young people," State's Attorney Gregg Bernstein said in a statement. "I thank the police and prosecutors for their unrelenting commitment and tireless work to bring this case to justice."
>
> The victims were "boys who had done nothing wrong," Assistant State's Attorney Thiru Vignarajah said during opening arguments. "They were young boys who paid in blood in a war among men."
>
> Sean Johnson, a standout student with a promising future, was killed after being shot twice in the head, once in the neck and once in the leg. Another teen in the group was shot nine times, but survived.
>
> None of them had ever been arrested; one of the surviving

---

[236] http://articles.baltimoresun.com/2005-12-12/news/0512120104_1_gladden-young-men-young-people

victims now works as an usher at the Baltimore Symphony Orchestra; another is attending college, and the other is about to graduate from high school.

Sean's mother, Shawnta Little, sat in on the trial and said she was pleased the case was concluded "so I can start the process of healing, all over." The neighborhood has been quiet since the shootings, she said, though it is less common to see children outside playing anymore.[237]

But it's white people today who must continually pay for the actions of their ancestors, despite the present being nothing more than an endless series of black-on-black misery, crime and murder.

Even the approbation surrounding the relatively meager milestone of "less-than-three-hundred-murders" hide the ugly truth of life in a majority black city, where black leaders constantly carp about white supremacy and lynchings of the past while remaining willfully ignorant about black destruction of civilization in the present. [Fewer than 300 homicides at last: Crime: For the first time in more than a decade, Baltimore's toll for a year breaks a barrier that it had seemed impossible to breach only months ago., Baltimore Sun, 1-1-2001]:

> But statistics hardly matter to the families left to grieve. Rosalind L. Knott, 45, has lost two sons to shootings - and a third wounded by eight bullets - since April 1998.
>
> "Every time I turn on the TV, they are telling me that crime is down," Knott said. Her son Ernest L. Knott III, who was shot and killed Dec. 6, would have turned 23 the next week.
>
> "It's all lies," she said, crying as she sat among family members in her Northeast Baltimore home recently. "No mother should have to mourn like this. You tell me why I have two sons taken by gunfire, lying side by side in a grave."
>
> Baltimore has experienced more than 300 murders each year

---

[237] http://www.baltimoresun.com/news/maryland/crime/blog/bs-md-sean-johnson-trial-20140316,0,7768884.story#ixzz2wF8OOEqn

since 1990. Most are blamed on the city's volatile cocaine and heroin trade fueled by an estimated 60,000 addicts who stumble around desolate neighborhoods pockmarked by boarded-up rowhouses, vacant lots and trash-filled alleys.

Police officers had T-shirts emblazoned with "The city that bleeds," mocking the city's old slogan, "The city that reads."

With each violent death, a family mourned, most having gained little public attention. Rosalind Knott said she doesn't like the preoccupation with the numbers that shroud the names.

Her sons Daniel P. Smith, 22, and David Smith, 16, were shot April 2, 1998, as they stood on their porch in the 1100 block of W. Saratoga St. The elder brother died; the younger was hit eight times. He survived, but has three bullets lodged in his chest.

Police said four assailants rode down the street shooting from bicycles. No motive has been discerned, nor has any arrest been made.[238]

A lynching by any other name.

By blacks on other blacks.

No outrage, because it's such a common occurrence.

So to recap:

Between 1882 and 1968, there were 4,743 lynchings in America; of those, 3,466 were black and 1,297 were white.

Between 2007 and 2013 in Baltimore alone, there were 1,629 murders, of which 1,492 (or 91.5 percent) were black – almost all murdered by other blacks.

---

[238] http://articles.baltimoresun.com/2001-01-01/news/0101010157_1_homicides-baltimore-norris/2

No need to mention the rate of black-on-white homicides in the city, but we all remember what Zach Sowers widow endured.

Baltimore is a majority-black city because white people no longer feel safe to raise families there (white flight wasn't because of racial hatred, it was because of legitimate fear of blacks), with the remaining whites scared to even mention the racial "elephant in the room" when discussing crime, homicide, diminished property values, and/or why so much real estate is still unsafe for gentrification.[239]

The black community, meanwhile, collectively "lynched" white civilization in Baltimore, turning once-thriving public housing buildings into "concentration camps",[240]and remaking the city in their image. Every week, another horrific crime occurs – such as the execution-style killing of five black women in 1999, three generations of a single family wiped out by black male ⋯ that does far more to threaten the stability of Baltimore than those two lynchings did back in the 1930s. [A race against time, revenge: Police scour city for two suspects in rowhouse slayings, U.S. marshals join hunt, Baltimore Sun, 12-9-1999][241]

The names Matthew Williams and George Armwood have far more political equity behind them, than Mary McNeil Matthews, Levanna Spearman, Mary Helen Collien, Makisha Jenkins and Trennell Alston do (whose executions were labeled a "local brush of evil") precisely because black life apparently has more value when it's taken by a white.[242]

---

[239] http://www.vdare.com/articles/tracey-halvorsen-turns-tail-but-that-won-t-stop-baltimore-or-something-breaking-her-heart

[240] http://articles.baltimoresun.com/1999-12-12/news/9912110095_1_o-donnell-heights-heights-home-army-barracks

[241] http://articles.baltimoresun.com/1999-12-09/news/9912090372_1_rowhouse-northeast-baltimore-five-women

[242] http://articles.baltimoresun.com/2001-09-25/news/0109250233_1_sentences-quarles-sensibilities

Black-on-black crime?

How boring.

For blacks in power now, black-on-black crime is a minor annoyance at best, as it reinforces all those fears white people had for their civilization long ago.

Blacks may continue to lynch civilization in Baltimore, yet the only story we ever hear about are the lynchings of two blacks back in the 1930s.

Life During Wartime: The Conditions of 83 Percent Black Baltimore City Public Schools... America's Most Dangerous School System

Eric "My People" Holder won't like this.

Not one bit.

Neither will Arne Duncan or Barack Obama.

Ever wonder why white people fled a school system like Baltimore City Public Schools?

A school system under black control since the early-1980s (as you'll see, black political elites 'jealously' guard this control because it ensures a steady flow of money into their pockets...)?

One reason...violence.

Black violence.

There is no "school- to-prison pipeline"; just black individuals being punished for breaking school rules (rules that protect both their classmates teachers alike) at a collective rate far, far beyond that of all other racial groups.

It's funny: Baltimore City Public Schools enrollment in 1923 was 83 percent white; 10 years later it was 77 percent white; it dropped to 71 percent white in 1943 and 62 percent white in 1953; by 1963, it was 43 percent white and by 1973 it was only 30 percent white. [*Brown in Baltimore: School Desegregation and the Limits of Liberalism*, Howell S. Baum, p. 225]

Today, Baltimore City Public Schools (BCPS) is 83 percent black and eight percent white; 84.5 percent come from low income families (based on eligibility for Free or Reduced-Price Meals).[243]

Most importantly, the BCPS system is one of the most violent in all of America.[Student on teacher assaults on rise, ABC 2, 2-26-2013]:

> BALTIMORE - We first showed you the most recent video in November; students at Digital Harbor High School in Federal Hill taunting, bullying, assaulting a substitute teacher at the front of the classroom.
>
> Taken with a student's cell phone, the video pulls back the curtain on a bigger issue many simply don't want or won't talk about.
>
> "It's just a tremendous amount of stress and anxiety. Literally, I have to force myself out the door."
>
> Baltimore city school teacher Jeffrey Slattery wants to talk about it because he still literally feels it.
>
> It was December 2010 at Baltimore Community High School on the east side when he stopped a student without a hall pass.
>
> The student got physical and Slattery let him go.
>
> "He walked down the hallway, I turned around and went back to my classroom and he came up from behind me and once I was on the ground, he's basically standing on top of me. He struck me multiple times. When my jaw broke, I went unconscious and I don't remember anything after that."
>
> The Social Studies teacher would later learn it took four other teachers to pull the student off him.
>
> Slattery broke his jaw, it was wired shut for weeks.
>
> He pressed charges and the student was convicted.
>
> Slattery's assault by a student was just one of seven hundred that school year in Baltimore City Public Schools where its own data shows an average of four school personnel were assaulted each day in 2010.
>
> ABC2 Investigators found that average holds true through the past five school years with a total of nearly four thousand

---

[243] http://www.baltimorecityschools.org/domain/5

assaults by students on personnel, with noticeable increases in the last two years.

Broken down by grade level, it is evident seventh, eighth and ninth graders commit the assaults more often.

[Do those numbers shock you?] "No," responded the President of the Baltimore Teachers Union, "In fact, I am very surprised they are that low."

Marietta English says it was after an attack on city art teacher Jolita Berry in 2008 when assaults by students raced to the top of mind for most educators.

The story went national, fueled by the video posted to myspace back then.

Berry's story was the impetus for the union to start keeping its own records by imploring teachers to fill out a form reporting abuse; documentation to lobby for more support to stem this violent tide.

"They should not come to work fearing they will be attacked. They should not come to work fearing they are going to be verbally abused. This is not what we should be coming to work and face on a daily basis. [*The reality of it is they do though?*] That's the reality of it, unfortunately yes," responded English.[244]

Just how violent is the 83 percent black school system (remember, it's been *at least* 70 percent black since 1973... that's forty-one years)? Just ask Baltimore's risk management office, which tracks assaults and attacks on teachers in the 83-percent-black school system. [Painful Lessons: Run-ins with students take toll on teachers, city finances, Baltimore Sun, 2-16-14]:

> Jennifer Jones' school day started with her standing in front of her class of third-graders at Harford Heights Elementary, and it ended with her flat on her back in the East Baltimore school's hallway.
>
> She lay there surrounded by colleagues and students at dismissal time, injured by a boy who grabbed her leg and pulled it out from under her. His resolute stare, she says, was as frightening as the assault on that day in January 2013.

---

[244] http://www.abc2news.com/news/region/baltimore-city/student-on-teacher-assaults-on-rise

Soon she was on a stretcher, headed to Johns Hopkins Hospital, hoping she would not be paralyzed.

Jones is one of hundreds of city educators whose violent and traumatic encounters with students have led them to seek — and often receive — compensation for mental and physical injuries, a Baltimore Sun investigation of workers' compensation claims has found. Those claims provide a behind-the-scenes look at violence that is rarely documented in school system reports.

School employees report more injuries than those in any city agency except the Police Department. In the last fiscal year, more than 300 claims were related to assaults or run-ins with students — more than a third of the school system's total claims.

And such claims are costly. School employees account for an estimated total of $4.6 million in medical bills and other costs related to workers' compensation claims in that year, according to records obtained by The Sun in a Maryland Public Information Act request.

For officials in city government, the school system's claims signal a troubling pattern of teachers being attacked or serving as buffers in fights.

For teachers like Jones — whose workers' compensation payout will total an estimated $20,000 — the claims reflect a part of the job that leaves them feeling less like educators and more like punching bags.

"Every day it hurts like hell, and my life is forever changed," said Jones, 31, who remains out of work and is fighting to obtain other benefits. "I can't walk my dogs. I can't do laundry. You eventually start to give up on the dishes. Every time I think about it now, I think the same thing when I was laying on the floor: Why?"

The school-related payments are a significant part of a large and growing expense for taxpayers, who foot the bill for workers' compensation payments for medical bills, lost wages and permanent disabilities that can stretch for years.

In the last school year, the district logged 873 suspensions for physical attacks on staff — nearly triple the number of workers' compensation claims labeled altercations and assaults.

"We know that's not what teachers signed up for," Edwards said. "They want to go into a school where they can be in a healthy, respectful environment, and we have an obligation to help them create that environment in our schools."

'Epidemic-like' fighting

City government officials say that as they look for ways to trim workers' compensation costs, they have urged the school system to help reduce expensive injuries — which usually result from educators breaking up fights, confronting disruptive students or being attacked.

Of the system's anticipated $4.6 million bill for the last fiscal year, the city has paid out about $2 million so far for injuries that range from assaults to accidental falls. The largest single category: assaults and altercations. The city anticipates paying $1.4 million for claims in that category; it has already paid out about $615,000, records show.

Of the school district's 866 workers' compensation claims in the last fiscal year, 293 were labeled assaults or altercations, and eight were referred for criminal charges.

The highest award for a teacher injured in school was an estimated $192,793 for a man who reported that he fractured a leg while breaking up a fight between students; $44,822 of that claim has been paid, city records show.

About 45 more claims related to fights or interactions with students were listed in other categories; the city estimates that those claims will cost more than $270,000.

For instance, a fall that cost about $1,500 was summarized this way by a claimant: "Two students were fighting and they fell on teacher, and all fell on top of an overhead projector injuring [teacher's] neck, shoulder, and upper back." In an "overexertion" claim, for which the city has paid roughly $21,000 of an estimated $33,000, a teacher injured her knee breaking up two fighting students.

And such incidents can leave other scars. One teacher filed a claim for psychological stress after witnessing a student assault another; the city has paid $2,300 of an estimated $9,050 for it.[245]

---

[245] http://data.baltimoresun.com/workers-comp/

Do you get why white parents don't want to send their children into these glorified daycare centers, where a student population, almost entirely dependent on the state for their existence, has declared war on the teachers merely trying to occupy their time for a seven hours? [Baltimore Schools Among Most Dangerous In U.S., CBS Baltimore, 7-21-2011][246]

In many cases, the public schools in Baltimore are little more than prisons, with students forced to walk through metal detectors (not including those handheld by police officers), drug sniffing dogs, and a full-time police presence [Minority pupils more likely to face metal detectors, Education Week, 8-29-2011][247]

Ask Baltimore city school teacher Jeffrey Slattery why all that might be necessary. He can talk now. His jaw is no longer wired shut.

No, the 83-percent-black BCPS is nothing more than a war zone. And the blacks in charge of the system - enjoying the job security this control ensures - have little regard for school reform (the only way for reform to occur is to increase the white proportion of the overall enrollment).

Baltimore's first black mayor, Kurt Schmoke, spent years fighting and ultimately defending black political control (attempts to reform the system compromised black control...):

> Kurt Schmoke's leadership in school affairs and his efforts toward reform were also constrained by the city's dominant political culture. In 1990, when interim superintendent Edward Andrews pressured several principals to resign, retire, or accept reassignment to a lesser post, Mayor Schmoke summoned him to city hall and asked him to back off. Schmoke cut short the city's experiment with private management after black church leaders and union officials, fearing the loss of jobs, mobilized to end it. Schmoke again wavered on the city-state partnership after other African-American leaders complained that he was relinquishing

---

[246] http://baltimore.cbslocal.com/2011/07/21/baltimore-schools-among-most-dangerous-in-us/

[247] http://www.edweek.org/ew/articles/2011/08/31/02security.h31.html

procurement contracts, employment opportunities, and other material reward accrued from black control of the school system.

From birth in a hospital designated for African Americans to burial in a black cemetery, black Baltimoreans lived an almost entirely separate existence bounded on all sides by racial discrimination. The city is very much the product of a past that emphasized racial issues.

By the 1980s Baltimore had shed most of its southern orientation. Given a history of white domination and control, today's African-American leaders view recent gains, especially black administrative control of the school system, as long in coming.[248]

In 21st century America, blacks are judged (always positively) by the color of their skin; as the pernicious influence of white privilege teachings demonstrates, whites will also be judged negatively *by both their character and the color of their skin.*

There is no reforming this system; there is merely surviving this system until it inevitably collapses.

Blacks will continue to leverage old racial resentment to justify their reasons for ignoring black dysfunction and promoting black interests; conversely, the continued refusal to admit the reality of black dysfunction only showcases why a pre-Brown vs. Board of Education world was necessary in America.

The pendulum will swing back to the future.

---

[248] Marion Orr's *Black Social Capital: The Politics of School Reform in Baltimore 1986- 1998, p. 191-192*

The State of Baltimore in 2014: What We "Celebrate" When We Cheer the Civil Rights Act of 1964

It's as if a great flood came and washed away all that was good, leaving behind fragments of a civilization barely resembling the conservative society of the antediluvian time period.

No life raft was available, with people forced to flee for higher ground.

Blockbusting in Baltimore: The Edmondson Village Story is W. Edward Orser's story of a racial change in an almost entirely white area of Baltimore, with its transformation into just another black slum.

This story is not just of Baltimore, but could be Newark, Camden, Philadelphia, Detroit, Atlanta, Birmingham, Memphis, Charlotte, Dallas, Houston, Milwaukee, or Chicago. It's a story of Anywhere, USA.

Once again, W. Edward Orser's book offers the powerful lesson that "race is all that matters: adherence to this principle should be the basis for crafting all laws guiding public life."

We start with this passage from the book:

The Trauma of Racial Change

The recent reflections of two women illustrate the poignancy and complexity of their experience in the west Baltimore neighborhood of Edmondson Village when racial change began to occur on a massive scale in the late 1950s, early 1960s. In an interview I conducted with a white former resident, Marilyn Simkins sought an explanation for the response of whites who panicked and fled the neighborhood: "They saw a very secure world changing very drastically," she said, " and they couldn't accept it. This was distasteful, and in some respects it was forced down their throats, and they felt they had no other choice, I guess."

In a separate interview session, Margaret Johnson, a pioneer from the era of initial African American settlement in the same neighborhood, described her own feeling about the flight of her white neighbors: "They were friendly, but they were prejudiced. They didn't want to live where colored people did... They don't have to say it... They'd didn't tell you [why they moved]; they just moved."[249]

We'd hear from Simkins again in the final pages of the book:

---

[249] Orser, W. Edward. *Blockbusting in Baltimore: the Edmondson Village story.* Lexington, Ky.: University Press of Kentucky, 1994. p. 1

White Attitudes and the Trauma of Change

Edmondson Village's white expatriates dispersed along the
natural corridors of suburban migration westward, some to
nearby neighborhoods, others throughout Baltimore County's
general Catonsville area and beyond to Howard County.
Many friendships and family networks persist, and people
often encounter old neighbors on visits to regional shopping
centers, churches, or social organizations. The experience of
uprooting lingers as an unhealed wound, the source of mixed
feelings of nostalgia, bewilderment, bitterness, and social
learning. Some believe they have found new suburban havens
that provide the social homogeneity and insulation
Edmondson Village afforded for a while. But others view life
in their new neighborhoods differently as a consequence of the
Edmondson Village experience.

Interviews with white former residents of varying ages
inevitably evoke considerable nostalgia for the old
neighborhood and the lifestyle that accompanied it. Qualities
of closeness, neighborliness, commonality, and security
bubble forth unprompted in such discussions.

For example, Marilyn Simkins, who was a teenager in the
1950s, offered this summation of her experience: "Personally,
I would be satisfied if I still lived there, if things had stayed
the way they were. It wasn't exactly what you would call
paradise, but it was a nice neighborhood."

Some white former residents return periodically to see their
former houses and the neighborhoods, but frequently they
speak of feeling depressed by the changes they see, especially
by signs of deterioration. Simkins, for examples, said
wistfully: "It's just not taken care of anymore. I've driven
through the area since I've moved, and it depressed me so, I
don't go back anymore.[250]
Why is it those white people were so fearful of living near black
people? Why did they abandon Baltimore (or insert major American
city in Baltimore's place) for new real estate, uprooting their lives in
the process?

---

[250] Ibid., p. 163-165

In 1940, Baltimore had 692,705 whites and 165,843 blacks; by 1950, the city had 723,655 whites vs. 255,099 blacks; only a decade later, the white population had dropped to 610,416 to 328,608 blacks; by 1970, the city was nearly 50-50, with 479,837 whites to 425,922 blacks.

What scared whites away?

Kelvin Sewell, a black former Baltimore police officer, wrote a book with Stephen Janis that attempts to answer that question. It's called *Why Do We Kill? The Pathology of Murder in Baltimore.*

It should be titled *Why Do Black People Kill? The Pathology of Black Depravity in Baltimore.* Here's why Kelvin Sewell believes homicide is such a problem in Baltimore:

> Why do we kill?
>
> This is a question that goes to the root of why police exist at all, here as well as elsewhere, which is why I'm asking it. It asks why, in cities like Baltimore that spend a large portion of their budget putting officers with guns into the neighborhoods and communities, do people continue to shoot and kill each other with reckless abandon?
>
> Why, after spending millions of dollars on plainclothes units to disrupt drug dealers, using military-style tactics, does the shooting continue unabated?
>
> These are questions that I want to answer because I think in the end it matters. We have to ask "Why?" We have to think. Because without asking "Why?" we may continue on the same path that has done little improve the city where I was born, raised, and worked my entire life.
>
> Because for all the money and time that's been poured into policing Baltimore, the city is truly no better off. Hundreds of people year in and year out pick up guns and try and kill each other. Largely because of this, 30,000 citizens moved out of Baltimore over the last decade, a period when the population of the State of Maryland grew by nine percent.
>
> We've torn down housing projects and built new homes. Created empowerment zones and spent hundreds of millions

to try and breath new life into neighborhoods where much of
the killing is done. We've paid more than three billion dollars
over the past decade on direct costs alone fore aggressive
policing, arresting hundreds of thousands of poor, mostly
black men and boys. Homicide detectives in Baltimore City
have arrested hundreds of killers, even though, admittedly,
our clearance rate could be a whole lot better.

Yet if I stood today on the corner of Preston and Greenmount,
or Lombard and Carey, the Alameda and Belair, where we
have concentrated those resource, I can tell you without
question those neighborhoods and the people who still live
there are no better off. They are not happier or safer. Instead,
there is a sense of despair that has infected many parts of the
city, a sense of hopelessness that I know has much to do with
the reason people pick up a gun and aim it, with little
provocation, at another human being.[251]

The conditions black people have created in 63-percent-black
Baltimore are the same conditions that whites fled to being with,
knowing the racial transformation of their neighborhoods would
mean lowering of community standards.

Whites didn't vote for these changes on Election Day; instead, they
voted with their feet, heading for the peaceful exurbs once the
formerly all-white neighborhoods tipped black. Sewell continues:

If you walk down the 3500 block of West Garrison Avenue on
any given day, you'll see distinct types of people: menacing
young men in white T-shirts drifting up and down the streets,
and old ladies sitting on the porches of worn-down row
homes.

Both, in a sense represent the contradictory forces that enable
the most desolate parts of the city to survive while remaining
for the most part dysfunctional.

The old women are a vestige of the city's past, the sinew,
strength and bedrock of what remains of the generations of

[251] Sewell, Kelvin, and Stephen Janis. *Why do we kill?: the pathology
of murder in Baltimore*. Baltimore, MD: Baltimore True Crime, 2011.
p. 9-10

African-Americans families that came to Baltimore to work in the Sparrows Point steel mill and Dundlack-area auto factories.

Spend some time in District Court on any given day and you will see old black women sitting on the benches, watching grandsons and great-grandsons being ferried in and out of courtrooms in shackles.

And on Garrison Avenue in Northwest Baltimore you will see them sitting on their porches, sitting and the young men, in many cases their grandsons and great-grandsons, hustling, selling drugs, doing whatever it takes to survive.[252]

Quite the legacy these black grandmothers left in Baltimore, the arrival of blacks nothing more than a harbinger of destruction as evidenced by the sorrowful state of the city. The condition of Baltimore today is a direct result of those black grandmothers' generation driving away white people, thereby ensuring the city would endure an Apocalypse that God himself wouldn't condone.

And yet, Sewell leaves us with an interesting hypothetical, a seemingly unanswered question in his book that white flight from the city (well, mainly black people) powerfully is the answer:

Why do people behave so differently 20 miles north of Baltimore City? Why don't people in Hunt Valley or Monkton shove babies into bags? Are people really that different in essence? Or are we essentially the same, just shaped by our environment or by the neighborhood we live in?

This is not a complicated question, but is has some important implications.

People kill regularly in Baltimore. Twenty miles north they don't - at least not regularly. What should I conclude from that? What type of boundaries of the land have we created that also take hold of the mind?

But Baltimore is apex of that violent strain. And thus the city begs the question: Are these people naturally amoral or prone

---

[252] Ibid., p.49

to violence? Or, and this is a thought that bothers me more, is the violence I see here simply a payback for the years of neglect and cruelty we inflict upon the less fortunate?

Better put, are we civilized or can we ill afford to be civil?[253]

By the standards of civilization set by white people, black people in Baltimore are not civil; they are the population in Baltimore from which is birthed the violence that drives away white people and the necessary capital to keep alive the flame of a 1st World Civilization.

Were those dangerous black neighborhoods, where menacing black people walk (with black septuagenarians rocking on porch swings), to be filled with white people - you know, the type of people who once lived there but feared raising families around black people who birthed menacing black males - the violence in the city of Baltimore would end overnight.

Overnight.

Wherever white people fled, they created prosperous communities; whatever black people inherited from white flight, they regressed to the black mean.

Businesses fled, where they once flourished; school test scores plummeted, necessitating measures like No Child Left Behind; property value collapsed, where once it seemed destined to only appreciate.

Such is the nature of racial change from white to black.

And it isn't just Baltimore.

It's not just Newark, Camden, Gary, Milwaukee, Chicago, Birmingham, Memphis, or Charlotte, either.

It's not just Atlanta, Rochester, Jackson (MS), St. Louis, or Kansas City.

It's America.

---

[253] Ibid. p. 77

The lesson of Baltimore will empower a new generation of leaders to reassess the trajectory of this country, because our current path is paved with aging black women and menacing black men loitering in white t-shirts.

The Civil Rights Act of 1964 ensured the Baltimore of Marilyn Simkins would turn into the Baltimore of Kelvin Sewell.

This is not worth celebrating.

Son of "No Snitching" DVD Creator Gunned Down in Baltimore

Peter Moskos is a Harvard-trained sociologist who spent a year as a cop trying to bring law and order to the 63-percent-black dystopia that is Baltimore. He wrote a book about his experience, *Cop in the Hood: My Year Policing Baltimore's Eastern District*. The book offers one excuse after another for why civilization has regressed to the black mean. But there's one fantastic, illuminating portion of the book that deserves reprinting.

In light of Baltimore's "No Snitching" King, Ronnie Thomas, losing his son to the black violence[254] driving away those capable of sustaining civilization in the city, Moskos only interesting portion of *Cop in the Hood* is highlighted here:

Thug Life

---

[254] http://newamericamedia.org/2010/07/stop-snitching-creator-sentenced-to-20-years.php

While poverty is unquestionably rampant, many police (often using their own economically poor upbringing as evidence) are convinced the poverty does not create the ghetto. Rather, a ghetto culture of violence, sex, and drug use creates poverty. One officer told me, "You've seen what it's like. Can you imagine what it would be like if your professors knew what really goes on here? I don't see them walking down these alleys or spending time in one of these houses. They read about 280 murders, but they don't know about the thousand shootings, the cuttings, the assaults where people don't die. Those don't make the papers. If people saw how fucked-up everything is, they'd stop blaming poverty or racism and just want the whole place torn down."

Most police, both white and black, believe that the social problems in the Eastern District [PK NOTE: an entirely black area of Baltimore] are hopeless. One black officer said, "It's hard not to think that this is a jungle here. People running around in the street at all hours. Getting high, acting like fools... They ought to tear everything down. All of it!" A white officer echoed this belief: "I'd like to napalm the whole area. Wouldn't that be beautiful? Just come in with air strikes and watch the whole thing go up in flames... I don't know what else you can do. If people want to live this way, I say fuck'em."

A black officer proposed similar ends through different means. "If it were up to me," he said, "I'd build walls and just flood the place, biblical-like. Flood the place and start afresh. I think that's all you can do." When I asked this officer how his belief that the entire area should be flooded differed from the attitudes of white police, he responded, "Naw, I'm not like that because I'd let the good people build an ark and float out. Old people, working people, line'em up, two by two. White cops will be standing on the walls with big poles pushing people back in."[255]

The Eastern District of Baltimore is a dystopia, a mini Port-au-Prince, Haiti, in a once thriving American city.

Baltimore's skyline, built by a people far different than those creating

---

[255] Moskos, Peter. *Cop in the hood: my year policing Baltimore's eastern district.* Princeton: Princeton University Press, 2008. p. 39-40

the culture of death in the Eastern District, stands as a silent witness to the black-created misery in the city.

Moskos, trained to blame all black dysfunction on either vestiges of white racism, Jim Crow (which was created to protect whites from the very conditions thriving in the all-black Eastern District), and/or white privilege, lacks the ability to discern the misery of black Baltimore as a creation of their own making.

Law and order was established to protect the civilization whites built; "no snitching," as popularized by Ronnie Thomas in Baltimore, was built to protect the civilization blacks built. Thomas, aka "Skinny Suge," was featured in *Stop Fucking Snitching Volume 1*.[256] Well, now his son is dead, a victim of the exclusively black violence tearing away at the foundations of Baltimore white people erected long ago (and ultimately abandoned via white flight). [14-Year-Old Shot In The Head Was Son Of 'Stop Snitching' DVDs Creator, Baltimore CBS, 4-23-14]:

> Save our youth—that's the mission of city leaders, including the Baltimore City Police Department, after seven teenagers have been murdered this year.
> Rochelle Ritchie reports the most recently slain teen is the son of the man who created the "Stop Snitching" DVDs. Fourteen-year-old Najee Thomas was fatally shot in the head Monday night while inside his Cherry Hill home in the 600-block of Roundview Road.
>
> He is the son of Ronnie Thomas, also known as Skinny Suge, who created the "Stop Snitching" DVDs that gained national attention. The first video surfaced in 2004 and was followed by a sequel in 2007. Police believed the DVDs were a form of witness intimidation and popularized violence in Baltimore.
>
> Skinny Suge was sentenced in 2010 and is now serving nearly 20 years in federal prison. Now stuffed animals and balloons hang from the fence of the home where his son was shot and killed. His murder makes the seventh teen killed this year in Baltimore City.
>
> The violence against Baltimore's teenagers is a major concern for parents with teens of their own.

---

[256] http://www2.citypaper.com/news/story.asp?id=17202

"I have a 13-year-old girl and 12-year-old boy to be concerned about. They were playing basketball with [Najee] the same day he passed away," said Rozonia Bunch, neighbor. Last week, 17 year-old Michael Mayfield, a student at Edmondson-Westside High School, was shot and killed. No arrests have been made in either of the boys' deaths.

As summer break approaches, the mayor is stepping up her efforts to make sure Baltimore's kids have the right leadership and a safe place to go. "That's why it was so important for me to do the work, the youth connection centers that I spoke about in my state of the city," said Mayor Stephanie Rawlings-Blake. "We are working to make sure we have year-round protection."[257]

There is no coordinated violence against the black youth of Baltimore; it's just outbursts of spontaneous blackness, the kind found in other black areas of America like the south side of Chicago, all of Newark and Camden, Philadelphia, and New Orleans.

Gun crime in Baltimore is a uniquely black phenomenon, though the same problem can be found in Gary, Fort Wayne, and Indianapolis, Indiana, as well as Macon, Atlanta, Savannah, and Columbus, Georgia.

The Eastern Establishment, from which Peter Moskos was educated, has failed in addressing the cause of the violence in Baltimore and other American cities.

It's simply blacks.

---

[257] http://baltimore.cbslocal.com/2014/04/23/14-year-old-shot-in-the-head-was-son-of-stop-snitching-dvd-creator/

Longtime White Mayor of Baltimore William Schaefer: "He was certain [Kurt] Schmoke ... wanted to make Baltimore an all-black city."

It was something gleaned from C. Fraser Smith's book *William Donald Schaefer: A Political Biography.* The last white mayor of Baltimore – before the black voting bloc of a city rapidly losing its white population (fleeing black crime for the safe suburbs) made the executive seat a black seat of power - Schaefer had spent almost his entire life in the city, working to make it a better place for every citizen.

Not just white, not just black, but for every citizen.

He was the proud mayor of Baltimore from 1971 to 1987, until he abdicated the position to become the governor of the state of Maryland. Kurt Schmoke would become the first elected black mayor of the city of Baltimore in 1988.

Schaefer was born into a Baltimore that was 80 percent white; by the time he died in 2011, the city was less than 29 percent white.

It's in Smith's biography on the long-time Baltimore public servant, where we learn this:

He spent a fair amount of time complaining publicly and privately about the Schmoke administration, sounding cranky and bitter or worse. He was certain Schmoke and [Larry] Gibson wanted to make Baltimore an all-black city. The old integrationist ideal was fading under Schmoke's housing and neighborhood revitalization policies, Schaefer thought, and he resented it. He resented Schmoke personally because he thought his successor had not paid his dues and had not accorded Schaefer the honor of recognizing that the job was a hard one, one that had to be learned. Schmoke was, in a sense, an accident of history, a man whose resume made him the ideal bridge from Schaefer's era to a new one. Schmoke had enormous promise, education, and charm, but he was not in a job he seemed particularly well suited for or one he might have chosen for himself on the basis of his talents or interests. History had chosen him... [258]

William Schaefer was certain Schmoke and Gibson wanted to make Baltimore an all-black city... not exactly a theory that got much airtime in David Simon's critically-acclaimed documentary on black dysfunction, *The Wire.*

But the consequences of an all-black city (one where the burden of funding the city government and public institutions falls squarely on the dwindling white tax-base) is obvious in stories such as the push by the majority-black city council of Baltimore to "Ban the Box" and make it illegal for employers to force predominately black ex-offenders to check on application designating them as ex-cons. ['Ban the Box' bill advances over opposition from businesses: Legislation intended to help ex-cons find work could get final vote this month, Baltimore Sun, 4-7-14]:

> Supporters of a proposed law to help more ex-convicts land jobs in Baltimore scored a victory Monday when they fended off efforts by the business community to block the measure indefinitely.
> The protracted debate over the so-called "Ban the Box" legislation — which would remove the box ex-offenders must check on job applications — underscores a sharp divide among city leaders over how to help those with criminal records become gainfully employed.

---

[258] Smith, C. Fraser. *William Donald Schaefer: a political biography.* Baltimore: Johns Hopkins University Press, 1999. p. 367-368

The issue has had resonance in Baltimore, with its sizable population of residents with a criminal record and relatively high unemployment.

Council President Bernard C. "Jack" Young said city leaders have spent enough time talking about the problem, and need to take action. Young said he is especially concerned about the hardships faced by African-American men with criminal records.

"I am tired of people who look like me continuing to be discriminated against," said Young, who is black. "They paid their dues by serving their time. When is enough enough?

"I see it every day. I get the calls to my office every day. I get stopped on the street every day by people who want a second chance."

The measure would forbid an employer from searching a job candidate's criminal history until after a conditional job offer has been extended. The legislation would expand upon a similar restriction that prevents city agencies from running background checks on candidates for some government jobs.[259]

How dare prospective employers force ex-cons to note on applications that they once broke the law? Don't they know Baltimore is destined to be an all-black city, where even black ex-cons are free from being subjected to the white man's law?

What could clearly illustrate Baltimore becoming all-black city, where anarchy - instead of law – rules the day than the story of black teenage bikers who terrorize the street, with police helpless to do anything about it? [Baltimore Bikes: 12 O'Clock Boys is a better preface to a longer story than a stand-alone film, Tucson Weekly, 1-30-2014]:

> In inner-city Baltimore, it's a tradition and rite of passage for African-American men to ride dirt bikes through the streets. It's illegal, and that's at least part of the point. The police are forbidden from pursuing the riders because, when there are dozens of bikes going every which direction, it's simply too dangerous. So the cops have to track the dirt bikes with

---

[259] http://www.baltimoresun.com/news/maryland/baltimore-city/bs-md-ci-ban-the-box-update-20140407,0,5600295.story#ixzz2zlQPjy7X

helicopters, catching only a few, and the attention hooks kids such as Pug.

The documentary *12 O'Clock Boys* traces the culture but not much of the history, focusing more heavily on Pug and his family. We meet him at age 13, in 2010. Within a year or so, he's got gold grillz, a few arm tattoos, and finally his own bike. Says one of the veteran riders, "The thing about Pug, he's a real cool dude. Little dude; I think he's gonna grow up to be something."

The question, as a viewer, is whether Pug will grow up at all. A former Baltimore P.D. officer and independent security contractor says street racing kills about 15 people a year, a high number when fewer than 100 people participate. Most of the fatalities are riders, but some are bystanders. And the more the cops try to take it away, the more the community grows.[260]

Anarchy - a retreat from the law and order that was once the hallmark of civilization - is the new norm for majority black Baltimore.

Black individuals' collective footprint on the city of Baltimore is to trample - to the roots - the civilization whites had planted in the city.

The dangerous conditions black people create in any zip code, neighborhood, or community they claim as "theirs" within the city makes Baltimore incredibly unsafe for either walking or bike riding. Mike Bowman, a white 32-year-old, was attacked by more than 10 black kids while he was biking through the city recently. Thankfully, he had a camera on his helmet, which captured the vicious, unprovoked assault. Most peculiar in the situation was the fact that Bowman's attackers didn't even steal anything from him.

They just assaulted the white guy on the bike. [Police Investigate After Bicyclist Attacked By Group Of Teens, CBS Baltimore, 4-14-14][261]

---

[260] http://www.tucsonweekly.com/tucson/baltimore-bikes/Content?oid=3953600

[261] http://baltimore.cbslocal.com/2014/04/14/police-investigate-after-bicyclist-attacked-by-group-of-teens/

Perhaps the experience Bowman had while "biking while white" through majority-black Baltimore is why so few people dare to bike to work in the *Charmless City?* [Can Cities Change the Face of Biking?: There's a growing trend of teaching young people (especially those from demographic groups that historically haven't embraced biking) how to repair and ride bikes., Governing Magazine, 3-24-14]:

> Of the few workers in Baltimore who commute by bike, a disproportionate share -- about 87 percent -- are white, according to aggregated five-year estimates by the Census.
>
> More than three-quarters have a bachelor's degree or higher. In contrast, the overall population of city workers is 39 percent white and about one-third have a bachelor's degree.
>
> Commuting to work by bike, "while not massively popular among any subset of Baltimore's population, is even less-so among low-income and black citizens," [Chris] Merriam said. "To be blunt, it is seen as a white, middle- and upper-class thing."[262]

Mr. Merriam, who serves as the executive director of Bikemore, can be forgiven for his faux pas.

It's civilization that is a white, middle and upper-class thing. It's even a white lower-class thing as well.

But as we can see with majority black Baltimore in 2014, the civilization whites created and eventually abandoned (entirely due to the black crime and property devaluation that came with it) is dead. In its place, something else has grown on the same grounds and land where a young William Schaefer grew up.

Baltimore was once a great city.

When it was majority white.

Baltimore is now a failed city.

---

[262] http://www.governing.com/topics/urban/gov-can-cities-change-face-biking.html

When it is majority black.

Memo to Tracey Halvorsen: Hiroshima Recovered from an Atom Bomb; Baltimore Will Never Recover From Losing its White Majority

Names like Zach Sowers,[263] Jon Fogg,[264] Stephen Pitchairn,[265] John Mason,[266] Aysha Ring,[267] Alex Ulrich [268](as well as Jason Curtis,

---

[263] http://www.jhu.edu/jhumag/0608web/sowers.html

[264] http://www.wbaltv.com/news/maryland/baltimore-city/suspect-arrested-in-canton-assault-of-baltimore-sun-editor/24099372

[265] http://articles.baltimoresun.com/2010-07-27/news/bs-ci-md-homicides-stabbing-2-20100726_1_robbery-drug-related-arrests-and-convictions-detectives

[266] http://www.wbaltv.com/news/maryland/baltimore-city/2-men-arrested-in-November-beating-in-Baltimore/17988650

[267] http://www.amnation.com/vfr/archives/014129.html

[268] http://www.baltimoresun.com/news/maryland/crime/blog/bs-md-ci-mt-vernon-shooting-vigil-20120814,0,6357923.story

[269]who was injured in the same "horrific" shooting)[270] and Kimberley Leto will be little remembered outside their peer circles.

The Baltimore Police Department even took the uncharacteristic step in releasing pictures of Ulrich and Curtis,[271] ostensibly because unlike most homicide/nonfatal shooting victims in the city, they didn't have prior records. To the chagrin of Baltimore *City Paper* Editor Evan Serpick, people were actually momentarily shocked and saddened by the murder of Ulrich (the incessant black-fueled crime/homicide/misery is like water warping the foundation of the city, with citizens willingly blind to the elemental change taking place... better not to notice black dysfunction than call it out!).[272]

No children will ever hear their names in classrooms, where the history of an "oppressed" group is told in tale-of-woe interconnected stories woven together in a tapestry of eternal white guilt.

---

[269] http://www.baltimoresun.com/news/maryland/crime/blog/bs-md-ci-double-shooting-20120810,0,451838.story

[270] http://baltimore.cbslocal.com/2012/09/13/nc-man-arrested-in-fatal-shooting-robbery/

[271] http://www.baltimoresun.com/news/maryland/crime/bs-md-double-shooting-victims-20120812,0,5471724.story

[272] http://blogs.citypaper.com/index.php/2012/08/every-murder-is-a-tragedy/

Laura @Laura_Rhymes   08 Feb
I know @TraceyHalvorsen can't control how ppl use her work, but I'm
sure she doesn't love the fact that @sbpdl embraced it.

Tracey Halvorsen
@TraceyHalvorsen

@Laura_Rhymes @sbpdl my opinions and my article
have nothing to do with race and I don't appreciate my
content being used to promote racism.

4:58 PM - 8 Feb 2014 from Delaware, US, United States

2 FAVORITES   ← ⎘ ★

Baltimore may be breaking her heart, but daring to point how who is
breaking Baltimore is beyond the pale... Wonder what Jon Fogg
would say?[273]

Sylvester Stallone may have a movie franchise with the title
Expendables, but the expendability of the white population of rotting
black-majority urban areas like Baltimore proves reality is far more
despondent than any fiction peddled by Hollywood.

It's becoming one of the more amusing rituals of American political
life: a naïve white liberal notices (or even implies) the Hatefact that
crime is disproportionately black, and is instantly lynched by his/ her
own kind. Last year, it was *Philadelphia* Magazine's Robert Huber,
whose *Being White in Philly* cover story actually caused the black
mayor of the city, Michael Nutter, to write to the Philadelphia
Human Rights Commission demanding action be taken. This year,
it's Tracey Halvorsen, a white Baltimore woman who just published
an article [*Baltimore City, You're Breaking My Heart/ This is why
people leave*, Medium.com, February 7, 2014] in which she went to
the very edge of the racial abyss in describing why the 63.5 percent
black city is dying—only to turn tail under pressure.

---

[273] http://www.wbaltv.com/news/maryland/baltimore-city/suspect-
arrested-in-canton-assault-of-baltimore-sun-editor/24099372

Halvorsen appears to be the epitome of Stuff White People Like liberals. Her Twitter profile reads: *President & Chief Visionary Officer at Fastspot. Artist, animal lover, writer, joker, traveler. Life's short, have fun.* Perhaps to establish her PC credentials, she made it clear that she's a lesbian.

Maybe Halvorsen's passionate philippic was provoked by the murder earlier in the week of 51-year-old Kimberley Leto, a white female bartender. Leto was murdered in her home by two black males, aged 16 and 14—the 14-year-old, only an eighth-grader, asked the judge to be allowed out on bail to *visit his daughter*. [*Police arrest teenagers in Ellwood Avenue homicide: Kimberly Leto found dead inside Patterson Park home*, WBALTV.com, February 3, 2014]

Halvorsen's piece didn't even mention race, but it's 100 percent about the problems the black community causes in Baltimore, exacerbated by black control of City Hall[274]:

> Life takes you places, you follow a course that isn't completely of your own making. One day you wake up, and it's really all up to you. So where do you want to live? I happen to live in a city. Baltimore, to be specific.
>
> And I'm growing to absolutely hate it here.
>
> I'm tired of hearing about 12 year old girls being held up at gun-point while they walk to school.
>
> *http://www.baltimoresun.com/news/maryland/crime/blog/bs-md-ci-12-year-old-girl-robbed-20140206,0,5595591.story* [VDARE.com note: *URLs in original*]
>
> I'm tired of saying "Oh Baltimore's great! It's just got some crime problems."
>
> *http://baltimorecrime.blogspot.com/*
>
> I'm tired of living in a major crime zone while paying the highest property taxes in the state.

---

[274]http://msa.maryland.gov/msa/mdmanual/36loc/bcity/html/bcityl.html

http://www.foxnews.com/politics/2013/02/06/city-baltimore-is-on-path-to-financial-ruin-report-says/

I'm tired of hearing about incompetent city leaders who are more fixated on hosting the Grand Prix than dealing with thousands of vacant buildings that create massive slums, and rampant crime.

I'm tired of being looked at like prey.[275]

Halvorsen went on to supply more devastating details.

They don't call it "The City that Bleeds" thanks to voluntary Red Cross blood donations.

Halvorsen's piece went viral. The *Baltimore Sun* ran an article. [Rash of crimes in Southeast Baltimore sparks new debate over public safety By Carrie Wells, February 8, 2014]

In a response piece, WYPR producer Lawrence Lanahan contended that "white privilege" was really to blame: *"Whose Heart is Baltimore Breaking, Really?",* February 7, 2014.

The joy of our interconnected world meant that I could take to Twitter and engage our latest celebrity in conversation, pointing out that she forgot to mention the world "black."

Halvorsen tweeted back to @SBPDL:

> @Laura_Rhymes @sbpdl my opinions and my article have nothing to do with race and I don't appreciate my content being used to promote racism.

Remember, this is the same city where the zero-tolerance crime policy of a white mayor (Martin O'Malley 1999 to 2007) was denounced as "racial profiling" by black leaders like the Rev. John L. Wright, who revealingly said: "The common denominator is 'lock up Negroes.'" [*Black officials raise zero-tolerance fears: O'Malley tells group that enforcement will not be race-based,* By Ivan Penn, *Baltimore Sun* December 21, 1999]

---

[275] https://medium.com/p/1873a505ce2a

(After O'Malley was elected governor of Maryland in 2006, Baltimore's first black female mayor rescinded its "zero-tolerance on crime" order almost immediately upon taking office [*Baltimore mayor to Announce Leonard Hamm's resignation* | Mayor Sheila Dixon successfully sought police commissioner's resignation, July 18, 2007]

In 2010, the city of Baltimore resolved its suit with the NAACP and the ACLU over its foolhardy, racist efforts to restrict crime . [*City approves settlement with NAACP, ACLU in 'mass arrest' case; Agreement calls for auditor to review 'quality of life' arrests by city police, Baltimore Sun*, June 23, 2010])

Forget for a moment that homicide in Baltimore is almost exclusively a black-on-black problem, with 'disrespect killings' (not drugs) one of its primary motivations. [*Bill Bratton hired to review Baltimore Police Department:'Respect crime' fuels most violence in city, Bratton says*, WBALTV, July 25, 2013]

Forget for a moment that Baltimore is a place where high-profile black-on-white assaults/murders are routinely covered-up by the Baltimore Sun (e.g. on St. Patrick's Day 2012) *St. Patrick's Day violence exceeded initial reports, police dispatch tapes show*, April 10, 2012–which then editorialized that it was irresponsible to notice "*Black Youth Mobs Terrorize Baltimore on Holidays*"–and is downplayed by the police department. [*Bealefeld: Downtown beating not a hate crime*, April 10, 2012]

Halvorsen herself, of course, failed to mention that Leto had been murdered by blacks (what she called the "pack of kids") or that the murderers who curb-stomped Zack Sowers were also black; and she didn't mention the notorious 2010 killing of breast cancer researcher Stephen Pitcairn was at the hands of blacks. [*Hopkins researcher's promising life cut short in robbery: Two arrested in connection with crime robbery charges against suspect were dropped in May*, By Justin Fenton, *Baltimore Sun*, July 27, 2010].

No wonder she assumed her PC credentials would protect her.

Violence is such a fact of life in Baltimore that a black mayoral candidate's idea of a $1-per-bullet tax on ammunition purchased in the city to reduce crime was widely supported, rather than denounced. [*'Bullet Tax' Proposed By Mayoral Candidate: Otis Rolley Running In September's Primary*, WBALTV.com July 28, 2011]

Back in 2002, when a black man firebombed the house of a black family, killing a mother and five of her children because they had reported drug activity to the police, even black legislators called for the deployment of the National Guard. [*Man, 21, charged in fatal city fire: Police say he was angry with neighboring family for reporting drug activity; 'This is terror, too,' official says; Outraged lawmakers seek to call in state police, Guard to help fight crime, Baltimore Sun,* October 18, 2002].

However, consistent, effective action would require blaming black people. And that can't be done in modern America—as evidenced by Halvorsen's tail-turning tweet.

Though she initiated a conversation about crime and race in another dying, bankrupt, majority-black city, Halvorsen is a card-carrying member of a vast coalition of people united by their contempt for traditional American values.

To Halvorsen, being seen as sympathizing with traditional Americans is a fate worse than being the victim of black crime in Baltimore.

Zach Sowers, Jon Fogg, Stephen Pitchairn, John Mason, and Kimberley Leto thought the same way; it's just their black attackers didn't feel the same post-racial thoughts.

The most important (and salient) point of the piece at VDare was this passage:

> And back in 2002, when a black man firebombed the house of black family, killing a mother and five children, because they had reported drug activity to the police, even black legislators called for the deployment of the National Guard. [*Man, 21, charged in fatal city fire: Police say he was angry with neighboring family for reporting drug activity; 'This is terror, too,' official says; Outraged lawmakers seek to call in state police, Guard to help fight crime,Baltimore Sun,* October 18, 2002].[276]

---

[276] http://articles.baltimoresun.com/2002-10-18/news/0210180471_1_dawson-state-police-city-police

But effective action would require blaming black people. And that can't be done in modern America- as evidenced by Halvorsen's tail-turning tweet.

After the horrific firebombing of a black family in Baltimore -- by a black male who took offense that they "snitched" on drug dealers, black political leaders dared suggest an Israel-like solution was needed (if not the US Military itself) to make the city safe:

> Members of the City Council and state House and Senate delegations criticized the system in a closed-door meeting with Norris yesterday morning at police headquarters, participants said. Yelling and cursing at times, they called for drastic action, including calling in state police and even the National Guard to patrol Baltimore's streets.

> They compared the fight to reclaim the city from drug dealers to the battle against international terrorism and the hunt for the Washington-area sniper.

> "I know that we do not have the manpower on the Police Department to man every corner. That's what we've got the military for," said City Councilman Melvin L. Stukes, who called the governor's office with a request to send in the Guard. "The military is being used on the sniper, with the spy plane. Well, this is terror, too."

> State Sen. Nathaniel J. McFadden said the idea of calling in the Guard was "not

> over the top for me."

> "We have terrorist cells of juvenile drug dealers," McFadden said. "We liken it to al-Qaida and Osama bin Laden. Same kind of thing. And it's all over the city. And they have no fear of retribution. It's just a brazen attack when you firebomb a person's house two times within a month. ... We want to respond just like the Israelis would respond when they're bombed. You bomb them one day, they take action the next day."[277]

---

[277] http://articles.baltimoresun.com/2002-10-18/news/0210180471_1_dawson-state-police-city-police

Who exactly are represented in these "terrorist cells of juvenile drug dealers" that black leaders likened to al-Qaida and Osama bin Laden responsible for brazen attacks in the city of Baltimore?

Blacks. ["Like Him Right There": What does the random murder of Zachary Sowers tell us about urban violence? And what does a widow do in the aftermath?, Johns Hopkins Magazine, June 2008]:

> Last year, more than 8,000 juveniles were detained or arrested in Baltimore City, most often for assault or drug charges. Eight in 10 were male, and more than 90 percent were black, though blacks make up only two-thirds of the city's residents.
>
> Dozens of others are regularly charged with crimes as adults, usually for serious offenses. Roles as victim and perpetrator seem interchangeable at times — a victim often later victimizes others. Baltimore children are eight times more likely to die from homicide than are kids nationwide, according to a study released in February by the city health department. From 2002 to March of this year, 172 city youths 18 or younger were victims of homicide, and hundreds of others had been shot.[278]

The National Guard can't be used to subdue the black population of Baltimore, for people like Tracey Halvorsen would scream "racism"; though such an action would make the streets of the dying city safe again for commerce (perhaps even persuade some convenience store owners to remove the Plexiglas surrounding their employees and goods?).

Back in 2012 during St. Patrick's Day at the Inner Harbor in Baltimore, black mobs brutalized holiday revelers trying to enjoy a pint, disrupted commerce, and attacked several white people. The Baltimore Sun editorialized this for those who dared notice it was black people:

> Race is simply irrelevant in this instance. That those involved in the St. Patrick's Day incidents at the Inner Harbor were black is no more pertinent than their height, weight or eye color.[279]

---

[278] http://www.jhu.edu/jhumag/0608web/sowers.html

[279] http://articles.baltimoresun.com/2012-05-17/news/bs-ed-mcdonough-20120517_1_baltimore-county-delegate-criminal-

If a volcano suddenly emerged from the ground in Baltimore, spewing lava, ash, and debris into an already-devastated city, would the *Baltimore Sun* choose to describe the lava, ash, and debris spewing from the volcano (further ruining an already ruined city) as "irrelevant?"

Would the temperature of the magma (or is it lava?) be considered no less pertinent a fact than a black criminal's height, weight or eye color?

I know, I know: why care about a failed city like Baltimore? Because no one else, outside of the family members and friends of Zach Sowers, Jon Fogg, Stephen Pitchairn, John Mason, and Kimberley Leto, will remember how they lived.

Will remember their hopes, dreams, and ambitions.

The population responsible for crushing these hopes, dreams, and ambitions, and for how these good people died (or were put into a coma and forced to pay huge hospital bills)... though the *Baltimore Sun* would claim otherwise, is directly related to white, tax-paying citizens' unwillingness to live in majority- black Baltimore.

Hiroshima was rebuilt and thrives today despite an atomic bomb falling from the Enola Gay in 1945 and leveling the city; yet Baltimore has never recovered from the 1968 black riots, when the city went from being majority-white to majority-black.

Tracey Halvorsen... it's all about race.

---

behavior-baltimore-officials

"Primal anger over dubious acts of disrespect": The Fate of Baltimore Captured in Seven-Words from the Baltimore Sun

Low impulse control.

A lethal case of poor future-time orientation.

An average IQ incompatible with maintaining a long-ago-abandoned civilization decaying all around them; a civilization that was bequeathed to them when white people (the very people responsible for creating civilization) ran from the black newcomers "like they were the plague", a group of people, on average, one standard deviation (15 points) less intelligent than whites.

Unknown to geneticists at the time, these Nubian settlers held the potential in their own DNA to creating a far different community than the one revealed in the manicured lawns, safe streets, and thriving economy of the now-departed white population.

Once they successfully drove away whites, the city was remade in their black image, with government and city jobs going to black individuals in positions no private company would ever consider creating. But the Baltimore that grew around this new black majority was just an outgrowth of the DNA inherent in the blacks who lived there. [His gospel preaches teaching, not jailing Corrections chief: At 70, Bishop L. Robinson continues to argue for keeping people in school, not prison., Baltimore Sun, 3-11-1997]:

> Bishop Robinson was born Jan. 16, 1927, into a Baltimore vastly different from the one whose citizens he imprisons at alarming rates today.
> Back then, you could sit and visit in the courtyard of the McCulloh Homes where he grew up in West Baltimore.
>
> "Nobody was running through the neighborhood with a Tec-9," he said.[280]

Maybe now it makes sense ethnic white people "ran like the plague" (*White Working-Class Politics in Baltimore, 1940-1980: Behind the Backlash*, by Kenneth D. Durr, p. 101) from black people, knowing the truth of this racial transformation would unleash a far less desirable neighborhood/community than the one television would produce in the 1980s sitcom *The Cosby Show*.

The *Baltimore Sun's* Don Rodricks' shed some light into the type of community black people created in Baltimore, when he wrote of the plague of "disrespect" that causes far more damage to the city than drug wars. [The insanity of Baltimore's 'disrespect' killings: Verdicts take two killers off street, but how do police prevent such murders?, Baltimore Sun, 1-19-14]:

> Two years after someone fired 18 bullets into his body, we finally know the reason Gregory McFadden died such a brutal death at the age of 27 in West Baltimore. He turned his back on a guy.
>
> It was disrespect, a malady that inflames the male ego and makes young men do terrible things. Disrespect has been around for centuries, of course, but its consequences have been particularly lethal in the age of the high-powered handgun.

---

[280] http://articles.baltimoresun.com/1997-03-11/news/1997070112_1_robinson-prison-education-and-crime

Killing someone because he disrespected you is a phenomenon that no amount of police power or community vigilance can seem to stop.

Some interventions — Safe Streets in the Leon Faruq days — have been effective when beefs between young men became known. But what do you do to stop a killing like McFadden's?

All of the following facts come from testimony in a murder trial last week in Baltimore Circuit Court.

The shooting occurred on Tuesday night, Nov. 15, 2011, in Harlem Park.

McFadden was part of a group of young men on the street at 11 p.m. in the 700 block of N. Carrollton Ave., near a beautiful old stone church.

Maybe it's not a good idea to be on Carrollton Avenue at that hour, but until we declare martial law, a citizen is allowed to visit with friends on the sidewalk. That's what McFadden was doing.

The problem developed when a couple of guys approached him on the sidewalk.

One was Melvin Baker, 34, the other Antonio Moore, 22.

Baker had a brother named Neal Hunt, and Hunt had a girlfriend.

McFadden had flirted with the girlfriend a couple of weeks earlier, and now Baker wanted to have a word with him about that on Carrollton Avenue.

McFadden declined the opportunity for conversation and turned his back.

Baker took offense. So did Moore.

They felt they had been disrespected.

Instead of cursing McFadden or even engaging him with their fists, they reached for guns.

Baker started shooting. McFadden started running.

Baker chased him, shooting as he ran. Some of the shots hit McFadden. He collapsed in the street.

Baker and Moore fled into an apartment building, but moments later Moore re-emerged on Carrollton Avenue. He found McFadden prostrate on the asphalt, stood over him and fired more shots into him.

The medical examiner later found 18 wounds on McFadden's body, one from a close-range shot to the head. The detectives who worked the scene found 26 shell casings in the street.

The facts sound insane — primal anger over dubious acts of disrespect (in this case, flirting and spurning a confrontation about it) leading to a vicious death — but I hardly think this is an unusual story. In fact, I think it's more common than we generally believe.

We think of Baltimore homicides as drug-related, stemming from a turf war or an unpaid debt; we think of them as gangland killings.

But a bunch of them happen because of stupid human stuff, and the availability of guns.

You wonder how, in such cases, police ever manage to make arrests — how they get witnesses to come forward, how they separate facts from gossip — and how prosecutors manage to get convictions from juries that include some citizens who have low opinions of police and jaundiced views of the criminal justice system.[281]

Don't blame the gun; a gun is an inanimate object, a tool that can hardly be blamed for performing its duty when an individual pulls the trigger.

Low impulse control, poor future time orientation, and low IQ combine to create a situation where fatal incidents of "primal anger over dubious acts of disrespect" ignite into spontaneous blackness.

It is now this community who elects the people in charge of Baltimore (and sit in almost all-black jury pools that acquit civil rights heroes like Davon Neverdon of murders)[282], convincing those remaining white people to continue to "run like it was the plague." [Denial of black racism denies justice to Joel Lee, Baltimore Sun, 1-19-1997]:

We find ways anew to kill Kenneth Lee.
In September of 1993, Lee's oldest son, Joel Lee, was killed during a robbery in Northeast Baltimore. The elder Lee -- a Korean immigrant -- probably died a little that day, as all

---

[281] http://www.baltimoresun.com/news/maryland/bs-md-rodricks-0119-20140118,0,4286204.column#ixzz2qtoBBheB

[282] http://archives.nbclearn.com/portal/site/k-12/flatview?cuecard=759

relatives and friends of homicide victims do.

Baltimore police arrested and charged Davon Neverdon in the slaying. In July of 1995, Neverdon was tried in Baltimore Circuit Court in Joel Lee's slaying. A predominantly black jury acquitted Neverdon, who is also black, eliciting charges of racial bias from Kenneth Lee and others. On a radio talk show a few days after the verdict, one of the jurors said none of the six prosecution witnesses was credible.

When asked if she thought Neverdon had in fact murdered Joel Lee, the caller answered, "He probably did, but the evidence was weak."

Other callers took to the airwaves, chastising those who criticized the verdict. How dare they question the intelligence of black jurors? (As if a jury that doubts the credibility of not one, not two, not even three, but six prosecution witnesses is not in some way cognitively challenged.) How dare they imply that the verdict was racist? Black people, it was repeated ad nauseam and for the umpteenth time, couldn't be racist.

Purveyors of this fiction insist that in order to be racist, you need power. Blacks have no power, the argument goes, hence they cannot be racist. It's an attempt to invoke black moral superiority, but in the process those who use this reasoning end up conceding black inferiority. It's a subconscious admission that blacks are powerless and will always be so.

But in Baltimore blacks have power aplenty. The executive and legislative branches are run by blacks. There are black judges and a black state's attorney. There is adequate black representation on juries. We do, indeed, have power.

What, then, do we call it when we use that power to acquit a black man of murdering someone of another race despite overwhelming witness testimony indicating he did so?[283]

We call it a city powered by the idea of Black Supremacy, where no law can interfere with the right of every black individual's cup of "primal anger over dubious acts of disrespect" to runneth over, submerging the decaying remains of Baltimore in their image.

---

[283] http://articles.baltimoresun.com/1997-01-19/news/1997019151_1_joel-lee-kenneth-lee-elder-lee

Low Impulse Control + Poor Future Time-Orientation + Low IQ(x)Jury Nullification (black political control)² = Baltimore in 2014

It's not drugs.

No matter what you saw on *The Wire*, drugs are not the root cause of the violence in Baltimore. The *Baltimore Sun's* Don Rodricks' shed some light into the type of community black people have cultivated in Baltimore, when he wrote of the plague of "disrespect" killings that causes far more damage to the city than drug wars. [The insanity of Baltimore's 'disrespect' killings: Verdicts take two killers off street, but how do police prevent such murders?, Baltimore Sun, 1-19-14]

One of the latest homicide victims in Baltimore is just another black male, allegedly murdered by another black male.

Well, in virtually every homicide in 63 percent black Baltimore, the murderer and victim share the same racial lineage: black.

Whether the year was 1990,[284] 1999,[285] or 2009,[286] the story remained unchanged: black male found dead from multiple gunshots in Baltimore and a black male suspected in the shooting.

But it's too easy to just blame drugs as the reason behind the exclusively black violence found in the city.

It creates a boogeyman, against whom an eternal war must be waged (a war on drugs) in a vain effort to liberate the city of Baltimore from its invisible grip. Rodricks' piece isn't far off the mark, with "disrespect" homicide likely the primary cause of the homicide problem in Baltimore.

Though blaming drugs for the body count in Baltimore has worked for years in garnering sympathy for an entirely unsympathetic population (whose role in the demise of the city's fortune is entirely due to their inherent genetic code), a simple formula emerges that helps explain the conundrum of black casualties:
Low Impulse Control + Poor Future Time-Orientation + Low IQ (x) jury nullification (black political control)^2 = Baltimore in 2014

It's this formula that helps drive down property values and convince potential owners to invest elsewhere.[287]

It's this formula that helps explain why "primal anger over dubious acts of disrespect" is unravelling the fabric of civilization in Baltimore. [Man charged with fatally shooting neighbor after Sunday cookout: Brandon Stanfield felt 'disrespected' when victim left before

---

[284] http://articles.baltimoresun.com/1990-12-24/news/1990358017_1_homicide-city-murder-1990-murder

[285] http://articles.baltimoresun.com/1999-01-03/topic/9904280932_1_baltimore-s-homicide-baltimore-city-time-baltimore/2

[286] http://articles.baltimoresun.com/2009-06-03/news/0906020063_1_baltimore-decline-in-homicides-city-homicide-rate

[287] http://articles.baltimoresun.com/2001-02-11/news/0102100094_1_criminal-justice-unchanged-deliver-justice

his family arrived, according to court documents, Baltimore Sun, 4-22-14]:

> A Woodlawn man was charged Tuesday with fatally shooting his neighbor, saying he felt "disrespected" when the victim left a Sunday cookout early, according to charging documents. Police said Brandon Jerome Stanfield, 30, shot and killed Michael Jefferson Jr., 39, inside his home on Rocky Brook Court after Jefferson left a cookout before Stanfield's family arrived, one witness told police, according to documents filed in Baltimore County District Court.
>
> Officers found Jefferson dead from multiple gunshot wounds inside his home shortly after midnight Monday after receiving reports of shots fired.
>
> Several witnesses told detectives that they were with Stanfield and Jefferson at a cookout earlier that day and that the two men went inside Jefferson's home.
>
> Once inside, one witness told police that Stanfield pulled out a .40 caliber Glock and placed it on the kitchen table, and Jefferson told Stanfield he didn't want guns in his home, the document said. Stanfield then began shooting, and Jefferson tried to flee, running toward the front door. The witness escaped down the basement and left through the back door.[288]

"Disrespected" over a guest leaving your cookout early?

So you *shoot* him? This is the rationale for your typical black homicide in Baltimore.

Not drugs.

Oddly, this was never covered in an episode of David Simon's *The Wire* or discussed in either of his books *The Corner* or *Homicide*.

---

[288] http://articles.baltimoresun.com/2014-04-22/news/bs-md-co-homicide-arrest-20140422_1_cookout-court-documents-multiple-gunshot-wounds

Where the little tax revenue generated by the majority black population should be going - city beautification projects like enhancing parks for the enjoyment of families, fixing potholes on streets, improving existing infrastructure like outdated water pipes, or making public transportation more convenient and affordable - instead must go to policing the black community and staffing the support system required to populate Baltimore's prison-industrial complex.

[Baltimore homicides for 1991 reach 304, 1 under '90 record Shooting of woman marks first of '92, Baltimore Sun, 1-2-1992]:

> In this majority-black city, young black men have dominated the homicide roster in recent years, and 1991 was no exception.
>
> As of Nov. 30, when The Sun put the year-to-date killings at 269, 62.8 percent of homicide victims -- or 169 -- were black men between the ages of 20-39. When blacks between the ages of 10 and 20 were included, the percentage of victims who were black and male increased to 75 percent.
>
> All of the slain children were black. Among them was 6-year-old Tiffany Smith, who was killed late one summer evening when she was visiting a young friend overnight in the Walbrook area of West Baltimore. She stepped into the path of a shootout between two men. And there was Renae Hicks, an 11-month-old baby allegedly beaten to death last month by her mother and her mother's boyfriend.
>
> In the final two months of 1991, devastating budget cuts hit Baltimore. Although the Police Department was spared layoffs or furloughs, other areas of the criminal justice system suffered. City prosecutors had to take six furlough days, which in turn meant that the business of bringing criminals to trial didn't get done for at least a week.
>
> With the city anticipating yet another loss of state dollars -- this time perhaps $13.3 million -- the prospects for more police or prosecutors in the new year are dim.
>
> "We need more dollars for chemists, analysts, detectives and attorneys," said Baltimore State's Attorney Stuart O. Simms.

"Dollars are something we don't have a lot of at the moment."[289]

Civic enhancements are not a priority in a majority-black metropolis where continually hiring new police department support staff is a major fiduciary concern.

Just one generation ago, the first elected black mayor of Baltimore, the Ivy League educated Kurt
Schmoke, burst onto the national scene with the hopes of saving his beleaguered city.
Branding Baltimore as the "City That Reads", Schmoke hoped to erase the formula (quoted above) already turning much of the white-built housing stock in the city into nothing more than blight, crime infested neighborhoods.

Initially it was greeted with national praise. [Baltimore Targets Its High Rate of Illiteracy; Schmoke Pushing Programs to Make 'City That Reads' More Than Just an Idle Slogan, Washington Post, by Paul Valentine, 8-27-1990]:

> You see it everywhere, at bus stops, on park benches, on bumper stickers, on city trucks: a silhouetted figure poised over an open book next to the motto "Baltimore, the City that Reads."

> Not exactly a glitzy slogan, Baltimore Mayor Kurt L. Schmoke acknowledges. But in a city of 720,100 where up to 200,000 adults are functionally illiterate, he says, "it shows where our priorities are."

> On second thought, Schmoke says, literacy is more than a priority. It's a matter of survival. Yet, of the 200,000 illiterates, only about 3,700 are enrolled in literacy programs at any given moment, according to city estimates. Absenteeism runs high.

> And 70 to 90 percent of participants are welfare recipients, mostly women, a kind of captive group that must enroll in education or job training programs to maintain welfare eligibility.

---

[289] http://articles.baltimoresun.com/1992-01-02/news/1992002004_1_homicide-detectives-number-of-homicides-homicide-rate

Baltimore, like many older "smokestack" cities with a fading industrial base, is moving rapidly to a service economy-banking, insurance, tourism, health care-where the need for greater literacy and technological savvy grows daily.

"We need to adjust to the economic realities of the future," says Schmoke, 40, one of the new generation of young black professionals who have become mayors of major U.S. cities. "That's why these {literacy} programs are so vital."

"At the receiving dock, it used to be the guy would just unload the truck," Westinghouse executive Charles Zimmerman says.

"Now he has to enter the information into a computer. "Unless we improve the literacy levels of the people coming into the work force," says Zimmerman, a board member of Baltimore Reads, a private support group of the city's literacy campaign, " . . . these people don't have a prayer."

Behind the barrage of slogans, "readathons," car wash fund-raisers and other promotional gimmicks since Schmoke became mayor in 1987, he has established a new Cabinet-level literacy office and assigned it the Herculean task of teaching legions of people not only to read but to cope with high-tech America.

The numbers are daunting. About one-third of the city's population above age 16 is functionally illiterate, that is, unable to read at a ninth-grade level.

While that standard may seem high, officials say many have difficulty performing common tasks like reading bus schedules or filling out job applications. Uncounted thousands cannot read at all. Many of the people in literacy programs come from neighborhoods wracked with crime, drugs, teenage pregnancy, unemployment and poverty, problems that hinder attendance, officials say.

Of 5,409 enrolled in programs during the year ending June 30, up to 40 percent dropped out at one point or another.

Almost 37 percent were unemployed. Fourteen percent were nonreaders. "They're prisoners in their own neighborhoods," says Maggi Gaines, the city's literacy boss.

"They can't read bus and street signs. They can't read medicine bottles." "I never worked a job in my life," says Annette Shellington, 30, a mother of three who completed the eighth grade at age 17 but until recently read at second-grade level.

"I never filled out a job application. I was scared . . . . I was embarrassed."

Enrolled in a city program, she now reads at fourth-grade level.[290]

It is this black population that gave birth to the de facto moniker of Baltimore: "*The City that Bleeds*."

Black women like Annette Shellington birthed the new Baltimore, enabling the formula to become more than just a mathematical theory on a blackboard; ultimately drowning the civilization that whites had created in generation after generation of poor, unintelligent, welfare-dependent blacks, until white civilization was no more.

No, it's not drugs.

It's this:

Low Impulse Control + Poor Future Time-Orientation + Low IQ (x) jury nullification (black political control)^2 = Baltimore in 2014

---

[290] Baltimore Targets Its High Rate of Illiteracy; Schmoke Pushing Programs to Make `City That Reads' More Than Just an Idle Slogan, Washington Post, by Paul Valentine, 8-27-1990

ABOUT THE AUTHOR

Paul Kersey is the author of the blog SBPDL.com. His writings have appeared at VDare.com and Takimag.com. He is the author of *Escape From Detroit, Black Mecca Down,* and *The Tragic City.*

Works Cited

Alvarez, Rafael. *The wire: truth be told*. Rev. ed. New York: Grove

Press :, 2009. Print.

Baum, Howell S.. *Brown in Baltimore: school desegregation and the*

limits of liberalism. Ithaca: Cornell University Press, 2010.

Print.

Beilenson, Peter L., and Patrick A. McGuire. *Tapping into The Wire:*

the real urban crisis. Baltimore: Johns Hopkins University

Press, 2012. Print.

Bell, Madison Smartt. *Charm City: a walk through Baltimore*. New

York: Crown Journeys, 2007. Print.

Fee, Elizabeth, Linda.. Shopes, and Linda Zeidman. *The Baltimore*

book: new views of local history. Philadelphia: Temple

University Press, 1991. Print.

Gomez, Marisela B.. *Race, class, power, and organizing in East*

Baltimore: rebuilding abandoned communities in America.

Lanham: Lexington Books, 2013. Print.

Hayward, Mary Ellen, and Charles Belfoure. *The Baltimore*

rowhouse. New York: Princeton Architectural Press, 2001.

Print.

Ifill, Sherrilyn A.. *On the courthouse lawn: confronting the legacy of lynching in the twenty-first century.* Boston: Beacon Press, 2007. Print.

Kennedy, David M.. *Don't shoot: one man, a street fellowship, and the end of violence in inner-city America.* New York: Bloomsbury USA, 2011. Print.

Kennedy, Liam. *The wire: race, class, and genre.* Ann Arbor: University of Michigan Press, 2012. Print.

McDougall, Harold A.. *Black Baltimore: a new theory of community.* Philadelphia: Temple University Press, 1993. Print.

Moskos, Peter. *Cop in the hood: my year policing Baltimore's eastern district.* Princeton: Princeton University Press, 2008. Print.

Orr, Marion. *Black social capital: the politics of school reform in Baltimore, 1986-1998.* Lawrence: University Press of Kansas, 1999. Print.

Orser, W. Edward. *Blockbusting in Baltimore: the Edmondson Village story.* Lexington, Ky.: University Press of Kentucky, 1994. Print.

Pietila, Antero. *Not in my neighborhood: how bigotry shaped a great American city.* Chicago: Ivan R. Dee, 2010. Print.

Potter, Tiffany, and C. W. Marshall. *The Wire urban decay and American television.* New York: Continuum, 2009. Print.

Sewell, Kelvin, and Stephen Janis. *Why do we kill?: the pathology of murder in Baltimore.* Baltimore, MD: Baltimore True Crime, 2011. Print.

Simon, David. *Homicide: a year on the killing streets.* Boston: Houghton Mifflin, 1991. Print.

Simon, David, and Edward Burns. *The corner: a year in the life of an inner-city neighborhood.* New York: Broadway Books, 1997. Print.

Smith, C. Fraser. *William Donald Schaefer: a political biography.* Baltimore: Johns Hopkins University Press, 1999. Print.

Stegman, Michael A.. *Housing investment in the inner city: the dynamics of decline; a study of Baltimore, Maryland, 1968-1970.* Cambridge, Mass.: M.I.T. Press, 1972. Print.

Vicino, Thomas J.. *Transforming race and class in suburbia: decline in metropolitan Baltimore.* New York: Palgrave Macmillan, 2008. Print.

41088642R10164

Made in the USA
Lexington, KY
29 April 2015